SENSE AND SINGULARITY

Sense and Singularity

JEAN-LUC NANCY AND THE INTERRUPTION OF PHILOSOPHY

Georges Van Den Abbeele

FORDHAM UNIVERSITY PRESS   NEW YORK   2023

Copyright © 2023 Fordham University Press

All rights reserved. No part of this publication may be reproduced, stored in a retrieval system, or transmitted in any form or by any means—electronic, mechanical, photocopy, recording, or any other—except for brief quotations in printed reviews, without the prior permission of the publisher.

Fordham University Press has no responsibility for the persistence or accuracy of URLs for external or third-party Internet websites referred to in this publication and does not guarantee that any content on such websites is, or will remain, accurate or appropriate.

Fordham University Press also publishes its books in a variety of electronic formats. Some content that appears in print may not be available in electronic books.

Visit us online at www.fordhampress.com.

Library of Congress Cataloging-in-Publication Data available online at https://catalog.loc.gov.

Printed in the United States of America

25 24 23   5   4 3 2 1

First edition

Contents

LIST OF ABBREVIATIONS   vii

Introduction: From the Interruption of Sense to the Poetics of Finitude   1

1   Descartes's Iterative Cogito, or the *Sum* of Each and Every Time   23

2   *Monograms*: Writing Singular Plural   49

3   The "Singular Logic of the Retreat": Interruptions of the Political   78

4   *Corpus Interruptus*: Uncommon Sense and the Singular Crossings of *Eros*, *Logos*, and *Tekhnè*   115

ACKNOWLEDGMENTS   163

NOTES   167

BIBLIOGRAPHY   197

INDEX   209

Abbreviations

Alquié René Descartes, *Oeuvres philosophiques*, ed. Ferdinand Alquié, 3 vols. (Paris: Garnier, 1963–73).

AT Rene Descartes, *Oeuvres de Descartes*, ed. Charles Adam and Paul Tannery, rev. ed., 11 vols. (Paris: Vrin, 1964–76).

BSP Jean-Luc Nancy, *Being Singular Plural*, trans. Robert D. Richardson and Anne E. O'Byrne. (1996; repr. Stanford, Calif.: Stanford University Press, 2000).

C Jean-Luc Nancy, *Corpus*, trans. Richard Rand (1992; repr. New York: Fordham University Press, 2008).

CMS René Descartes, *The Philosophical Writings of Descartes*, trans. John Cottingham, Robert Stoothoff, and Dugald Murdoch (Cambridge: Cambridge University Press, 1984).

CW Jean-Luc Nancy, *The Creation of the World, or Globalization*, trans. François Raffoul and David Pettigrew (2002; repr. Albany: SUNY Press, 2007).

ES Jean-Luc Nancy, *Ego sum: Corpus, Anima, Fabula*, trans. Marie-Eve Morin (1979; repr. New York: Fordham University Press, 2016).

GS Sigmund Freud, *Gesammelte Werke* (London: Imago, 1940–52).

IC Jean-Luc Nancy, *The Inoperative Community*, trans. Peter Connor (1983; repr. Minneapolis: University of Minnesota Press, 1991).

SE   Sigmund Freud, *The Standard Edition of the Complete Psychological Works*, trans. James Strachey (London: Hogarth, 1953–74).

SW   Jean-Luc Nancy, *The Sense of the World*, trans. Jeffrey S. Librett (1993; repr. Minneapolis: University of Minnesota Press, 1997).

SENSE AND SINGULARITY

Introduction
From the Interruption of Sense to the Poetics of Finitude

Somewhere, somehow, a horizon has been lost, a limit retraced, a way of knowing altered—in short, an interruption or disruption of some kind has occurred, leaving us exposed together on the edge of the unknown. Something has come to an end, even if it be an end that takes the form of a certain endlessness. Such is the ever strange yet strangely familiar opening to many a text signed by Jean-Luc Nancy. For this most exigent of contemporary philosophers, however, that "sense of an ending," to repurpose the title of Frank Kermode's celebrated work,[1] might be more like the ending of a sense or even the end of sense altogether. An *end* of sense, both aim and closure.

What appears as the contemporary withdrawal or retreat of sense, its definitive interruption, however, is neither a redemptive opening onto some infinite beyond of sense nor a cynical occasion to bask in a nihilistic acceptance of the absurd as commonly understood. Proposing neither mysticism nor insensibility, neither "God" nor "clod," transcendentalism nor immanentism, Nancy instead urges us toward an edgy reckoning with the retreat of sense as the urgency of a critical thinking always to come, as what matters *today* for what we still call philo-sophy, that vaunted *love* of knowledge, or the salutary openness to the unheard-of that he calls "adoration," and after Jacques Derrida, the *salut* of "a salutation without salvation."[2]

There is, of course, nothing particularly "Nancean" in the assertion that we are witnessing an ending of one kind or another. Such assertions can take the form of nostalgia, melancholia, or even "irony" and, as such, are the staple of a certain post-Rousseauian romanticism, what Jacques Derrida channeling Kant called "a certain apocalyptic tone formerly adopted in philosophy."[3] As the coeditor of *The Literary Absolute* and the author of a two-volume

Deconstruction of Christianity, Nancy knows well the derivation and lure of this commonplace: "Nothing is more familiar to us than to lament the threat hanging over the world and existence."[4] For Nancy, however, such proclamations of finitude or de-finitude—that is, the dislocation of stabilizing bounds, the utter *débordement* of which leaves us all exposed together on the limit and the liminality of our being, both being on the limit and on the limit of being—such proclamations appear as the pretext for something much more peculiar and strange, singular even. They allow for an avowedly apocalyptic reversal of the possibilities of thought, if not of the very condition and urgency of thinking anew. "Our time is the time of a disappropriation," he writes in *Adoration* (6), and "our suffering" comes from the fact that "we know that we are bereft of horizons" as we experience the "self-dissolution of the West" (73–74), and yet in contemplating the very nadir of this negative infinity, something else can be sensed, a salutation without salvation perhaps, or the singular ecstasy of an unprecedented exclamation. The very loss of any horizon would seem to be the current horizon of philosophy, and it demands a thought that is always still to come: an interruption of philosophy that is also a recognition of philosophy *as* interruption. Philosophy, or thinking, to be more precise, only takes place in or as this interruption, as "the opening of an always unheard-of sense," an "attentive listening, sensitive to the inaudible that speaks itself," but always only after what effectively happens. It is only in the aftermath of a certain *Wirklichkeit* that knowledge can occur, as Hegel famously notes with regard to the owl, that ancient symbol of wisdom associated with Minerva, that only takes flight after the sun has set, an image that recurs under Nancy's pen in recalling the philosophical exigency of hearing the unheard: "The odds today are more than ever with what is unheard of. More than ever, the owl of Minerva spreads its wings at dusk. A world is coming to an end."[5] Such is the characteristically Nancean moment, and such perhaps is his ongoing appeal today in the dusk we call the anthropocene, *after* modernism and after postmodernism, after communism and after neoliberalism, after structuralism and after post-structuralism, after Foucault, Deleuze, Lyotard, and Derrida.[6]

In his epigraph to the 1993 special issue of *Paragraph* dedicated to his work, "You Ask Me What It Means Today . . . ," Nancy writes, after listing a number of the better known "trouble spots" that surfaced in the immediate aftermath of communism's collapse in 1989 and the concomitant triumph of globalist neoliberalism, from Bosnia to Somalia to Central Asia (many of which remain just as troubled in the "today" of decades later):

> We'll not come to the end of the list of places and marks of uncertainty, of helplessness, of anguish. There is something like a general

loss of sense. Sense, that's the word that matters to me today. A general flight of sense, whether it occurs in a political or esthetic or religious or whatever other form. Sense matters to me, since "philosophy" deals with nothing else but sense. Absolutely nothing else. If sense is screwed to hell everywhere . . . this is obviously a philosophical concern, and also because philosophy is screwed to hell everywhere.[7]

The "end of philosophy," Nancy concludes, is "what we have at present, very concretely before our eyes" as the "sense of words like "nation," "people," "sovereignty," . . . "community," . . . and so many others . . . are leaking out of so many cracked vessels" (108–9). And with regard to such leaked and leaking meaning, even earlier, in the 1977 first version of "Exscription," Nancy, with reference to Georges Bataille, similarly evokes "the limit where all sense spills out of itself, like a simple ink stain on a word, on the word 'sense.'"[8] But in the kind of reversal familiar to readers of Nancy, such a "stain" on sense that overflows the very meaning of meaning turns out to be not just the revelation of some postmodern historical moment, but the very apocalyptic condition of sense itself—namely, "the pain and pleasure that result from the impossibility of communicating anything at all without touching the limit where all sense spills out of itself. . . ." Meaning can only occur as spilling out, as the overflow that stains out onto the very word of "sense," but that is also the only sense we can ever know, if not *all* of the senses by which we can sense: "Thinking, language, affect: a thrusting that overflows itself. Sense, sensation, sentiment."[9]

Adorno-like in his evocation of the demise of philosophy in the context of a world that has lost all sense, Nancy nonetheless springs a characteristic move, possibly the only move left at this presumed "end" of philosophy. Returning to the text from *Paragraph*, we can see this move in action: "Here is what matters to me: far from considering this general flight of sense as a catastrophe and a loss, I want to think of it as the event of sense in our time, for our time. It is a question of thinking sense in the absencing of sense. . . . It is a question of thinking what 'sense' can be when one has come to the end of sense understood in that fashion" (109). Philosophy can no longer be, as it once was, the very "giver of sense," nor can it even continue to be, as it has been since Kant, "the philosophy that does not want to give sense but to analyze the conditions for delivering a coherent sense" (109)—that is, philosophy as critical, as the critique of sense in every sense.

But if philosophy today can no longer be the mere giver of sense or the explication/deconstruction of the conditions for there to be any sense, what can it be? Quoting Nietzsche's injunction "to introduce a new sense—it being understood that this task itself has no sense," Nancy closes this short text with what seems to be at least two answers, whose compatibility or incompatibility remains to be scripted or ascribed, and whose sense thus remains in suspense. On the one hand, the Nietzschean response to the end of sense "is revolution itself: the destitution of the authority of sense or of sense as authority, and the entry into the unheard-of. For the unheard-of, one has to get one's ears ready" (109). In its anarchistic zeal and postmodern aesthetics of the unpresentable, this statement sounds like Nancy talking Lyotard. The other answer, in its enunciation of a constitutive absence that maintains a certain senseless sense, might then sound like Nancy talking Derrida: "But today this is where there is some sense: in saying sense is absent, in saying that this absence is what we are exposed to, and that this exposition constitutes what I will call not only our present history but with Rimbaud, our refound eternity" (110). Perhaps this is Nancy's way of doubly tracing a certain limit or horizon line of contemporary philosophical discourse caught between the poetic evocation of a necessarily inchoate outside of philosophy and the philosophically eloquent pronouncement of the end of philosophy. The tracing of this line is perhaps the practice of a certain *exscription* in Nancy's work: a writing that is not so much on the limit between a supposed inside and outside of philosophy, but one that *exposes* philosophical thought to its unheard-of outside *in* the very act of speaking the end of philosophical thought as the internal limit to its sense. The contemporary event of sense that is the absencing of sense, its apocalypse, is the unheard-of that philosophy tries to let speak within it as what speaks the end of philosophy, an unheard-of that speaks perhaps in the voice, not of a philosopher but of a poet, say Rimbaud (whose name often recurs as the very example of the poet for Nancy, not unlike the way Hölderlin does for Heidegger), who speaks what is at once "present history" and "refound eternity."

The apocalypse of sense is similarly evoked by the ambiguously termed "forgetting of philosophy"—both subjective and objective genitive in its formulation—in his 1986 work by that title.[10] On the one hand, there is the contemporary grumbling (perhaps even louder today) that philosophy has lost its way in a world without sense and is no longer fulfilling its duty to provide sense in such a world. On the other hand, as Nancy retorts, such a call for philosophy to return to itself is to forget philosophy's own tangled relation with sense, its own constitutive forgetting of sense and consequent "surprise" before the arrival of sense elsewhere. This sense is not, he qualifies, the already determined, located, or pinpointed sense (*sens repéré*) that we understand more precisely as signification. Rather, Nancy proposes that "sense resides perhaps only in the coming of a possible signification" (14) before concluding more definitively that the loss of sense or of meaning should be understood as "that withdrawal [*retrait*] of sense by which sense arrives" (108). That withdrawal or retreat of sense as the condition of the sense that comes to us is also, for him, one way to understand the "origin" of philosophy: "In this sense, sense needs to abandon us for us to be open to the very opening up of sense. And this, henceforth, cannot be forgotten: this abandonment is our history" (108). Philosophy, in its origin as well as its end, is not the provision of sense but the very surprise of encountering sense in its appearance/disappearance, a surprise that can only happen by our being open or liable to its possible arrival in or as its vanishing. Meaning must be spilled for the stain of sense to appear.

Two issues confront us, then, in Nancy's reformulations of what sense and philosophy can mean today. One is the question of the sense of sense itself, which I propose somewhat polemically to translate consistently as "sense" rather than trying each time to decide, as most translators do with varying levels of assurance, to render it as *either* sensation *or* meaning, or even for that matter as direction (as in that lovely French expression for a one-way street: *sens unique*). All three English words render French *sens* more or less correctly, while systematically concealing the commonality of the French word, although English "sense" can with varying degrees of appropriateness stand for *all* those various French meanings, as well. Such a dilemma is not an uncommon translation challenge, but in the case of Nancy's thinking it risks blinding the English reader to the ways the word "sense" is deployed in ways that question cardinal philosophic presuppositions about the difference between sensation and meaning, or between the sensible and the intelligible, foundational to the oppositional structure of Western metaphysics. By tracking Nancy's use of the word in its unitary form, I hope in this work to manifest the radicality of his thought from his early, devastating rereading of Descartes through his later inquiries into the body, sexuality, aesthetics, politics, and technology. Readers are free to substitute "meaning" or "sensation" or "sentiment" or "direction" as they deem fit throughout this work, but my aim is to unravel a set of interconnections and dissonances only possible by rendering *sens* consistently as "sense." Finally, Nancy has himself explicitly insisted on translating the French *sens* as the English *sense*.[11]

The second issue has to do with what in an older vocabulary was understood as the difference between structure and history. Is the retreat of sense, its withdrawal and unexpected arrival, its comings and goings, an event, something in the moment of our times, something happening *now*? Or is it merely the recurrence of an eventuality always already inscribed in its being as sense? As with his treatment of the word "sense," Nancy relentlessly questions the ease of such oppositional thinking. The question of sense appears and reappears as a problem of the moment, as what we experience as our contemporary lived reality now, and then now again, each time as "present history" and "refound eternity." But this ontological conundrum also highlights the adventurous ways Nancy writes both abstractly *and* in the concreteness of any given moment and its historical contexts. From his early "monograms" through his philosophical "chronicles," and from the "hot spots" evoked in the *Paragraph* piece to the Fukushima disaster ("the catastrophe of sense") and the COVID-19 pandemic ("an all too human virus"),[12] Nancy's work is genuinely remarkable for its intervention *as* philosophy in the events and contexts of the day not as mere occasion or editorial moonlighting, but as a form of what I would call a "philosophy of the actual." "Actual" here is best understood not only in the Hegelian sense of *Wirklichkeit*, commonly rendered in English as effective reality, but also in the colloquial French sense as what is current or happening now, what French news calls "*les actualités*." A philosophy of the *actuel* triggers for Nancy both an impressive array of formal experimentations for whatever we can term the genre of philosophical writing, on the one hand, and a thinking grounded in the particularity of the moment, in the singularity of the event, again not as the mere occasion for philosophical thinking but as its very openness or liability for sense to come, as the very basis for its recurrent "surprise" before the fact that sense somehow does arrive. This "retreat" of sense, at once withdrawing and retracing, is what Nancy calls the "singular logic" that guides much of his thinking of the historical and the political. Both these consequences, formal and conceptual, will be explored in this work, hence the title of "sense and singularity" to designate the guiding threads of this study into the extraordinariness of Nancy's capacious and challenging philosophical project.

I think we can see, though, that such a project does not simply define a new horizon of philosophy. The lines Nancy's texts trace in *and* out of philosophy do not open up some new vista or territory for philosophical exploitation but expose philosophy to the singular *actuality* of its context, to the contemporary absencing or exempting of sense—that is, to the threshold of its being nonetheless a sense-making discipline, a practice of thinking that demands that thinking always begin anew. Rather than a retreat from the classic philosophical commitment of the Sartrian kind, Nancy's calls for a "finite thinking" actually deepen philosophy's critical engagement in and with the world. The trope of finitude, as it appears in Nancy's texts, is not a simple one of enablement whose dialectical reversal/sublation would renew the possibility of philosophy, thus allowing it to remain selfsame in the face of the vicissitudes of sense. Nancean finitude is not a negativity to be overcome, but the *interruption* of an event to dwell in and upon, the very advent of a thought that can only, in his terms, exscribe its compearance, or write itself as exposed to and with its others. The lost horizon of sense becomes the liminal space from which the sense of the absence of sense can be thought, but only to the extent that the horizon is indeed "lost"—that is, opened up onto the unheard-of of sense rather than the comforting contours of a world closed unto itself. In this way, the thought of finitude also opens onto the infinitude of sense, the limitlessness by which sense can always be made.

We can track another such apocalyptic twist of sense near the beginning of *The Inoperative Community* when Nancy cites Sartre's declaration that "communism is the insuperable horizon of our time,"[13] a quotation placed with no small irony within the book's opening evocation of the end of community (and *a fortiori* the end of communism as utopian ideal) as that to which our time bears witness. Again, though, the issue is not to mourn the loss of community—or of communism—nor even to celebrate that loss, but to lose the very concept of horizon:

> *Communism* can no longer be the insuperable horizon of our time. And if in fact it no longer is such a horizon, this is not because we have passed beyond any horizon. Rather, everything is inflected by resignation, as if the new insuperable horizon took form around the disappearance, the impossibility or the condemnation of communism. Such reversals are customary; they have never altered anything. It is the *horizons* themselves that must be challenged. That ultimate limit of community, or the limit that is formed by community, as such, traces an entirely different line. This is why, even as we establish that communism is no longer our insuperable horizon, we must also establish, just as forcefully, that a communist exigency or demand communicates with the gesture by means of which we must go farther than all possible horizons. (8–9; translation modified)

The loss of community is posited as an absence all too easily sublatable by any immanentism bemoaning that loss and trumpeting a so-called return to communal values as seen in so much political discourse today, right and left. What Nancy seizes upon rather is a kind of communism or communality that would be not itself a horizon, but the undoing of all horizons—namely, a community founded upon the appearing together or "compearance" of singular beings in the incommensurate commonality of their *difference*.

Much later, in the concluding chapter of *The Dis-Enclosure*, Nancy returns to the contemporary question of the horizon: "This is our situation: no more horizons. From all directions horizons are asserted in the modern world, but how can we grasp what I would call 'horizontality'? How can we grasp the character of horizon while we are on a ground that is not a ground of horizon(s), a ground without ground of indefinite opening?" (145). This opening, Nancy further specifies, is nothing less than "the structure of sense itself," both "as horizon of sense *and* as a rending of the horizon" (156), its interruption. To the extent that sense is implied in its own sensing—that is, in its own sending—it presupposes an opening or a spacing that enables that sending that sense is, the limit or finitude that opens onto the possible infinity of sense making, literally inter-mittent, a sending that is by definition interrupted and interrupting. As such, the horizon emerges "as a proper noun for the finitude that turns toward its own infinity." The horizontality of sense means both its limit and its endlessness, a horizon perpetually circumscribed and perpetually breached, interrupted, which also means that sense is never fixed but always to come, always coming, in *differance*. Finalized signification, on the other hand, as in Christian theology, would attempt to "undo" this horizontal *differance* by "mak[ing] it pivot into a verticality: the present instant like an infinite breakthrough" (156). Whence the stakes of philosophy come down to "a matter of thinking the limit (that is, the Greek sense of *horizô*; to limit, to restrict), the singular line that 'fastens' an existence, but that fastens it according to the complex graph of an opening, not returning to itself ('self' being this non-return), yet, again, according to the inscription of a sense that no religion, no belief, nor any knowledge . . . can saturate or assure" (157).

While these particular comments appear by way of Nancy's deconstruction of Christianity in *Dis-Enclosure*, we can also follow such a thinking of the limit and the concomitant "undoing of all horizons" by considering the example of the assumed immanence of communal identities to demarcated geographical spaces in the form of towns, lands, or nations. In its most vulgar formation, this relation appears, of course, as the nationalist ideology of blood and soil. But the equation between land and ethnicity demands the installation of the literalized horizon that is the border, the institutionalized inscription of a cartographical divide that *defines* all those within as ethnically, culturally, and linguistically identical and all those without as different, barbarous, savage, and inimical. This inscription of cultural identity onto or into topography, however, can only ever protect the differential undoing of that identity by the reinforcement of the inscription as violence. The greatest fear today among nation-states is that of "losing control" of their borders, a cry echoed today with the most ominous of reverberations from eastern Europe to southern California. What is this seemingly omnipresent fear all about? What is so different after all about Ciudad Juárez and El Paso, or Tangiers and Cadiz, for example, and what is the fear—beyond all the hypocritical talk about administrative and economic complications—except that the supposed difference is *not* a difference, and that difference occurs both on this side and that side of the border, and in wanton disregard of the border. Perhaps the fear is that no "reinforcement" of border patrols, no institution of crossing fees, no control of identity papers, no linguistic legislation, no interrogations or agreements, no "big, beautiful wall," can stem this becoming unbordered of the border, its insuperable *débordement*. And indeed, that fear is justified (the border is out of control because no border can ever be successfully controlled), but its consequences may not be as bad as all that, and certainly not as bad as the bloody and brutal efforts to redefine and maintain borders.

What the loss of borders exposes is the contingency of the nation's existence upon a certain *areality*—a word Nancy uses throughout his work but that begs to be applied to the immanence of nationhood as community with its longstanding use of corporeal metaphors (notably that of the "body politic") in its legitimating discourses. "*Aréalité*," Nancy writes in *Corpus*, "is an antique French word, signifying the nature or specificity of an *aire* ("area"). By chance, this word also serves to suggest a lack of reality, or rather a slight, faint, suspended reality."[14] The areality of the nation is what suspends or interrupts the myth of the land as a nation's substratum or *subjectum* [*hypokeimenon*], that which literally lies or is thrown below the feet of a certain community understood as a sort of vegetative immanence: what sprouts or springs from the soil as its natural outgrowth, the indigenous agro-cultivation of a "culture" that sees itself as the "natural" possessor of the land from which it comes. The nation as subject, the common ground as the founding locus of a "common sense": the dangers of this myth are well known, but sadly still bear repeating. Nancy, to be sure, has been one of the most trenchant articulators of the perils of nationalist or communitarian mythmaking.[15]

The arealization of the nation leaves it in place but suspended, (un)bordered in its expanse, exposed on the limit between spatial, ethnic, and linguistic differences. Perhaps it is such a becoming areal of the nation that provokes such dismay today, the disappearance of its sense as the contemporary event of sense, despite its being the very condition for there to be any sense of the nation. Nancy would, I believe, be the first to point out, though, that geographical identity is not the only, or even the most insidious, form of communal immanence. Indeed, the apparently worldwide implosion of borders experienced as the post-communist (or neoliberal) crisis of globalization bears eloquent witness to the obsolescence of the old nation-state snugly or smugly confined within its borders amid the postmodern plethora of telecommunicational networks and unprecedentedly vast diasporas and collective migrations that would seem to shatter any last illusions about the *sense* of place and community, while reducing all such sense to the general equivalent of exchange imposed by capital. Yet the metaphysics of presence and the ideology of cultural separatism have perhaps never been more manifest than in the contemporary situation where collectivities of all sorts can be convoked in the near instantaneity of (social) media (mis)representation.

And here perhaps is where the becoming senseless of the nation can occasion a Nietzschean new sense, or at least a philosophical point of entry into the unheard-of. Having become irrelevant in its areality, the nation remains the uncommon ground of difference. And by "ground of difference," I refer to the vertigo of difference within its supposed confines, as well, of course, as the difference it marks or demarcates from other nations. As *areal*, the nation is exscribed: not just uncommon ground but ungrounded community. How can we philosophize then in this space without a horizon, or perhaps that is nothing but horizons? How can we get our ears "ready" for the unheard-of? How can we think the utopics of difference that is post-national space? Or resist the simultaneous siren call of renewed and hyper-nostalgic nationalism?

For Jean-Luc Nancy, there seems to be a name for such a thought, and that name again is "poetry." In a short text published in 1983 in *Poësie* and translated and reprinted in *The Birth to Presence*, he specifies that "poetry is a cadastre, or else a geography"[16]: "The poet can be recognized," he writes, "by a certain surveyor's step, by a certain way of covering a territory of words, not in order to find something, or to plant a crop, or to build an edifice, but simply to measure it" (308, translation modified). But if the poet is a geographer of words, could there not be a geography that is poetic, an experience of spatial and communal differences that *qua poetry*, to quote again from Nancy, "takes the form of an effacement: a gesture which itself is, after all, commonplace, which indicates your place, mine, yet another's, and which withdraws" (308–9)? Such an indication of place(s) is also the event of a kind of *mitsein*, of being in common as different, of being together as apart, of a spacing and finitude that is the unheard-of condition of community. Poetry, as described here, exists precisely in what semioticians would call its pragmatics, the compearing of singular beings at loose ends that Nancy calls the inoperative community, the *communauté désoeuvrée*, not the opus of its own immanence but the undoing of itself as itself. But then the poetry in question cannot be one that issues forth in a work, but one whose gesture must also be irretrievably singular, finite, the indelible stain of a sense that overflows the bounds of its meaning. Poetry too cannot be a new kind of insuperable horizon. Indeed, while the metonym of the nation-state as people grounded in a land demands the horizontality of topographical and discursive borders, of frontiers and myths, poetry since at least Rimbaud (and perhaps that is part of his significance for Nancy) is what speaks the unheard-of verticality or vertigo of sense, not as the apotheosis of signification, but what gives new direction or *sens* to sense, a direction that is none other than the other of direction. In the words of Rimbaud, the poet who most exemplarily works at and toward the very limit of sense, this would be the *"dérèglement de tous les sens,"* the unruling or unruliness of every sense/meaning/direction.[17] It is the coming to presence of the unforeseen and the unheard-of not only in language but also in our difference from each other, from our history, from the spaces we inhabit. Such a *poein* in its root sense is a "making" that is simultaneously an unmaking, a co-appearing or "compearing" of community that is also its withdrawal, an advent of sense in which sense is eclipsed, a speaking of what cannot be heard—in short, what Nancy calls elsewhere a "creation of world." This is not to say that Jean-Luc Nancy is a poet rather than a philosopher, or even that he is a philosopher rather than a poet, or even that there is something especially "poetic" about his philosophical prose, but that philosophy as it is written by him is a *poein* of thought exposed upon its limit, with no comforting horizon in view, only the endless exscription of sense in retreat: the "commonplace" of a "gesture which indicates your place, mine, yet another's, *and which withdraws."* What we can call, in other words, a poetics of finitude, or the kind of poetry he sees as "inevitably attained by a philosopher who cannot be satisfied with philosophy."[18]

And yet, this commonplace or *locus communis* of poetic sense is always—each and every time, if you will—resolutely singular. Its commonplace is the ascription of places in common—"your place, mine, yet another's"—the punctuality of their indication, the fleeting deixis of an indexing, a momentary pointing out of what only comes to be in its being with (*mitsein*) a set of other points, in the poetics of its community as *constellation* (to evoke Benjamin's concept of the idea as the articulatory function of thought).[19] But how are we to understand the as yet indeterminate relation of these singular *points* to the poetic ensemble? And what is the sense of their singularity as charted by the poet/geographer/astronomer?

We can get some help here if we turn back to *The Inoperative Community* at the point where Nancy interrupts his opening analysis of the ways the concepts of *both* "individual" and "community" remain grounded within "the general problematic of immanence" (6). Whether the community magically precedes its members through immanent self-engenderment or whether immanently self-engendered "individuals" contractually agree to join together in a community, what is missed is the very thought of how it is that we are together as such. The importance of Nancy's interruption is doubly marked by its being framed (in the French text) by a white space with asterisks *and* a set of parentheses. A "reservation" is noted,—and as any reader of Nancy (or of Derrida) knows, such a reservation is not to be taken lightly. Nor is it simply "parenthetical." Such reservations are never mere local objections but a first sounding of a crack or *faille* in the armature of a text, the seemingly quiet and innocuous *locale* where the seismic upheaval of a deconstruction is about to take place, where something radically other comes to be heard, or at least to disclose some trace of itself.

Nancy's reservation here bears upon the "theme of the individual" behind which lurks the "question of singularity":

> What is *a* body, *a* face, *a* voice, *a* death, *a* writing—not indivisible, but singular? What is their singular necessity in the sharing that divides and that puts in communication bodies, voices, and writings in general and in totality? In sum, this question would be exactly the reverse of the question of the absolute. In this respect, it is constitutive of the question of community, and it is in this context that it will have to be taken into account later on. But singularity never has the nature or the structure of individuality. Singularity never takes place at the level of atoms, those identifiable if not identical identities; rather it takes place at the level of the *clinamen*, which is unidentifiable. It is linked to ecstasy: one could not properly say that the singular being is the subject of ecstasy, for ecstasy has no "subject"—but one must say that ecstasy (community) happens *to* the singular being. (6–7)

One would be ill-advised to assume that "singularity" is merely or just the deconstructed term for individual via an easy substitution of names. Rather, singularity haunts Nancy's text as the mark or stain of a certain limit to philosophy, as the name of what can only remain untheorizable yet that demands to be thought, and so can indefinitely generate philosophical sense—not through the immanence of a creation or some *point* of identity, but instead through the singularity of an *event*, the oblique ricochet of its clinamen—that is, through the graphic swerve of a certain untoward trajectory. Singularity is a philosophical curve ball that wreaks havoc in the game of logic and the play of concepts. In mathematics, singularity occurs when a function reveals an anomaly whose derivative cannot be differentiated, such as in the case of $1/x$ when x equals zero; in astrophysics, it is technically defined as the ultimate geometrical curve, where the curvature of space-time "becomes infinite."[20] Philosophically, the risk, however, is to turn singularity apocalyptically into "exactly the reverse"—namely, the absolute, be it divine, or communitarian, or even literary—that is, to turn the singular into the universal of a principle. The question, then, is whether the singular in Nancy is allowed to pursue its work of collision and repartee, or whether its swerve is dodged by its conceptualized rebound as absolute.

The general risk of the singular's sublation into universal can be gauged by a glance back at the discourse of Renaissance cosmography, where singularity first appears in Western thought as a scandalous anomaly in knowledge. One of the many early modern genres grounded in the practice of compilation, cosmography claimed to describe a given part of the world (or, in the case of "universal" cosmography, the whole world) by detailing its "singularities" or "curiosities"—namely, whatever the compiler assumed to be most remarkable or noteworthy in a given locale: monuments, customs, flora, fauna, and, of course, all manner of monsters and "prodigies." Among the best-known exemplars of the genre, André Thevet's *Singularitez de la France Antarctique* (Paris, 1557), with reference to the land of Brazil, includes, among others, chapters on cannibals, toucans, tree sloths, and tobacco. Obviously, an early attempt to classify knowledge by geography, cosmography also strove to overcome the singularities it pinpointed by trying to relate them to some other, more familiar, and less singular objects. Hence, most singularities were made out to be remarkable or unusual yet already duplicated or replicated somewhere else (whether in the book of the world or the world of books): the cannibalistic Tupinamba fight, for example, just like the ancient Romans. For the Renaissance cosmographer, true singularity, as opposed to these somewhat duplicitous singularities, was always a sign of the absolute, an awesome index of God's omnipotence and ability to defy or overturn whatever humans thought might be the "natural order" of things, the singular disturbance of which portends a sequence of dire events, such as in the unfolding of Shakespearean tragedy, for example. Whence, too, the combination of fear and wonder evoked by the occurrence of portentous events or monstrous beings. For a compiler of human miseries and misfortunes such as Pierre Boaistuau, in his widely reprinted and translated *Théâtre du monde* (Paris, 1558), such occurrences are so many cases that point to and show (*monstrare*) God's will at work. Singularities may be epistemological scandals, but they can be typically recuperated, either by reference to already familiar categories or as the very sign and sense of the absolute, the dis-enclosure that marks the discourse of Christianity.[21]

On the one hand, all singularities must have something remarkable, some way in which they are marked as distinctly different from what surrounds them and so designatable *as* singular in their anomaly. On the other hand, something that makes sense of the singularity occurs only by the resending or repetition that sense necessarily enacts. Attributing sense to singularity is thus to deny its singularity as such. While the singular is necessarily particular, it is—mindful of the adjective's second meaning—a unicity that is also *peculiar* in some way: not just single but *singulare*. It is *unique* in the strong sense of the word, what the linguists call a "hapax," or a word defined as having only a single occurrence. And yet nothing is more common or more universal in its dispersion. Indeed, one could hazard that the universe itself is nothing but an infinitely vast collection of singularities, if what we call the universe is not in and of itself an immense and all-encompassing singularity, the initial singularity, if that makes any sense. Alternatively, singularity reveals the end of sense itself, its apocalypse. The singular is the vanishing point of every nominalism, *viz*, the infinite curvature of thought and language, the *clinamen* that endlessly deflects the claims of every realism (realism understood here in the medieval universalist sense as per Duns Scotus). That deflection or curvature is not without its trace or mark: the ex-stasis or exscription by which it marks and remarks itself, retracing itself in its very withdrawal or *retreat*.

If, moreover, the singular is necessarily *remarkable*, it must be inscribed with the capacity to be indefinitely remarked upon, to open onto an incessant remarkability as the very (lost) horizon of its sense, as the overflow of its stain. The singular thus necessarily inscribes and is inscribed or exscribed in/as the plural—there is never a question of there being *a* singularity but only of singularit*ies*. This is one of Nancy's most important contributions and an indication of why the ecstatic "question" of the singular is crucial to his elaboration of a community "at loose ends";[22] it bears no relation to the atomistic concept of the individual as that autonomous entity who would preexist all communal formations and would enter into community only after contracting with other supposedly preexisting autonomous individuals. Rather, what Nancy focuses on is the *relation* (of *mitsein* or togetherness) between singularities and community that is the necessary condition of their coming into being in the first place. In other words, the singular can only occur as what (re)marks itself within the plural—and the plural as what demarcates a world of singularities, flash points in *constellation*. Singularity and community appear as co-posited, as called together (*comparues*) in the relation of togetherness, in the being together or *mitsein* that is the only way for singularity to be singular and for community to be communal.

Of course, the countless ways in which singularities are together in or as community remain to be determined. If the remarkability of the singular necessarily implies its plurality, *how* singularity is remarked remains obscure—especially if it is one of those massive singularities contemporary cosmology names as the (non)entity at the core of a black hole. According to the theory, a black hole is formed when a star collapses under its own weight with a gravitational pull so great as to prevent even light from escaping, whence the name "black hole" to designate the invisibility of this phenomenon, which is irreducibly *non*-phenomenal in itself (even if its existence can be indirectly deduced by the adjacent warping of space-time). Not only, however, is a black hole remarkable by its very invisibility but also, so say the cosmologists, by its virtual absence: that which lies beyond what is called the "event horizon" of a black hole "is not part of our universe."[23] Space and time both come to an end at the point of infinitely massive density and immeasurable pressure that defines the singularity as that single point into which the enormous mass of an entire star has catastrophically imploded. That point is called a singularity by mathematicians and astrophysicists alike because that is where "the theory itself breaks down."[24] Black holes are therefore, to no surprise, not the only phenomena to pose the problem of singularities. The currently canonical big bang theory posits an originary singularity, out of whose virtual nothingness the universe would have exploded (in a reverse movement to a black hole's implosion). Contemporary astrophysicists, like the cosmographers of the Renaissance, would prefer to find a way to explain away singularities—some are even said to find "the whole idea of singularities repugnant."[25] Once an advocate of singularity who even hypothesized a universe full of tiny "primordial" black holes, Stephen Hawking pivoted away from such thought to seek a GUT (or that supreme cosmological good called a "Grand Unified Theory") that would explain a universe "without singularities or boundaries."[26] A "naked singularity" such as that of the big bang is also susceptible to a theological reinterpretation, as were the prodigious singularities of the Renaissance, since the very lack of theoretical explanation curiously rebounds as proof of a divine creator. While the Catholic Church—no friend of revisionist science—only recently rescinded its censure of Galileo, it has had no problem accepting the big bang theory as in conformity with scripture and has endorsed its teaching since 1951.[27] Indeed, the positing of a single point as the singular origin from which the creation of the universe takes place *ex nihilo* is the very example of the dis-enclosure that, according to Nancy, defines Christianity itself.

Still, singularity remains in contemporary cosmology a theoretical concept at the very limit of theory. Indeed, that is what makes for the *singularness* of singularities. The various implosions and explosions in which it is implicated by astrophysics also have led that discipline to draw adventurous and speculative fictions about passages to alternative universes as well as the birth and death of our own. *Et tout le reste est littérature.* Yet what is ultimately most interesting about cosmological singularities is that, philosophically speaking, they can only be when they are not: Hawking argues that they "always lie either entirely in the future . . . or entirely in the past" (89). Singular being is utterly and radically ecstatic, never "present," occupying neither space nor time, yet with the most manifest effects on space and time, conditioning its very possibility. Singularity is the retreat of space-time, what marks and remarks its limits in the endless play of explosions and implosions, of big bangs and "big crunches." Singularity is the very existence of Being, of the very possibility of their being beings, of the singularity of being as existent. As such, singular being cannot even be said to be, except when, ex-posing itself as what is or was or will be outside of itself (although as a *point* of infinite density it could never be said to have had any inside at all)—that is, by its existence in a space-time whose limit it exscribes, it is then always already a community of beings as the mere being-together of the singular, already more than one in the already expanding or the not yet contracted. It only comes to be as plural; as one, it is nothing. In a sense, the singular is not. Hence, the necessary remarkability of its trace, of its endless "retreat" at once redrawing and withdrawing, the (in)finitude of sense in every sense.

Now, this discursive interlude might seem a rather fanciful cosmological fable, perhaps even a questionable allegory of Nancean community in the terms of contemporary astrophysics, were it not that Nancy himself dedicates an entire section of *Corpus* to the specific subject of black holes. What he there describes, though, by the stellar metaphor is the body as the black hole of meaning. Sense, like space-time, comes to an end as whatever corporeality is retreats into itself, a movement Nancy also refers to as an "infinite intussusception, the *proper* devouring itself, all the way to the void at its center" (77). Is this center the singularity of sense or meaning (which is to say no meaning, *because* it is single—that is, in relation to nothing, which is to say literally *senseless*) and the ultimate particularity of the body, of matter as infinitely receding particle? Or are we talking about the point of infinite curvature between body and sense as the kernel or clinamen of that singularity that is of a completely different order from that of the putatively atomistic individual? Is the singular what one would find in the heart with its contractions and expansions, or rather in the nethermost pit of the cavity (that the fullness of the body seems to have become) of the Cartesian entity who there or here, now or once or henceforth says that it is, *ego sum*, at the vanishing point of its fictive or feigned trajectory of self-inquiry or self-doubt? Is it the inescapable gap (or gasp), that heart-stopping syncope, that rhythms the abyssal flights of a logodaedalus? Speculative remarks or sophistic ventriloquism? Nancy's early works already offer an adventurous exploration into some philosophical singularities (named Plato, Descartes, Kant, Hegel) where "sense," "body," "subject" are bracketed and scrambled by the necessity of their exposure onto what they are not. The singular as singular is not; only in its ex-position can something be said to have happened, can something be said to be there, the *seiend da* of *Dasein*. Nor is this exposition a matter of choice: it rejoins what Nancy describes as the very *experience* of freedom in the necessity of exposure, which is to say, of course, the necessity of a community that is always already at loose ends:

> . . . difference is not opposed to identity: difference makes identity possible, and by inscribing that possibility into the very heart of

identity, difference exposes it to the following, namely that its meaning cannot be identical with it. Our identity is us, and *we* designates—once again in the simultaneous and non-decidable reference to our "singularities" and to our "community"—an identity necessarily divided and shared among us and between us. Difference takes place in this dividing and sharing [*partage*], at once the distribution of sense among all significations and the retreat of sense from all significations—a retreat that every signification indicates, at the limit. (*L'oubli de la philosophie*, 98–99; my translation)

We are, only as exposed together to each other and to ourselves on the limit of our singularities, which only are insofar as we are exscribed, each and every time, at the limit of what we are (not).

Such singular being is not to be confused with the perhaps more fashionable term of subject position inspired by Jacques Lacan and popularized by Ernesto Laclau and Chantal Mouffe,[28] a notion that, however fractured or fractal, still bespeaks a certain anatomy of identity as divisible "parts" of a psychic or social formation, which are themselves available for the suspect alignments of identity politics with the disastrous consequences we see all around us today: resurgent nationalisms, ethnic separatisms, religious fundamentalisms of the most varied kinds. Perhaps the singular name that a quarter century ago most distressingly evoked the impasse of positional or territorial identity formation is that of Bosnia-Herzegovina, a veritable vortex of conflicting languages, creeds, and cultures, the violence of whose clash no simple repartition into autonomous regions seemed at the time able to contain. Today, we may add other names, such as Iraq, or Syria, even Belgium, or Catalonia, or post-Brexit, the so-called United Kingdom. No response to such strife can be just that does not begin by jettisoning such idealistic and geographical identities and by recognizing the virtuality and retreat of singularity that makes us ourselves only by our being together as singular in community, by all the ways in which we are the same alone, by our being inextricably together at once as singular and communal, in our shared exposition or coposition, in what Nancy calls the *comparution* of beings.[29] *Le partage des voix*, or the "sharing/splitting of voices," is the title of one of Nancy's earliest works, dating from 1982.[30] Not only does this partaking name the literary communism of being together in difference, but also evokes one of Nancy's defining attributes as a thinker, specifically his penchant for writing not only under his own name but in collaboration with others: not just his long-term partnership in writing with Philippe Lacoue-Labarthe, but his coauthoring of works with Jean-Christophe Bailly, Jean-François Bouthors, Aurélien Barrau, Mathilde Monnier, Abbas Kiarostami,

Federico Ferrari, Adèle Van Reeth, and Jérôme Lèbre, among many others, as well as countless "dialogues," interviews, and other works best described as collective or collaborative.

Nancy thus exemplifies the inoperative community in his writing practice as well as in his so-called finite thinking. We appear together in this poetics of finitude at the limit of ourselves, at or as the frayed edges of a community that can be nothing but frayed edges, at loose ends. What Jean-Luc Nancy has taught us is to begin to think our being together, to think an ethics and politics of singularity from those edges. There, the singular endlessly re-marks itself in its resolute unthinkability as the utter necessity of its being thought, whatever the stain on sense. The spill or swerve that thus defines the event of sense marks its own singularity even as sense in its fundamentally iterative structure of re-marking cannot help but efface the very singularity it would target. We can thus conclude, in response to our initial query, that *singularity is the apocalypse of sense itself*, the revelation of its "end"—namely, the senselessness that is the limit of sense, what it inescapably fails to grasp. What sense does is to perform the singular, but only as iteration, as the end of its revelation as no longer singular but indubitably multiple. The making or coming of sense thus constitutes the poetics of finitude, each time singular in the plural of its iteration, each time plural in the singularity of its (re)marking.

The following study comprises four distinct but interconnected essays to examine Nancy's expansive understanding of *sense* (perception, meaning, direction) and restricted definition of *singularity* (co-posited with plurality)[31] as key to his radical revisions or interruption of philosophy, in a broad set of works across his career. The aim here, however, is not that of a comprehensive or even selective overview of Nancy's work, nor of an attempt to situate his contributions within a historical context, nor to chronicle his manner of reckoning with other thinkers (with one major exception).[32] Rather, the approach taken here is that of a critical reading or commentary that explicates given texts or problems in Nancy's corpus to highlight philosophy's interruption in and through them. Four different paths are taken to examine (1) how he rereads a foundational philosophical text against the grain of tradition (Descartes); (2) how he experiments with an intermittent genre of interventional philosophical writing (the "monograms"); (3) how his deployment of a critical and contradictory term (*retrait*) frames his analyses of politics and community; and finally, (4) how the interruption of sense and singularity in his writings on the body, sensuality, and sexuality underwrites a poetics, and even an ethics, of finitude, what he calls, "finite thinking."

Chapter 1, "Descartes's Iterative Cogito, the *Sum* of Each and Every Time," explicates Nancy's radical and foundational rereading of Descartes, first in the

1978 monograph *Ego sum*, then over the course of the rest of Nancy's work. Nancy reads Descartes's *cogito* as singularly interrupted, or "iterative." He urges us to grasp the foundational statement, *ego sum, ego existo*, as necessarily iterative, as having to be repeated in its singularity, "each time." Far from the continuity of a self-actualizing subjectivity, we encounter the endless interruption of self-evidence, of self-sensing, that can never be fully evident beyond the singular event of its utterance. The analysis enabled by this perspective opens a set of figures that will stake out the senses of the scene of writing, of philosophy's self-presentation, of world-making or "fabling," and of corporal areality. All of these emerge in later works as prominent concerns of Nancy's capacious philosophical attention. Most importantly, Nancy's subsequent deconstruction of the opposition between body and mind (or the sensible and the intelligible) derives from this same thesis of interrupted consciousness while revealing that relation as an *unum quid*, or "as-if one," that unravels the ways in which thinking and perceiving, meaning and sensation, are differing but interrelated forms of cogitation, differing kinds of sense-making as a practice of difference.[33]

Chapter 2, "Monograms: Writing Singular Plural," critically details Nancy's experiments as a philosopher with an interruptive genre of short, occasional writings that model an engagement with the current context or "actuality" of their composition. The term "monogram" derives from Kant's concept of the schema as a hinge between the sensible and the intelligible. Nancy explicitly takes up the term, expands upon its implications, and galvanizes it into a thinking that tries to make sense of the singular, including the singular events of our time. This is a claim that goes to the heart of Nancy's career-long reflection on the form as well as the content of philosophical writing as a mode of critical intervention. As such, the monograms propose a new (or perhaps merely renewed) genre of philosophical writing that is punctual, fragmented, and interrupted, corresponding to a thinking inhabited and shaped by its finitude, a thinking that effectively questions the sense of philosophy's singular engagement with the world, with the unheard-of in philosophy. As a series, these writings emerge "each time" with a sense of plural singularity. Far from being simply "mono," the monogram appears to be irredeemably plural, as its each time plural title of *monogrammes* suggests. But then the monogram(s) cannot be a simple trait, not something simply singular but always already plural, repeated and repeatable as per the nexus of lines that contours or outlines a picture (the definition of a monogram). That picture is the pattern whose sense emerges from the retracing of lines whose linearity withdraws before the instance or instantiation of the image. The monogram is not a simple trait, but always already a complex *re-trait*, a redrawing that is a withdrawing, a retreat that is also an emergence, hence a figure of philosophy as complex *inter-vention*, literally a coming in-between or in the midst of a world it *inter-rupts*. Nancy's philosophical monograms thus model the interventionist, interruptive style found in much of his later writings on topics as diverse as the disaster of Fukushima, the COVID pandemic, or the foibles of French president Macron. They figure the interruption of philosophy in its actuality.[34]

Chapter 3, "The 'Singular Logic of the Retreat': Interruptions of the Political," follows chronologically with the germination of Nancy's political thinking by taking a close look at the senses of one of Nancy's guiding philosophical tropes, that of the critical and contradictory French word *"retrait,"* which is usually translated as withdrawal but which also implies a re-drawing or re-inscribing of a trait or trace, and which I choose after others to translate with arguable literality as "retreat" (following Simon Sparks in his translating *"le retrait du politique"* by "retreating the political"). The chapter will look at Derrida's similar use of the term in his early "The *Retrait* of Metaphor,"[35] which corresponds with Nancy's adopting the word in place of "retrenchment," which Nancy had previously used with roughly the same effect in *Ego Sum*. I then review and query the ways in which the concept of "retreat" is transformed from its inspiration in Derrida's discussion of metaphor, of all things, into a powerful engine of political critique articulated with Hannah Arendt's theory of totalitarianism, on the one hand, and Freud's analysis of mass psychology, on the other. The "retreat of the political" designates an essence of the political that is not actually political, something before or behind the *polis* that underwrites a form of *mitsein* or being together that seeks something more than mere life. Remarkably, it is the figure of the mother that appears as the very modeling of the retreat, as the sense of a withdrawal that is also the singularity of birth, which is the very corporeal interruption that defines the ethos of being both together and apart. The structured multiplicity of retreating, hesitating between with-drawing and re-drawing, emerges as a powerful articulator of sense and singularity.

Chapter 4, "*Corpus Interruptus:* Uncommon Sense and the Singular Crossings of *Eros, Logos, and Tekhnè*," builds on the preceding analyses to address the differential treatment of sense (sensation, perception, intellection) in Nancy via an analysis of *Corpus* and his subsequent writings on the body, aesthetics, and sexuality, notably *Sexistence*, as well as *Corpus II* and *III*,[36] and then revisiting some of his earlier writings on art and aesthetics. I show how Nancy's expansive definition of sense guides his broader analyses of sensation in his definition of the body as the "interval between two senses"—that is, the body as itself a space of interruption. Not the locus of some "common sense" but sense itself as uncommon. What he provocatively terms "sexistence," in the work by that title, matters, then, less for the analysis of sexuality per se than for Nancy's uncommon positioning of *eros* in relation to *logos* and *tekhnè*. For him, all three of these categories reinscribe the fundamental transcendence of existence or ek-sistence, literally standing outside oneself as what defines oneself as such. It is Nancy's triangulation of sex, language, and technology (including art) as mutually interruptive that brings the analysis of sense and singularity to a conclusion as the foundational articulation of the world we find ourselves in and whose patency remains the task of philosophy, and of the arts, to disclose as such. That disclosure, I would add, also takes place as sense's interruption by the singular in each of the three categories: language by the singularity of poetry, technology by the singularity of art, and sex by the singularity of birth either as creation or procreation, an outcome that conjures up again the curious "retreat of the mother," a theme that reappears in *Coming* and especially in Nancy's last work, *Cruor*, recently translated into English as *Corpus III*, thus extending a set of reflections on the body that spans the entire latter half of Nancy's career.

In particular, the *sense* of skin (experienced through the singularity of touching) as literal ex-position or exscription defines an ethics and aesthetics of exteriority and interruption in line with a finite thinking that is open to both the singular and plural, repetition and difference, open to the creation of world, and especially open to the singularly unheard, the unseen, the unsensed, the unknown. The *sense* of singularity and the *singularity* of sense together draw and redraw the lines of our *exposure* to what is finite, each and every time, yet endlessly, infinitely reinscribed, hence our exposure to or as the ecstasy of being drawn out, of a finite thinking that is *surprised* each and every time by its own freedom and the unsuspected inventiveness of its philosophical *poein*, by its "world creation."

The poetics of finitude senses and makes sense of the world in its infinite singularities, but that is also to come to terms with singularity as each time the beginning and/or end of sense. That precarious (non)relation of sense and singularity effectively challenges the traditional philosophical aims of either a return to origins or a proleptic teleology, hence disallowing the metaphysical ideals of either beginning or end. We are confronted with the necessity but also the freedom of a philosophy constantly interrupted and thus constantly recommenced. Nancy's consequent rethinking of what it means to do philosophy in and as interruption thus urges us, despite the daily apocalypse of a world reeling from disease, war, social unrest, and environmental catastrophe, to be attentive to thought that is necessarily still to come. For us, the necessity of the relation between singular and plural and the unsuspected convergences between sense as sensation/perception and sense as meaning mark and remark the finitude of a thinking exposed to the world, in- or ex-scribed on the limit as sense, as the limit of sense itself in the face of infinite singularity. The poetics of such finite thinking, or thinking with and within finitude, is also what makes for the very sense and singularity of Nancy's own philosophical enterprise.

1
Descartes's Iterative Cogito, or the *Sum* of Each and Every Time

All philosophers, at some point or other, must reckon with the work and legacy of René Descartes—and French philosophers, in particular, cannot forgo a determining encounter with the presumed father of modern philosophy. Jean-Luc Nancy is no exception, and his engagement with Descartes is both early and decisive in terms of the development of his own thinking. *Ego sum*, first published in 1979, is the third and final of a series of monographs where Nancy takes on first Hegel (*The Speculative Remark*, 1973), then Kant (*The Discourse of the Syncope: Logodaedalus*, 1976), before setting his sights on Descartes. One could view these three monographs spanning the decade of the 1970s, in fact Nancy's *first* three single-authored books, as a set of preparatory studies that enable his subsequent breakthrough works of the 1980s, none of which are monographs but rather problem-oriented studies: *Le partage des voix* (1982), *The Inoperative Community* (1983), *L'impératif catégorique* (1983), *L'oubli de la philosophie* (1986), and *The Experience of Freedom* (1988). While Nancy would occasionally return to the monograph in later years (Hegel, Heidegger, Derrida),[1] the shift from the early monographic triptych to a broad-ranging set of philosophical interventions remains striking.

It is certainly tempting to view *Ego Sum*, then, as a kind of *oeuvre charnière* in the development of Nancy's philosophical corpus, including the very corporal theme of the body itself, as well as that of the "world," the whole question of how philosophy *presents* itself, the structural aporias of finitude, singularity, and interruption, and even the thought of "thought" itself. Curiously, and despite these promising qualities, *Ego Sum* has received remarkably little attention over the years. While some excerpts were translated early on (*Oxford Literary Review*, *MLN*, *Glyph*), the book as a whole only appeared in English translation in 2016, nearly forty years after its initial publication.[2]

While Kant, Hegel, and especially Heidegger loom large in any consideration of Nancy's philosophical inspiration, the early monograph on Descartes should not be excluded simply because it would be absurd to claim a Cartesian dimension to Nancy's work. Rather, it is his powerfully critical and unconventional reading of the Cartesian text that should garner our attention to the extent that many of Nancy's signature terms, themes, and approaches find their earliest iteration in *Ego Sum*. No less an attentive reader than Jacques Derrida signals the importance of *Ego Sum* in Nancy's intellectual trajectory by starting his massive study *On Touching—Jean-Luc Nancy* with a reading of Nancy's reading of Descartes.[3]

Ergo ego

Let's start with the title, *Ego Sum*, at once pleonasm and figure of litotes, saying too much and not nearly enough. The classic expectation would have been for the title to read *Cogito ergo sum*, the Latin for the canonical "I think, therefore I am," which never actually appears per se in any Latin text by Descartes.[4] Instead, Nancy boldly draws the title explicitly from the following line of the Second Meditation, which he cites as an isolated epigraph following the title page: "Denique statuendum sit hoc pronuntiatum, *ego sum, ego existo*, quoties a me profertur, vel mente concipitur, necessario esse verum" [I must finally conclude that the proposition, *I am, I exist*, is necessarily true whenever it is put forward by me or conceived in my mind] (CSM II:7; AT VII:25). Nancy follows with his own expansive rendering to unpack Descartes's terse Latin: "Finally one must rule, establish, decide, erect as a statue and ground as a statute the fact that this pronouncement, the utterance, this statement, *I am, I exist*, each time I proclaim, propose, or pronounce it, each time I conceive it in my mind or each time it is conceived by my mind, is necessarily true" (*Ego Sum*, xxvii). Nancy's unpacking of this sentence from the *Meditations* opens up the questions that guide the subsequent chapters of *Ego Sum*, all likewise given Latin titles,[5] each taken from a different text of Descartes. Before broaching the specific readings of the chapters, it is worth lingering a little longer over the choice of this sentence from the *Meditations*, the implications of the title, and Nancy's gloss in the form of an expansive translation.

Ego Sum repositions the discussion of Descartes on ontological rather than merely epistemological grounds, following upon Heidegger's well-known critique.[6] It is the question of being rather than that of knowing that comes to the fore, with whatever we call "thinking" emerging as an outcome of being and indeed, of our specific being as *Dasein*, rather than the other way around, which is the canonical approach of Cartesian scholarship.[7] Nancy nonetheless takes a determined distance from a strictly ontological reading by "interrogating not the essence, but the *proposing* or the *proposer* [*le proposant*], so to speak, of the proposition: ego uttering itself. Which amounts to the same thing as interrogating the 'essence' (if there is still one) of the *first* proposition: 'ego sum'" (13).

The *first* proposition of *first* philosophy (*Meditations on First Philosophy* being the full title of Descartes's work), "ego sum," already says too little, as evidenced by the longer sentence within which it is embedded, and too much, since the "ego" attached to "sum" is redundant in Latin, where the personal pronoun is *already* implicit in the verb. This supplemental "ego" is, as Nancy states citing Nietzsche, already "an *interpretation* of the process and does not belong to the process itself" (15; Nancy's emphasis).[8] Latin grammarians, at this point, would probably retort that the "ego" of "ego sum" is less pleonastic per se than emphatic, as if to underscore the need to reaffirm the ego's stake in the issue, but that only supports even more Nancy's fundamental argument in the book: "*The Cartesian establishment of the Subject corresponds, through the most binding necessity of its own structure, to the instantaneous exhaustion of its essential possibilities*" (16; Nancy's emphasis). This unraveling of the "subject" in its very constituting is, of course, classic deconstruction, and the emphasis on the subject is framed by Nancy's opening remarks about a certain "return of the subject" in "contemporary discourses" of the time (1ff.).[9] But it is now quite a while since 1979, and it seems, on the one hand, like we have been subjected to countless and ongoing "returns of the subject," while on the other hand, Nancy's own truculent questioning in 1986 about "who comes after the subject?" still remains barely heard and with few attempts at an answer.[10] Unless, of course, we understand Nancy's whole trajectory past *Ego Sum* as his long and diligent attempt at an answer. Completing his early trio of philosophical monographs with a study of Descartes, the veritable poster child for the concept of the subject, Nancy goes on to engage a whole host of philosophical issues—community, world, the political, religion, art, the body—that require thinking past or at least through the deconstruction of the subject. But if the study of Descartes represents the very high point of this approach, its *nec plus ultra*, it is also the tipping point to something else. That something else is what remains to be explored.

Cogito interruptus

The *de trop* status of the "ego" in *ego sum* is the most evident sign of this tipping point, but even more glaring is the ego's ontological vulnerability in the sentence Nancy chooses as his point of departure and title of the first part of his preface, *quoties a me profertur*. The canonical reception of the statement *cogito ergo sum* seems to imply the permanence and selfsameness of the thinking subject, the singular prize of Descartes's method of hyperbolic doubt, the "indubitable foundation" on the basis of which the remaining task of philosophy is merely to deduce progressively the rest of knowledge (in his time, the existence of God and of the world, and later the ongoing validity of scientific experimentation). But this sentence from the Second Meditation, arguably *the crucial* sentence of the *Meditations*, strikingly limits the applicable truth of the cogito to only as much as or as often as the subject reiterates it, as underscored by the Latin adverb *quoties*, which is typically and correctly rendered as "whenever," but I would like to emphasize the performative or iterative sense of the word, as qualifying the truth of the cogito as being dependent upon its actual use or utterance. *Ego sum* is true, whenever I say or think it—that is, *every* time I "proffer" it, *each* time it is uttered, an implication corroborated by Nancy's French translation as *"toutes les fois,"* an expression that also recalls the Latin ecclesiastical expression *toties quoties*, which applies to the granting of generalized indulgences whose effects can be called upon whenever they are needed. To underscore the weight of the word in this sentence from the *Meditations* and to emphasize its consequences, I am modifying the translation of *quoties* to "each and every time." This adjustment also underscores Nancy's interpretation of the cogito as an early version of the *"à chaque fois"* or "at each time" that marks his later reflections on time as the very *difference* that is time, to the very unexpectedness or surprise of time as event, as the incessant "coming to presence of another present"—that is, in its very eventfulness *as* event.[11]

But if the ontological state of the subject is only "necessarily true" each and every time he "proffers" it, then what happens when *"ego sum"* is not being said or thought, whenever it is not "cogitated"? One is reminded of the old joke about Descartes in the bar: noticing his glass is empty, the bartender asks the philosopher if he would like another drink. "I think not," Descartes responds and instantly vanishes into nothingness. Do I have to keep thinking myself to be in order actually to be? The question is not trivial given Descartes's explicit formulation of this crucial sentence as the "indubitable foundation" of his "first philosophy." If we are to follow Descartes here *à la lettre*, then the so-called cogito, or even just the expression *"ego sum,"* is no longer a constative utterance (or a statement of fact) but a performative one that must be repeated endlessly, "each and every time [*quoties*]," to secure the truth of the subject.[12] But then the cogito is also iterative in the sense Derrida gives to the stem, *iter*, whose Sanskrit root *itara* means "other," hence an iteration or reiteration is a difference marked in/as repetition, a repetition marked in/as difference.[13] In Descartes's case, we need look no further than his reiterating the cogito first as *ego sum*, then as *ego existo*. What this implies is a discontinuous performance of subjectivity, a subject ceaselessly "inter-rupted" in its being, a being interrupted—to use still another term Nancy will mobilize to great effect in his subsequent work—as the essence of a distinctly finite subjectivity. "Thus is not the one who says *ego sum an other* than the one who says *sum certus me esse rem cogitationem* ("I am certain that I am a thinking being") at the beginning of the Third Meditation" (118n; translation modified). If there is cogito with or without *ego sum*, it is a cogito radically interrupted, a *cogito interruptus*.[14]

This *cogito interruptus*, though, is not just some bathos of illogicality (by design or not) or the tedium of distraction (whether constructive or not) but the very condition of subjective being, the chasm of the subject, *sub-jectum, hypokeimonon*, the absence upon which its presence is staked: that "deep whirlpool" described by Descartes at the very beginning of the second *Meditation*, "which tumbles me around so that I can neither stand on the bottom nor swim up to the top" (AT VII:23–24; CSM II:160). But it is that watery abyss *posited as itself—ego sum!—that posits* the subject on/as the sought-for Archimedean "firm and immovable point," that "certain and unshakable" foundation, from which all of "first philosophy" can be securely derived or deduced. Floundering, co-agitating (as per the etymological sense of *cogitare*), in boundlessly deep waters is where the subject always already finds itself, performing the solid ground of its being in the slippery, endlessly, ever-repeated iterations of its own *summation*, or *con-summation* as being whenever or each and every time it is said or thought, *ego sum, ego existo, quoties a me profertur vel mente concipitur*. And complicating this self-positing of the *ego* that thinks itself *sum* is the passive voice of the verbs *profertur* and *concipitur*, as if the very speaking and conceiving of the subject were something that happens to it, or befalls it, rather than the active work of a self-generating self.

This *interruption* of the subject per se is never named as such by Nancy in *Ego Sum*, even if it is repeatedly described. The word, as far as I can tell, never appears in *Ego Sum*, and certainly not as a conceptual operator of any kind. The concept of interruption does appear later in Nancy's work, and most notably with the chapter on "Myth Interrupted" in *The Inoperative Community*.[15] There, interruption is described neither as distraction nor as the kind of "disruption" that is synonymous in corporate environs with "innovation" (while surreptitiously belying new forms of performance enhancement, capitalist profitability, and exploitation). Rather, Nancy's interruption describes "the suspense and the 'difference' of sense in the very origin of sense" (178n), a formulation that explicitly recalls the Derridean notion of "writing" as well as, again, his concept of *iter* and *iteration* as the alterity of repetition. Interruption is the other of repetition, or repetition *as* other. Every interruption is different, but they are all the same *as* interruption. Interruption is not simply something that happens to an entity (sense, subject, myth, community, work); it is what constitutively suspends it in its claim to self-completion, what reveals the very lack of completion in its being, what reveals its finitude not just with relation to what stands outside of itself but in terms of its own inner constitution as such, the finitude by dint of which it shares being-in-common with others. Interruption is the structure of (in)completion that haunts the myth of self-sameness while enabling the supposed subject's ongoing reiteration, the finitude of its temporality, or the temporality of its finitude. As such, interruption hearkens back to Nancy's second monograph, on the "discourse of syncope" in Kant, a.k.a. Logodaedelus, which a note in *Ego Sum* (120n) reveals to be the source for another word, more in line with "Cartesian premises," that appears not only in *Ego Sum* but frequently throughout Nancy's work and to be construed in tandem with that of interruption—namely, "areality." The careful definition of this term in fact closes the second and final section of *Ego sum*'s "opening":

> What occurs to the subject, what befalls it—instead of supporting it with a sub-stance, and even instead of supporting it with a word—is the end, as we will see, its *areality*, . . . : both lack of reality (which is not an absence, and makes it impossible to carry out a negative egology in the fashion of negative theology), and area—*area* in Latin—the quality of space and extension prior to any spatiality. Areality is not the transcendental form of space either; prior to the transcendental regime (but only thinkable on the basis of Kant), more "primitive," areality extends itself as the unascribable place of the formless experience the "subject" has of its "own" chaos. Precisely because it has thought the absolute subjectivity of substance, Descartes's thought keeps, at every instant, seeing—without seeing anything—this experience befalling it unexpectedly. (19)

Areality plunges us back into Descartes's abyssal watery world, more of a submerging than a sub-jecting, a falling with no standing, and quintessentially the "unformed experience" of his "'own' chaos." Areality is both a nowhere and a distinct if "unascribable" place, a literal *u*-topia that appears as the spatial version of temporal interruption, the discontinuity of a spacing "prior to the transcendental regime," the marking of a prior or *a priori* difference before whatever can be said to constitute the subject, again a form of writing (*dum scribo*). But if areality is constitutive of subjectivity and of substance itself, then it cannot be simply something that "befalls" or happens to the subject "unexpectedly," since it would necessarily precede subjectivity, and for that matter, "experience." On the contrary, it would seem that the subjection or submersion into one's "own" chaos comes before the substance of experience—but how can a chaos be one's own? how can one "own" chaos unless it is through an appropriation that converts the chaos into form, submersion into substance, enabling a subject who can then experience that chaos as a mere accident of being, something that falls onto it or that it falls into with all the improvisational unexpectedness of a befalling? Areality is a happening before the subject, an a priori fall into being, the unexpectedness of a collapse prior to any erection, primordial castration, the (non)sum of *sum*. As such, the cogitation that proves the existence of that *sum* can itself only come after the ontological priority of being itself. Because I think, I know I am, but it is only because I am that I can think, and therefore know that I am. Areality, interruption, so many names for the retreat of thought itself. *Non cogito ergo ego sum interruptus.*

Singuli characteres in charta exprimuntur

Between areality/interruption, or between "between," we come across the scene of *dum scribo*, the first full chapter of *Ego Sum*, whose very typography and narrative voice interrupt the conventions of academic discourse (tacitly respected until this point in the book), first by typesetting the entire chapter in italics (except for quotations that then correspondingly appear in roman type), and second by seeming to speak in the very voice of Descartes in a most ironic adoption or adaptation of prosopopoeia. This chapter's very style thus figures an alternative space of visual, narrative, and conceptual disruption, a space in which Nancy appears to mimic Descartes's description of what happens "while I am writing" (*dum scribo*). This "scene" of writing, taken from the all-important Twelfth Rule, which resumes and concludes the first third of the *Regulae ad directionem ingenii*, also provides a foretaste of the famously reclusive philosopher's penchant for self-portraiture, later deployed on a grand scale in the *Discourse on Method*.

But this is not a simple moment of writerly self-reflection, a ready-to-hand pulling back of the curtain to reveal the writer in the privacy and retreat of his study. Rather, the entire scene is presented within the larger context of an analogy about the way we understand sensory impression. While Descartes subsequently cautions that "this should be understood *merely* as an analogy, for nothing quite like this power is to be found in corporeal things" (CSM I:42; AT X:415; my emphasis), the so-called analogy works in a very imperfect and limited way. Cognition, or what Descartes here calls, following the Aristotelian scholastic tradition, the "common sense," works for him in a manner utterly unlike that of a hand guiding a pen whose trail of ink cursively inscribes a set of letters and words. Rather, the tip of the pen, instead of actively projecting ink, is supposed to represent the body's passive reception of external stimuli "when an external sense organ is stimulated by an object" and "receives" it as a "figure." Descartes proposes a schema (to use a Kantian term) that is both more and less than a "mere analogy." On the one hand, perception occurs as the "imprinting" upon our senses by external objects "in exactly the same way as" a seal imprints its image on wax. On the other hand, the understanding, which corresponds to the other end of the pen, the intellection that follows directly upon the writing of the sensory imprint (*dum scribo, intelligo*) can either follow from the senses or affect them in turn. The "airy" writing—another instance of areality—at the upper end of the pen in motion immediately communicates with the sense impressions of the lower but can direct these in ways that are different. Nancy brilliantly seizes upon the fluidity and inconsistencies of Descartes's extended analogy ("this pen is unimaginable" [37]) to underscore that the pen's movement again is not a cursive movement at all but caught within a discontinuous structure of printing or imprinting: "While I am writing, at each instant, the distinctive mark of a phonematic unit of the language is imprinted: The printed whole of this phonography will not constitute a duration, since it will be a *sum* of characterological units. The *sum* will be characteristic: it will constitute the impression of the figure of thought expressed by language" (24; emphasis added). Like Descartes's metaphor of the wax and seal, the imprinting of each "unit" of language, each letter, corresponds to an instant, "at each instant while I am writing," or each and every time (*quoties*), but the instant, adds Nancy, "is not a chronological measure; it is quite evidently the achronic limit of such a measure" (23–24), again a certain interruptive areality. Note that Descartes speaks of individual letters being traced on the paper (*singuli characteres in charta exprimuntur*), or more properly, singular characters being "ex-pressed" or printed out (through a passivity not unlike in the earlier line from *Meditations* about the veracity of *ego sum* in the passive voice being put forward [*profertur*] or conceived [*conciptur*]). Writing is the metaphor of thinking being as imprinting/imprinted pen. As Nancy writing in the voice of Descartes specifies, "My model is a typographical one, like that of a printer—I am a writing machine, a typewriter" [*Je suis moi-même une machine à écrire*] (23). Or perhaps more like a film? Where the action of the "motion" picture happens through interruption and reprojection of *instantanés* or individual images (frames) and a projected areality: both lacking in substantial reality (even for so-called documentaries) and yet a recognizable space that is not itself spatially assignable. What appears as continuity is but a screen effect, with camera and projector functioning like the two ends of Descartes's pen. So too, the fragile sense of continuous subjectivity summed up by the iterative, interrupted, areal cogito, the work of understanding even as I write: *dum scribo, intelligo.* "My fundamental property lies in the immobility of my movement, in the death that in each instant interrupts and collects my writing gesture" (37). *Ego sum* is but the "sum" or *ad-sum (da-sein)* of every instant in its endless interrupting, in its ever-repeated death, *quoties*, each and every time. Playing on the Latin word Descartes uses to describe this perilous pen, *calamo*, Nancy concludes still in mimicry of Descartes's voice, "I am a calamity" (37), only to reiterate a few lines later: "Truth is a calamity" (38).

Cogitationes publicae

This screen effect, but also, to try and respect Descartes's text, the effect of the seal's imprinting onto wax, is also the calamity of a certain appearance or mask, the scripted entrance of the philosopher falling out onto the world stage, the *larvatus prodeo*, "I come forward masked," recorded in Descartes's early "*cogitationes privatae*" (CSM I:2; AT X:213), and the point of departure for Nancy's second chapter: *Larvatus pro deo*. What we could call Descartes's "coming out" will take place later and more dramatically in 1637 as the anonymously published self-portrait better known as the *Discourse on Method*, Descartes's first published book. But again, as with the analogy of the writing pen, the trope of self-portrayal is not as simple as it seems and freights its own set of inconsistencies and contradictions, "this complex and crafty device" [*ce dispositif complexe et retors*] (44; translation modified), which Nancy carefully again unpacks at length. The self-portrait turns out to be more of a screen, or mask, by which the "anonymous" author can judge the reaction to his method while (not) revealing his identity[16]: "I shall be glad to reveal in this discourse what paths I have followed, and to represent my life in it as if in a picture, so that everyone may judge it for oneself; and thus, learning from public response the opinions held of it, I shall add a new means of self-instruction to those I am accustomed to using]" (CSM I:112; AT VI:3–4). It is again a question of showing something, of making something seen—namely, the "paths" followed by the narrator in his intellectual itinerary and the *sum* of his life as if synoptically represented in a painting. In other words, a diachronic narrative of his ideas AND a synchronic self-portrait. It is not immediately clear, however, if there is any difference between these two. The problem is raised by the second moment in this pragmatic itinerary, when the addressee/spectator of the philosopher/addressor's self-representation is called upon to "judge" it. But what is being judged, the philosopher's thoughts or his life? The lack of distinction suggests that the judgment on the one is the same as on the other. This is where Nancy intervenes precisely to underscore the claim that "this method cannot be cloaked in an argument based on authority: It can be presented only according to what should be called an argument based on *authorship*: that of which *I* alone am the author can impose itself only upon the judgment that each *I* will be able to pass upon it" (40; Nancy's emphasis). But this authorial judgment in turn breaks down to the reader/spectator's recognition of the author's existence as such, to his self-presentation or de-monstration as author, to the mere verification of his ontological status as self-conceiving being: "Standing before the picture, then, and commenting on it, the viewer would perhaps verify not the resemblance, . . . but the very existence, the *sum* of the original. I am this thinking being that the other sees, or thinks s/he sees" (44; Nancy's emphasis). But what this means is that the very *sum* of the cogito depends upon a fundamental *mitsein*, or relation to otherness that both subtends (supports? subjects?) and undermines the very self-conception of the subject. The subject is literally ex-posed, or as Nancy puts it, "ex-cogitated": "The cogito, insofar as it has or makes a figure, is excogitated; it is only thought by exposing itself, by feigning to expose itself and by exposing its feint, its fiction, its extravagance" (50). The philosopher's cogitative self-positing necessarily and simultaneously co-posits some other: "A fictive viewer is thus everywhere necessary for the exhibition of the portrait, that is, for the *conception* of the *subject* of the picture, or again, for *truth*" (58; Nancy's emphases), on the understanding that "'fictive' here does not mean 'imaginary' but designates a position or a *role* that is structurally indispensable in the production of the *theoretical* truth of the subject" (59; Nancy's emphases).

This structural necessity of there being multiple subjectivities coterminous with any given subjectivity is given a further twist by Nancy, underscoring Descartes's theological reasoning: "The resulting situation . . . is homologous to the recognition of the existence of God by means of the vision of his idea (faithful copy) within me. The viewer of the picture sees Descartes as Descartes sees God . . . *larvatus pro deo*—I am masked in order to occupy God's place" (44), whence the word game that gives the chapter its title, from *prodeo* (to come forward, or proceed) to *pro deo* (for or on behalf of God). One is tempted to read out this structure in terms of Lacan's distinction between "other" and "Other," between the homologous other of mirrored spectatorship and the *sujet supposé savoir* of the paternal law. Or, for that matter, the homeosis that underlies the deconstruction of Christianity, as Nancy will later develop in *The Dis-Enclosure*.

Indeed, one can see an entire line of Nancean thought emerge from this de-structuring of subjectivity, from the very thesis of *The Inoperative Community* and the essays gathered in *The Birth to Presence* to the argument of *Being Singular Plural*, as well as much of Nancy's political thought from *Rejouer le politique* and *The Experience of Freedom* up through *The Truth of Democracy*.

Indeed, one of the key contributions Nancy has made is in his insistent thinking of community, freedom, and the political, not from the basis of subjectivity or as some expansion of it that retains all the problems of the subject, but rather by thinking the "we" before and as the condition of the "I" as a kind of a priori *mitsein*. Ironic that the first germination of this critical approach comes from the reading of Descartes, the thinker most frequently accused of a kind of intellectual solipsism and as an early exemplar for the ideology of individualism. As Nancy recapitulates in *The Inoperative Community*:

> ... before recognition [reconnaissance], there is knowing [connaissance]: knowing without knowledge, and without "consciousness," that *I* am first of all exposed to the other, and exposed to the exposure of the other. *Ego sum expositus*: on closer inspection one might discern here a paradox, namely that behind Cartesian *évidence*—that *évidence* so certain that the subject cannot not have it and that it need not be proven in any way—there must lie not some nocturnal bedazzlement of the *ego*, not some existential immanence of a self-affection, but solely community—that community about which Descartes seems to know so little, or nothing at all. In this respect the Cartesian subject would form the inverse figure of the experience of community, of singularity. The Cartesian subject knows himself to be exposed, and he knows himself because he is exposed (does not Descartes present himself as his own portrait?). (31; translation modified)

But, as we saw earlier, Nancy also offers another narrative for the emergence, the coming out, the processional entrance of the thinking subject, one that begins not with a foundational otherness or an immersive *mitsein* but with the foundational experience of the world as chaos: "The radical or even the original nature of the Cartesian enterprise requires that it begin with Chaos—inseparably, indistinguishably with chaos and with the subject. The minimal condition is at once the creation of a chaos by a subject, and the conception of the subject evidenced by the matter of this chaos" (54). Nancy playfully terms this version of cogito the *chaogito*: "To know chaos is to know oneself as such." This copresencing of subject and chaos evokes that other great strand of Nancy's thought, regarding the sense of the world, whose roots begin here and in the title of Nancy's third chapter from *Ego sum: Mundus est fabula*.

Mundus factum est

How can we reconcile this apparent divergence between community and world, between the cogito, as structurally implicit but unavowed *mitsein*, and the *chaogito*, as unacknowledged copresence of self and world? What matters here is less some conceptual difference between world and community, both of which terms Nancy has consistently tried to keep both as rigorous and as open as possible. "Community" is certainly not limited to *dasein* or to human beings, or even just to living creatures, but also potentially inclusive of inanimate objects, to all beings, in fact, to the extent that we and they are all with one another, co-appearing as being-in-common.[17] "World" too is clearly not to be understood merely as the geophysical sphere of the planet we inhabit, nor even in some restricted regionalist sense (such as the "worlds" of Louis XIV, of sports, of Islam, of night clubs) but simply as a totality or space of meaning (CW 41, 120n), as "a differential articulation of singularities that make sense in articulating themselves" (SW 78), "the being exposed of the ones to the others" (SW 71). And just as community should be understood neither as an organic unity nor as an aggregation of pre-existing individuals, so too does Nancy caution against "construing the relation between humanity and world as a relation between subject and object" (SW 56). Just as community can only ever appear within the context of a specific world or worlds, so too does the differential structure of a world imply the fundamental *mitsein* or being-with of beings that defines a community.

At issue, then, in Nancy's reading of Descartes appears to be two alternative ways of understanding the cogito that differ in significant ways from the traditional view of Descartes's grounding of philosophy in the subject's self-certainty, which *both* objectivizes the world *and* fails to think the reality of communal existence.[18] Nancy's careful reading instead argues the priority of both world and community in the very possibility of the cogito. Still, how are we to understand the relation between the *chaogito* of the metaphysician floundering in a bottomless watery world and the requisite enabling gaze of the other for the masked philosopher stepping out onto the stage or hiding behind his self-portrait? "*Mundus est fabula*" is the chapter of *Ego sum* that articulates this bifurcated narrative, interestingly not as one might anticipate, by directly unpacking the concept of world or *mundus*, but by focusing on the workings of *fabula*: fable making, storytelling, fictionalizing, feigning. Presumably, if we can understand "fabling," perhaps we can better understand "world," which, as the expression goes, is itself a fable. Descartes, as Nancy details, does not hesitate to describe his own work as a kind of fable, most explicitly in the unpublished *Treatise on the World*, which he explicitly designates as a fable about an imaginary world whose properties can be systematically deduced from first principles. The validity of that philosophical fable is supported by the demonstrable coincidence of the properties deduced with the properties observed in our own, actual world. Even more dramatically, he applies the term "fable" to the very discourse of the *Discourse on Method*:

> My present aim, then, is not to teach the method which everyone must follow in order to direct his reason correctly, but only to reveal how I have tried to direct my own.... I am presenting this work only as a story or, if you prefer, a fable, in which, among certain examples worthy of imitation, you will perhaps also find many others that it would be right not to follow; and so I hope it will be useful for some without being harmful to any, and that everyone will be grateful to me for my frankness. (CSM I:112; AT VII:4)

As Nancy remarks, this is a most unusual fable, which aims not to teach in the classical sense—*fabula docet*—of an instructive "moral" that serves as the soul for the fable's narrative, or body,[19] but merely to present examples that can be followed or not according to the reader's whim. The examples given turn out to be nothing more than the tale of the author's life and *his* search for truth, thus making of him an exemplary figure, the example of thought in action—that is, of a thought or rather a thinking that in fact corroborates the existence of the thinking being itself, here redacted in the French text of the *Discourse* with the classically received formulation, "I think, therefore I am [*je pense donc je suis*]."[20] But as Nancy observes, this reduction of moralizing fable to exemplary narrative to ontological claim makes of the *Discourse* no longer a simple case of exemplarity that may or may not be imitated: "The passage to the limit of the example is what cannot be imitated; it is the original—an original that anyone can produce (perhaps), but that no one can reproduce. Such is the *cogito*" (78).

Later in the chapter, Nancy invokes Benveniste's elaboration of the performative utterance to underscore *once again* the validity of the cogito only in its performative uttering, *quoties*, each and every time. No one can imitate this utterance or "reproduce" it: "The cogito cannot be said by an actor" (86). To utter the cogito is to produce it in and only in the actuality of its utterance. But if anyone can truthfully utter the cogito, can produce it as such, then the exemplarity of Descartes's fable is and is not "his," but the singular plural of any given being's being there, "that is, an ontology that blends with the invention of the discourse of my life, the invention of my life *as* discourse (or fable)" (83; Nancy's emphasis). Performing the cogito, like any other performance, is an event, but in the case of the cogito, "the event is here nothing other than the performance itself, or rather the *being* coextensive with this performance: *I am*" (85; Nancy's emphasis). The "performance" of the cogito is the event of being, the *(ego) sum* that happens each and every time it occurs, whether as "thinking," or more specifically in the course of the hypothetical doubting that leads to the advent of the cogito, as doubting, as feigning (to doubt), as fabling, or gearing all the way down to the etymological antecedents, as *fari*, *for* (to speak). The cogito is, as Nancy puts it, the "self-performation, even the self-formation through the statement [*énoncé*] of the being of the one who utters [*énonciateur*] as being of truth" (85). This "true being [*l'être vrai*]," Nancy continues, "does not consist in a statement [*énoncé*], any more than in the substance who utters, or in the position of an utterance [*énonciation*], for substance, position, meaning of the statement are all performed in 'cogito' [one is tempted to add, 'in-cognito'—GV]. Rather, it consists in an *uttering* [*énoncer*], in the *uttering* of utterance, of the one who utters, and the statement" (85, translation modified). And to the extent that, "as pragmatic linguistics asserts, all utterances are fundamentally performatives," cogito comes down to a "general or generalized '*for*'" (85). "I am" cannot be distinguished from "I say," *sum* from *dico*, but at the same time that this *cogito/for* is only true each and every time I "proffer [profertur]" it, "bring it forward," whether by "pronouncing or conceiving" it—that is, each and every time I *perform* the event of the truth of being there, *seiend da, da-sein, ad-sum*.

Nancy describes this conundrum as a form of retrenchment (*retrancher*), another word that anticipates his more widespread and well-known use of the word *retrait*: retreat, both re- and with- drawing. Retrenchment is a trenchant iteration that emphasizes the difference in the re-treat of repetition, literally a re-trenching that can mean excision, subtraction, or withdrawal as well as a "doubling down" or "digging in" that further entrenches whatever is trenched or trenchant but only at the cost of further diminution or withdrawal, literally digging out the ground from under one's feet, reemphasizing the subject by undoing the *sub-jectum*, in perhaps a slower, more arduous version of the plunge into bottomless waters. Each and every time I "pronounce or conceive" *ego sum*, I mark and re-mark myself as irretrievably different from myself in the very repetitive act of uttering (the same). And that "I" need not be even the "same" utterer/being at different moments, as *cogito interruptus*, but also a completely other uttering being. Already, Nancy suggested this possibility when he earlier stated that this is "what cannot be imitated; it is the original—an original that anyone can produce (perhaps), but that no one can reproduce. Such is the *cogito*" (78). *Sum* is true for *whoever* says it, each and every time, as the iterative event of being there, regardless of who is the being there. This is why the cogito is both inimitable and performable by each and every one of us, each and every time.

Later, in *Being Singular Plural*, Nancy will further unpack the cogito's implicit community: "The evidence for the *ego sum* comes down to, constitutively and co-originarily, its possibility in each one of Descartes's readers. The evidence as evidence owes its force, and its claim to truth, precisely to this possibility in each one of us—one could say, the co-possibility. *Ego sum = ego cum*" (BSP, 31). The *sein* of *sum* equals the *mitsein* of *sum cum*, it consummates it (*cum sum*), and unexpectedly reveals the subjacent community of our being-in-common: "The truth of the *ego sum* is the *nos sumus*: this 'we' announces itself through humanity for all the beings 'we' are with, for existence in the sense of being-essentially-with, as a Being whose essence is the with" (BSP, 33). Cogito, therefore, would be the very "dis-enclosure" (ES, 80) of community,[21] of *mitsein*, as the iteration of singular plural being, a certain "sharing of voices" not just for other humans, but, as Nancy specifies, "for all the beings 'we' are with." As Nancy further details in *Being Singular Plural*:

> critique absolutely needs . . . an ontology of being-with-one another, and this ontology must support both the sphere of "nature" and sphere of "history," as well as both the "human" and the "nonhuman"; it must be an ontology for the world, for everyone—and if I can be so bold, it has to be an ontology *for each and every one and for the world "as a totality,"* and nothing short of the whole world, since this is all there is (but, in this way, there is *all*). (51; emphasis added)

We come back, then, to the problem of the world, which is also the fable of a certain uttering, *mundus est fabula*, as Nancy tells us near the end of that chapter of *Ego sum*: "The world is the uttering, the *pure* subject is I who utters itself uttering" (86).[22] But "everywhere in this world," this subject "at the height of purity" retrenches and withdraws itself in the very uttering of its utterance, "within and from its *for*" (87). We are back to the *chaogito* as the copresencing of *sum* and world, but Nancy adds some precious qualifications to the *chaogito* that offers a parallel to the *cogito senso stricto*, whereas we remember the truth of the *sum* comes at the end of the process of hyperbolic doubt, as its extremity, where everything can be doubted, or feigned to be doubted, except for the I who feigns such a doubt: "You are, and you cannot not be, just as the chaos, from which the world—or its fable—can arise, cannot not be conceived" (83). The chaos from whence world can arise cannot not be "conceived." The *chaogito* "parallels" the cogito with I co-appearing in chiasmus with chaos: "*Chaos*—I am. I am—*chaos*" (83). And just as the content of feigned doubt at its extremity retrenches before the truth of the cogito, so too does the fiction or fable of the world find its truth in its very invention: "This truth is not only parallel or homologous to that of its content (the fictive creation): it functions only insofar as it invents itself—or invents itself as—the veritable creation, the unfictionable origin of a world in general. True or feigned, an invented world remains the invention of a world" (82–83). Nancy bases this startling conclusion upon his parallel reading of Descartes's *Treatise on the World* alongside the *Discourse on Method*, remembering that both announce themselves as "fables" whose pursuit in extremity leads to the retrenchment of their fictionality before a claim to truth. In the first case, the fable of an imaginary world leads to the summary description of the real world; in the second, the fiction of extreme doubt reveals the actuality of *sum*. Our previous questioning about the priority of world or community for the cogito seems to indicate the relation between cogito and *chaogito* as "parallel."

A further answer to the question regarding the relation between these unavowed encounters—*sum* and world, *sum* and community—can be found if we reconsider what happens between the end of the First Meditation and the beginning of the Second, where, as we recall, Descartes describes the result of his first meditation as a fall into a bottomless watery abyss. But how did he fall into this calamitous chaos, except through the final step in the hyperbolic doubt, which requires that he imagine some powerful entity able to deceive him in absolutely everything he might think to have been true, including "the sky, the air, the earth, colors, shapes, sounds, and all external things" or even whether he has "hands or eyes, or flesh, or blood or senses." The enabling figure for this most extreme doubt is not "God, who is supremely good and the source of truth, but rather some malicious demon [*malin génie*] of the utmost power and cunning [who] has employed all his energies in order to deceive me" (CSM II:15; AT VII:22). Only this fictional malicious or evil demon can drown the philosopher in a sea of doubt so deep and boundless, so chaotic, that the truth of *sum* can emerge. While Nancy's book-length study of Descartes is remarkable in many ways, it is also remarkable that this very figure of the evil genius, the very height of Descartes's feigned doubting, receives scarcely a mention, appearing only in a brief footnote that reduces that fiction to a mere reversal [*revers*] of the strategy of feigning doubt, a passive reversal of that feint: "I am tricked [*feinté*], and I am tricked by my *fiction* of an Evil Genius" (129n). A double (*diavolo*) to God, although one theologically empowered to do evil and wreak falsehood (a devil), the malicious genius not only enables the fiction of hyperbolic doubt to attain the extremity whereby the residue of what cannot be doubted comes to the fore, *ego sum, ego existo*, but he also *personifies* the chaos of a world where nothing is sure and as the very *face* of otherness itself, be it the faceless face of the divine Other—*larvatus pro deo*. As such, the malicious genius articulates the convergence of *chaogito* and cogito, or between world and community, appearing first at the very end of the First Meditation then reappearing near the beginning of the Second Meditation, right after the initial evocation of the chaotic watery abyss in which the philosopher finds himself after the encounter with the malicious genius and with no sure footing. This second appearance by the malicious genius leads straight to the sentence that is the starting point of Nancy's reading of Descartes:

> I have convinced myself that there is absolutely nothing in the world, no sky, no earth, no minds, no bodies. Does it now follow that I too do not exist? No: if I convinced myself of something [or thought anything at all—French translation] then I certainly existed. But there is a deceiver of supreme power and cunning who is deliberately and constantly deceiving me. In that case I too undoubtedly exist, if he is deceiving me; and let him deceive me as much as he can, he will never bring it about that I am nothing so long as I think I am something. So after considering everything very thoroughly, I must finally conclude that this proposition, *I am, I exist*, is necessarily true whenever [*quoties*: each and every time] it is put forward by me [*profertur*] or conceived in my mind. (CSM II:16–17; AT VII:25)

If "true or false, an invented world remains the invention of a world," wouldn't an invented other still be the invention of some *other*? The fiction of another— whether God or malicious genius—implies the other of fiction, not only for the "certain" existence of the *ego* that speaks *sum* and the truth of the utterance that says or thinks so, but also for the existence of others *tout court*, since the very positing of some other, whether "true or false," as heuristic ploy or as feigning fiction, reveals the structural necessity of there being some other or others in order for there to be *sum*, or stated otherwise, the necessary plurality of the singular.[23] The fiction of the malicious genius also forms the most minimal of communities, based here not on love (as per the Bataille of *The Inoperative Community*) but on mutual deception *and* presencing. But what do we make of the framing of the image of liquid chaos by the two evocations of the malicious genius? In fact, the resulting triptych articulates cogito with *chaogito*, the becoming community of or in the world with the becoming world of or through community, their mutual *iteration* and *retrenchment*: "The *self* becomes equivalent to *chaos*" (87). *Mundus est fabula* also means the coappearance of *sum* AND chaos, and of community AND world, where the face of the other is also the mask of the world in the etymological sense of Latin *mundus* and of Greek *cosmos*. Community and world join as the prosoppopeia of each other, *self* in the place of *chaos* and vice versa, leading to the question of what we mean by face if not essentially the mouth, *os*, that internal cavity whose retrenchment nonetheless "makes up the very act of *ego*, its self-position in the form of: it retrenches *itself*, and this *happens* to it, at the extreme point of its fabulation—of its *saying*—, like an accident through which the *self* [*auto*] becomes equivalent to *chaos*. As soon as I open my mouth, I retrench myself. The place of this mouth does not let itself be circumscribed" (87; translation modified).

Quasi permixtum

Circumscribing the place of this mouth puts us awkwardly between mind and body, another irreconcilable duality supposedly imposed by Descartes according to tradition. But where others claim a rigid distinction, Nancy sees "convulsion" as we move to the final chapter in *Ego Sum: Unum quid*. Although not as much a catchphrase as with the other Latin titles, the importance of this odd expression comes buried in a key line from the Sixth Meditation: "... *me non tantum adesse meo corpori ut nauta adest navigio, sed illi arctissime esse conjunctum et quasi permixtum, adeo ut unum quid cum illo componam*" [I am not merely there in my body as a pilot is there in a ship, but that I am most closely conjoined and, as if all mixed in, with it, so that I compose one thing with it] (AT VII:81; CSM II:56, trans. modified). In the book's most audacious move, one that effectively wreaks havoc with any concept of Cartesian dualism, *unum quid* posits a *single something* that "I" would "compose" with my body. To be sure, the composition of this *unum quid* is not a claim to some monism over and against Descartes's reputed dualism—far from it, as the very fact of its com-position attests. Nancy describes it as a "convulsion" in Descartes's thought, if not as the convulsion that is his thought, a "spasm of a system" that "tightens, ties, and contracts its parts as much as it disjoints or disarticulates them, . . . forcing the joint by tightening it rather than breaking it apart" (88). What brings together body and soul is what separates or distinguishes them, following the logic of retrenchment we've already seen at work. We can recall that *unum quid* is a legal term, by which is meant that various things are, for convenience or for some other reason, treated *as if* they were one. The oneness of body and soul is the act of treating them "*as one*" despite or because of the incommensurability of their difference, understood by Descartes as a radical gap between *res cogitans* and *res extensa*, or between the substance that "thinks" but has no extension in space and the one that extends in space but does not think.

Nancy contests the facility of this distinction while probing the instability of the *unum quid* as a com-position, or co-positing, co-appearing of what it brings together in difference. The "convulsion" in Descartes's thought will resound all throughout Nancy's subsequent thinking of the body, most notably in *Corpus* (whose textual corpus was itself published in various forms and editions from 1993 through 2006). For Descartes, as he stipulates in the passage from the Sixth Meditation, mind or soul is not something that is inserted into a body, like a boatswain in a boat, but rather body itself is conjoined or inextricably mixed in (*permixtum*) with mind. How does this work? To be sure, Nancy is not contesting that there is a difference for Descartes between mind and body, or between "thought" and extension, but what that difference is remains to be shown. Again rereading Descartes carefully and scrupulously, Nancy reveals that the difference between thought and extension is in fact the very condition for there to be a unity of mind and body, for there to be that *unum quid* that com-poses the two together, not as separate parts—*partes extra partes*—added to each other or the one inserted into the other, "like the pilot of a ship," which would imply some minimal "extension" for the thinking substance, be it the singular vanishing "point" of the pineal gland (as Descartes will later try to argue, less than convincingly).[24] Nor do these two substances—soul or mind and body, and I merely note the slippage between the two terms of mind and soul in Descartes and hence in whoever tries to explicate his thinking—form some new substance over and beyond the uneasy composition of this *unum quid*. The "union" of *unum quid* is no dialectic, no *Zauberkraft* of the negative. It is only because the two substances are *incommensurable* that they can come to occupy the same place in or as the living human being, as the *Dasein* or "*ad-sum*" of its existence: "*adesse* meo corpori . . . ut unum quid," being there in my body as one with my mind. Nancy concludes, "The proof of the distinction opens the space for what could be called a *singularly double* status of 'me'—of a strange couple of forces, disjunction and conjunction at the same time, exerting themselves on me" (95; emphasis added).

To this "singular duality" is added a fundamental divergence in cognition: the thinking substance knows itself through the meditating feint of doubting everything resulting in the irrefutable evidence of its own feigning/thinking, but as Nancy recalls from Descartes's June 28, 1643, letter to Princess Elizabeth, the practice of meditation, or directed cogitation, may *a contrario* work to obscure the innate evidence of one's own bodily existence: "But it is the ordinary course of life and conversation, and *abstention from meditation* and from the study of the things which exercise the imagination, that teaches us how to conceive the union of the soul and the body" (AT III:692; III:227; Alquié III, 46; emphasis added). Despite this evident contrariety between the truth acquired through meditation and the truth acquired by the absence of meditation, both the apperception of self, of ego, *and* of the union between body and soul impose themselves not as logical or argumentative proof based on prior principles, but as the incontrovertible (self) evidence of experience. But this "experience" needs to be qualified. Nancy writes:

The experience of the subject has nothing to do with the order of the empirical, nor with that of some existential intimacy. It builds the structure of the substance when the latter becomes the modern Subject. In this experience, the Subject apprehends its own *sub-stare* to the extent in which he does not grasp it as the *object* of an action, or a thought. . . . The evidence of the *cogito* stands underneath every faculty and every substantiality. Cartesian experience is the experience of the *sub* without stasis or stance. Up to the end and without reserve—*ex-perior*—the *sub* puts to the test what it can be. *Ego* is the proof of the *subex*. (107–8)

We seem to be back to the image of Descartes floundering in the depthless waters of uncertainty, the experience of being unsupported by anything below one's sinking self. As if afloat in a vast amniotic fluid prior to the birth to presence and/or calamitously drowning at the very point of absent expiration, the "antinomic" experiences of *sum* and of soul/body union, thinking and living, are the same "singularly double" experience (or being singular plural) of *unum quid*, "traversed by contrariety" and both "prior and subsequent to the distinction between substances" (108). Or, as Nancy will extrapolate in *Corpus*, which in many ways is an extended meditation on this final chapter of *Ego Sum*, "Experience is neither knowledge nor nonknowledge. Experience is a passage, a transport from border to border, an endless transport from shore to shore [I'm inclined to interpolate, from birth to death—GV], all along a tracing that develops and limits an areality" (C 113).[25] This areality traced or retraced, retreated and retrenched, by experience is that of the "constitutive instability"(102) that is *unum quid*: "Unum quid: a something that makes up a One without having any thingness, and hence without having any one*ness*" (109).

Indeed, Nancy explains that beyond the distinction between *res cogitans* and *res extensa* there is also necessarily the distinction between the subject or "subex" and the distinction itself between the two substances: "There is thus the distinction between substances, and the distinction between the subject and the distinction between substances" (97). *Unum quid* might thus read *ego sum distinctus* (96), as it is distinction itself that distinguishes the *sum* of each and every time, beyond the question of that incommensurable distinction between thinking and extension:

> . . . the distinction of *ego*, insofar as it is the distinction of what has, so to speak, no really substantial substantiality—but it is not a *what*, it is the *what* that is only *I*, that consists only in the *I* (who says I). This distinction, which is nothing other than the *distingo* of the *for*, raises (or, precisely, does not raise) the question of the existential status that *I* bestows upon itself, that *I* as such (or the *for* as such) consists in

bestowing upon itself. Therefore it raises (or does not raise) the question of a non-substantial *status*, of a constitutive *instability*. The instability, in sum, of the *sum* that grasps itself in the *for*. Yet, the status of this insubstantial substance is precisely identical with its apprehension: *ego sum* is true "whenever [*quoties*] *I* pronounce it or whenever *I* conceive it in my mind" (it is *I* who underline *I*). This "status"—that of evidence—necessarily has the structure of immediacy as *self*-relation. To this extent, it is not distinguishable—with regard to its structure— from the immediate apprehension of the union of soul and body. (102; Nancy's emphases; translation modified)

The "constitutive instability" of the "*sum* which grasps itself in the *for*" is what we have been calling the "iterative cogito," the "punctual identity" (104) of an uttering or a proferring that articulates itself "each and every time" and *only* "each and every time" as the evidence of itself as uttering being, as *for*. This iteration (re)marks itself, retrenches and redraws itself, interrupts itself, withdraws itself, every time, in distinction from any previous iteration. Nancy again proposes the metaphor of photography:

If *ego* sees itself in the snapshot [*l'instantané*] that allows the luminous trace of its unstable image to be inscribed (but is it an image? it is an utterance, an uttering, at most the opening of a mouth . . .), this vision and this inscription themselves depend on—in truth they do more than depend on it, they are "consubstantial" with—the instantaneous shuttering (the instant "is" also instability) of the diaphragm through which light passes. The evidence of the *cogito* has the nature of a *diaphragm*. It is what gets in the way of something, obstructing or obfuscating it." (103; Nancy's emphasis; translation modified)

Following this, we can see the cogito no longer simply as "interrupted," but also *as* interruption, but perhaps again, as I suggested earlier, less the isolated flash of a given snapshot than the repetitive or iterative workings of that series of snapshots or "frames" that define the *motion* picture or cinema, whose illusion of continuity, the "sum" of its *sum*, is as much a misprision as is the Cartesian subject's supposed sense of durable identity. Or, following Nancy (and Descartes) more closely in another register, the articulation/disarticulation of language in the proferring of *ego*, "each and every time I say it or conceive of it," be it most minimally the mere opening or closing of the mouth. And that is where we find the point of *unum quid*, where thought meets extension in the incommensurate *spacing* of the maw, the making space that is the internal cavity of the body, the *sum* of its *areality*.[26]

The overcoming of Cartesian dualism between mind and body does not mean the suppression of their difference but rather their indefinite and endlessly reiterated spacing and difference, the interruption of ceaseless (re)iterations, the stutterings of a vertiginous, invaginating exteriority: "The incommensurable extension of thought is the opening of the mouth. . . . But the human being is that which spaces itself out, and which perhaps only ever dwells in this spacing, in the *areality* of his mouth" (111–12).[27] But far from any comforting prosopopoeia, this mouth has no face, only a hole or holes for mouth/eye,[28] the mask again of *larvatus pro deo* that stages the dis-enclosure of a necessarily absent God.[29]

Unum quid tells us that the Cartesian body is not an interiority sheltering an even more interiorized mind/soul but a radical, incontrovertible exteriority, further exteriorized by the elucubrations of a thinking being that operates only iteratively to further exteriorize, differentiate, space out the "I" whose *sum* is coterminous with an incessant withdrawal, retrenchment, or retreat not *from* itself (which would presuppose a priorly existing self from which something could be taken) but *as* the very sense of self the "I" can claim—that is, as sense sensing itself. Taking us back again to the philosopher's watery doubt, Nancy concludes:

> The subject ruins itself and collapses into this abyss [*s'abîme en ce gouffre*]. But *ego* utters itself there. It externalizes itself there, which does not mean that it carries to the outside the visible face of an invisible interiority. It means, literally, that *ego* makes or makes itself into *exteriority*, spacing of places, distancing and strangeness [*écartement et étrangeté*] that make up a place, and hence space itself, primordial spatiality of a true *outline* in which, and only in which, *ego* may come forth, trace itself out, and think itself.
>
> It is this thought—*ego, unum quid*—that can alone find out that it does not give rise to any recognition of its subject, of the human being. This thought is always in advance withdrawn from the possibility of recognizing itself, and hence from the possibility of thinking. (112)

"*Ego* contracts thought to the point where it is wrenched away from itself," writes Nancy on the very last page of *Ego Sum* (112). Thought's greatest "advance" brings its own retreat. This retreat of thought, or its *"convulsion,"* that the thought of Descartes stages is nonetheless what is denied by the subsequent development of philosophical thought: "From Descartes onward, thought has refused to confront its own convulsion: violence is begotten in what one refuses to confront" (112).

Confusi cogitandi

We began by noticing the absence of the term *thinking*, or *cogitating*, from the title and theme of the book, the traditional *cogito ergo sum* reduced simply to *ego sum*. But now, at the end of the book, we are still left wondering what this "thought" actually is, or what this thinking is that can both tear itself asunder in its retreat and "refuse" to confront the convulsion that defines what it is, through a violence in denial of its retreat, of its retrenchment. Nancy, of course, will pursue the question of what thinking is elsewhere in his work (confirming again the importance of this reading of Descartes for Nancy's further philosophical development), although some intriguing hints already appear in *Ego Sum* itself. To begin with, the reduction of thinking and doubting to an activity of feigning (that there is no "sky, air, earth, colors, shapes, sounds, and all external things" or even that I have no "hands or eyes, or flesh, or blood or senses," that everything I sense is just the deceitful fabrications of a malicious genius) also paradoxically expands thinking to include sensory perception in general to the extent that what I *seem* to sense becomes indistinguishable from thinking and ipso facto from my being, as seen in this passage from the Second Meditation, cited by Nancy (*Ego Sum*, 46): "Nevertheless, at the very least, it is very certain that it seems to me that I see (*videre videor*), that I hear, that I feel hot, and that is properly what in me is called sensing, and that, taken precisely so, is nothing other than thinking (AT VII:29; CSM II:19; my translation). Again, later in the Second Meditation, "But when I see, or think I see (I am not here distinguishing the two), it is simply not possible that I who am now thinking am not something" (AT VII:33; CSM II:22, cited by Nancy, ES 72). And in a striking passage just following the line about *unum quid* in the Sixth meditation: "Sensations of hunger, thirst, pain and so on are nothing but confused modes of thinking (*confusi cogitandi*) which arise (*exorti*) from the union and, as it were, intermingling (*quasi permixtione*) of the mind with the body" (AT VII:81; Alquié II:186, 492; CSM II:56; *not* cited by Nancy).[30] The extremity of hyperbolic doubt ends up blurring the distinction between the two meanings of sense (as sensation and as meaning)—that is, between the sensible and the intelligible, or between "body" and "mind." Sensations may be "confused modes of thinking," but they are *still* a form of thinking, one that testifies to the "intermingling of the mind with the body," the *unum quid*. Or even hearkening back to the "calamity" of *dum scribo*, where a typography of sensation seamlessly connects with the imprinting of intellection, or cognition, the actual writing with its airy counterpart at the other end of the pen. A convulsive cogitating or co-agitating of the pen, *unum quid*, that is also nothing less than an ex-cogitating that marks a thought that is outside or beside itself:

> Thinking is not about a subject placing an object in front of itself to examine and evaluate it. It is what finds itself only in what it thinks. So it is, for Descartes, everything takes place in such a way that I find myself in it, or I touch myself in it, at the same time that I come up against something, a representation, a sensation or an affection. This is what makes it so that *ego sum* becomes equivalent to *cogito*: far from being able to establish an intellectual subject, this thought of *sum* accedes to a being that gives *itself* or that finds *itself* in as much as, infinitely, it wraps and unwraps itself (*s'enrobe et se dérobe*) with everything in the world. This is indeed why, as we know, the self-evidence of this *ego* is identical with its eclipse, and it too, as *res cogitans* withdraws in its nakedness. . . .
>
> What a thought that is stripped away (*la pensée dérobée*) thinks, it thinks therefore only as what is taken away from itself (*ce qui la dérobe à elle-même*). This is how it is "still thought." . . . An ex-cogitated *cogito*, a thinking beside itself [*pensée hors de soi*]. (*La pensée dérobée*, 12, 38; my translation)[31]

These lines emerge from a discussion about the paradox of thinking non-knowledge as differently thought by Sartre and Bataille, and so it is all the more strange to see Descartes emerge here as the exemplar of deconstructed thought, or as the deconstruction of thought that is its unraveling or disrobing, its being taken away from itself, its exposure that exposes us all, its exscription and retreat. It offers a vision of thought in its finitude, or as finitude, a finite or finished thought (*une pensée finie*), which Nancy elsewhere explains as follows: "A finite thought is one that each time thinks the fact that it is unable to think what comes to it. Of course, it isn't a matter of refusing to see ahead or plan. Rather, a finite thinking is one that is surprised each time by its own freedom."[32] It is a thought that "has to think itself as what loses itself in thinking—necessarily, if that sense it thinks is the sense of innumerable finitudes, . . . a thinking that can no longer impose itself, nor even propose itself, but that must, with all its resources, *expose itself* to what is finite about sense. Multiple, and each time, singular" ("Finite Thinking," 30). Thinking too, whatever we conceive it to be, necessarily still follows the logic of being/sensing singular plural, each and every time inside itself, outside itself, beside itself: ex-cogitated in its very cogitation.

What all this comes down to is an *ethics* of thinking, as inspired by Descartes as it is very different from the classical "Cartesian habits,"[33] very different from the innateness of what is clear and distinct, but very much a following out of the paths upon which we find ourselves, paths whose sense (in both the directional and the cognitive "senses") emerges only in its happening, in the openness toward what comes to it, each and every time.[34] The iterative cogito, the *sum* of each and every time, exposes us to ourselves and to each other in our finitudes, in our singularities, in our multitude, as the very sense(s) of our existence. Or, as Nancy will later conclude, "The act of sensing and the act of the sense are the same. Existence is the act internally differing from its own sense, its self-sensation as its own dehiscence. Nothing else is at stake, in the final analysis, in the *Ego sum, ego existo* of René Descartes, in the obscurity of its self-evidence and in the madness of its self-certainty" (SW, 28).

Nancy's Descartes, therefore, is "the founder neither of humanism nor of anthropology or the so-called human sciences" (ES, 109). Neither the hallowed source of rationalism nor the founder of some "idea of man," but rather, and dare I say, *simply*, the very *interruption* of thought, its finitude as its openness, its retreat that is, at once withdrawal and reinscription—*dum scribo*—, as masked dis-enclosure, stepping forth, stepping back, setting forth (*profertur*) setting back (*referitur*)—*larvatus pro deo*—, as world creation and *chaogito*—*mundus est fabula*—, as the areality of *unum quid*. In *sum*, as the ever-renewed (re)iterations of *ego sum*, whenever or each and every time it is set forth by me, whoever or whatever "I" may be. . . .

Descartes, the reputedly solipsistic thinker of *res cogitans*, becomes the surprisingly radical locus for rethinking body, community, world, and thought itself. As such, Nancy drives a durable wedge between the traditional "habits" of Cartesianism and the text of Descartes. Not that Nancy's critical interruption isn't also indebted to the examples of other key philosophers—Kant, Hegel, Nietzsche, Heidegger, and Derrida especially—and no doubt one could undertake an equally surprising journey through Nancy's readings of those philosophers, though I doubt any of them would emerge as irrevocably altered as Descartes, as exposing the areality of an "iter" marked by gaps, divergences, and interruptions, by *d'écartes*. I can only conclude in agreement with Antonia Birnbaum when she writes regarding Jean-Luc Nancy that "his passage through Descartes restores all its force to the strange method thanks to which a philosopher reinvented thought."[35] Perhaps it would be more apt, however, to speak of a mutual "being with," a dramatic compearance emerging from Nancy's *touching/reading* of Descartes that enjoins us—as they each in their own singular way explicitly invite us to do—to think thought anew, to "reinvent" thought *along with* them, which is with the classically (un)masked philosopher of body, community, and world and the contemporary thinker of finitude, dis-enclosure, and being *with* or *to*. Imagine Nancy/Descartes as *unum quid*, where the unity is that of incommensurable differences, the perpetual reiteration of a *sum* whose interruptions define the areality of an existence where thought is always still to come, a thinking/sensing singular plural, each and every time. . . .

Philosophizing is, then, in and as interruption, the intermittence of sense relaying the incessantly recurring but ever-vanishing punctum and punctuality of singular being. But that is also to demand a different way of writing philosophy. As such, the iterative cogito can offer a schema for making sense of singularity, a schema Nancy will try to actualize as the occasional, or interruptive, form of writing he calls his "monograms."

2
Monograms
Writing Singular Plural

Between June 1979 and December 1980, in the wake of having published *Ego Sum*, Jean-Luc Nancy pursued the exigency of doing philosophy differently by writing what we would have called in a pre-internet world a "column" or a regular contribution to a journal, something like what we now call a weblog or "blog." And while these periodic essays do function as a kind of log, or more precisely what Nancy refers to as a "chronicle," the experiment in this kind of writing comes to a halt after a short eighteen months with the demise of the periodical for which those pieces were written, *Digraphe*.[1] The series begins anew a dozen years later, in February 1992, for another journal, *Futur Antérieur*, only to end just as abruptly some twenty months later in October of 1993.[2] A full decade later, in February 2013, Nancy again relaunched the series of *monogrammes*, publishing three more installments in the journal *L'Impossible*. All told, seventeen of these pieces, to which Nancy gives the name "monogrammes," were published over a total of twenty-four years. Far from there being a continuous output over time (as the numerical equivalencies would suggest), they appeared unevenly in these three bursts of sustained activity broken by long hiatuses. After the last burst, they would disappear from his writing, never to be picked up again, at least as such.[3]

By "as such," I mean that Nancy is not necessarily a stranger to various forms of situational or occasional writing, and one should certainly note his many such contributions in this vein, including the series of radio lectures published in 2004 under the title *Philosophical Chronicles*, as well as some of his later monographs framed in response to specific events or circumstances: environmental disasters, pandemics, political developments.[4] A study of Nancy's *Monogrammes* is thus the occasion to broach a more general consideration of this untracked tendency in his work, not as a "break" or detour, or *détournement*, from his philosophizing in more traditional and abstract ways—viz. his monographs on individual thinkers, such as Descartes, Kant, and Hegel, or his theoretical works on such questions as community, democracy, and Christianity—, but as a *distinct* approach he charts for the practice of philosophy, a singular way of making sense, be it in the mode of intermittence or interruption.

It is not my ambition or intention to uncover the archaeology (historical, biographical, psychoanalytical) of this pursuit of a form of writing made more familiar in our current media-saturated world. And it is no doubt a symptom of the prescience of Nancy's monogrammatic forays that at least those essays published in the now defunct *Futur Antérieur* have themselves been collected and made readily accessible on the website of the successor journal *Multitudes*.[5] Rather, my interest has to do with coming to terms with the practice modeled by Nancy's *monogrammes* as a novel and experimental kind of intellectual intervention—and interruption—that is at the same time a continuing *philosophical* reflection on the sense of the *form* that this intervention takes and, more generally, on the singular occasion for the invention of *forms* that have creatively, and even classically, enabled the advent of certain ways of thinking (I'm tempted to say, certain *worlds* of thought).

Definitions: Singular Plural

So, what are these "monograms"? The first one begins with a triple definition, and subsequent installments will add further examples, specifications, and definitions of what a "monogram" is supposed to be. There is a fundamental pluralism here, not merely in the proliferation of formal definitions given at the beginning of each publication; each of the seventeen is itself given the "singularly plural" title of "monogrammes." And indeed, Nancy's approach is to include within each installment a number of different short texts on differing topics, separated by blank spaces and triangulated asterisks. Each of the "monogrammes" is itself a *set* of monograms, a collection of "singular remarks" bundled together and signed according to date and often place.

Of the three definitions proposed in the first paragraph of the first "monogrammes," the first is a personal one, to indicate what is meant *hic et nunc*: "Monogrammes: Ici, espèces de monologues écrits" [Monograms: *Here*, some kinds of written monologues]. The monogram is first and foremost a "kind" of *written* monologue, with the accent on the "mono" or single-voice aspect of the form; i.e., this would appear to be not a *dia*logue between speakers but the uninterrupted utterance of one. That monologue, however, does not exclude, and indeed *a contrario* the situational context of these "chronicles" demands, dialogue with real or potential readers. Indeed, many of the subsequent monogrammes include various responses by Nancy to readers whose messages and identity remain typically absent. The acknowledgment of such responses cannot simply be accidental. Why would one write such a chronicle if not precisely to elicit dialogue (like the "objections and responses" to Descartes's *Meditations*)? Or more boldly, to make operative a certain (philosophical) community, whether operative or inoperative? Either way, there is no "mono" without a "dia"; the plural singularity of the monologic monograms in turn implies the singular pluralities of dialogue (or a multi-logue). The "speaking with" precedes any "speaking to"; the colloquy comes before any soliloquy. It is as if the *monogrammes* presage or pre-stage the well-known theses of the *Inoperative Community* and of *Being Singular Plural*.

More tellingly, however, the *written* monologue is not a *logos* but a *gramma*, a mono-*gram*, the singularity of a trace, as suggested by the third of the three definitions Nancy provides at the beginning of *Monogrammes I*. This time the definition proposed is not a personal one, but the institutional definition given by a standardized dictionary—in this case, that of the French *Littré*: "Terme d'Antiquité. Qui ne consiste que dans les lignes, dans les contours. Peinture monogramme" [Term from Antiquity. What consists only in lines, in the contours. A monogram painting]. The *graphic* nature of the monogram is thus underscored by its *painting* a picture by the mere deployment of lines, by its consisting only of an outline, or a set of contours. But this is indicated as an outdated expression, a term from "antiquity" and one that would appear to be as far removed as possible from the contemporaneousness or *"actualité"*[6] Nancy otherwise embraces for his "monograms": that is, as a kind of "chronicle" where current events, book reviews, and philosophical reflections intersect, where the lines between them cross and cross again in a distinctive if undefined pattern, a monogram, a singular set of traces whose outline remains sufficient unto itself, while perhaps adumbrating something more. Far from being simply "mono," the monogram appears to be irredeemably plural, as its *each time* plural title of *monogrammes* suggests. But then the monogram(s) cannot be a simple trait, not something simply singular but always already plural, repeated, and repeatable as per the nexus of lines that outlines the picture. The picture is the pattern recognized from the retracing of lines whose singular linearity withdraws before the instance, the instantiation of the image, its sense. The monogram is not a simple trait, but always already a complex *re-trait*, a retracing that is a withdrawal, a retreat that is also an emergence.

Finally, a monogram is also something whose traces the signatory bears like a set of initials. It is both a decoration and a brand, or as *Monogrammes IV* states, "Ornament and signature at once." The monogram is also not a monograph:

"It is not a ciphered message, it's the Cipher itself, which does not cipher and thus does not decipher anything." The monogram both reveals and conceals the outline of a trace or the trace of an outline, an open "cryptography"—that is, "a secret displayed out in the light of day, or the light of day itself in its cryptic nature." As such, the monogram recalls the Heraclitan conundrum *phusis kruptesthai philei*, which Nancy translates and comments upon in detail as follows:

> *Phusis kruptesthai philei*—nature loves to hide itself, to encrypt itself—, this phrase which we cannot translate (but is Heraclitus himself able to translate it?), and which, for this reason, we cannot stop commenting on, speaks to the nature of the name as much as to the nature of light, or to the nature of nature. It speaks about what takes place in the light of day [*au grand jour*] in general, it speaks about the light of day. At Easter—in this moment—we learn anew the light of day, the bright, dawning light of the sky that has not yet installed its closed reign of heat, its calefaction and all the work of fructifications. In the sky and on the ground, everything withdraws [*recule*] before the evidence of a budding forth [*éclosion*]. For this budding forth is a withdrawing, rather than a manifestation, a cipher rather than a declaration. Except for a few runaway flowers, the plants are still only their monograms. The freshly planted sapling and the recently pruned tree are their own initials; they hold the evidence of their ciphers. And all evidence is a cipher.
>
> That's what Leibniz failed to understand, when he reproached Descartes for not having placed a sign upon the inn of evidence. Evidence is the contrary of publicity.

Leibniz notwithstanding, the "evidence" of the Cartesian *larvatus prodeo* is both a masking and an unmasking, the monogrammatic cipher that is both signature and evidence, the sign of spring and what it openly portends and secretly declares: the bud as monogram that brightly reveals what it ostensibly hides, a withdrawal or retreat (*recul, retrait*) that is also an emergence or advance, a ripening that redraws the contours of an outline in germination, a re-tracing or *re-trait* for that which "consists only in lines," the monogram. (As for the concern about distinguishing evidence from publicity, that remark too rejoins a number of comments in the early *monogrammes* about the contemporary media phenomenon of the so-called *nouveaux philosophes* and the wider problem of what Nancy describes in *Monogrammes I* as the suspect desire to present a certain "figure" of philosophy, "to pass oneself off as a philosopher," to pass philosophy off as what can be given a certain "figure," all of which fail, *on philosophical terms*, to understand "the very question of philosophy" as a relentlessly calling into question of "figuration" itself.)[7]

This set of monograms (*Monogrammes IV*) that so effortlessly evokes the Easter moment as the key to unraveling the meaning of monogram is dated April 15, 1980, just days after that year's Easter Sunday (April 6), thus situating the philosophical reflection within the ground of a particular place and time, a *hic et nunc* that is not coincidental but rather the contextual frame, the *contours*, if you like, that form the outline of the monogram.[8] Nancy signs his monograms with the date, his initials J.-L. N., and the place, his home/retreat at Les Ayes. When he doesn't make that location explicit, he often as not describes it, as in the final section of *Monogrammes III*, which is also a striking example of implicit dialogue *within* the monologue:

> Someone, a reader in sum, had asked me to speak again about nature in this chronicle. I will only tell him the following, today: winter is beginning, a little bit of snow has fallen, just now, while I was working in the garden. November 24, 1979, J.-L. N.

Instead of a philosophical reflection, we have the contours of the philosopher's dwelling, the outlines of his being in retreat, working à la Voltaire in his garden, cultivating what must necessarily already be at an end, with the growing season cut short by the winter's first snows. Although, to be precise, one cannot really say that the season is "cut short" since winter's advent points to the final completion of the ripening process, not a contingency or interruption except in the sense that all change is contingent interruption, the sign of finitude's inevitability, of the end always already inscribed in the beginning. And what could one possibly be doing by way of "work" in the garden at this time of year? Clearly, any effort at planting would be most untimely and literally "fruitless." But there does remain the job of clearing the dead vegetation and of making one's little plot ready for the next season's germination, ready for the return of Easter's daylight, which we will then "learn anew" along with its monogrammatic buds. Part of this preparation, as any gardener knows, is to prune or cut back any untoward branches or shoots to enable the new buds to succeed come their spring, come the eternal recurrence of their *Ur-sprung*. The growing season's growth must then indeed be cut short for it to grow again later. But just like the spring's anticipation in/of the bud ("Except for a few runaway flowers, plants are still only their *monograms*"), so too does the final autumn pruning leave us with nothing more than the outline of the plant, its contours or initials, its monogram again, which is not a cryptogram, but the "evidence of a cipher": "The freshly planted sapling and the recently pruned tree are their own initials; they hold the evidence of their ciphers." The monogrammes are thus essentially marked by a poetics of finitude: they chronicle a singular (outdated?, untimely?) time and place for philosophical reflections that themselves bear the potential for sense beyond as well as within the context of their germination.

Now and Then

Monogrammes XIV (the last in the second series) begins by reflecting precisely on this potentiality of sense given the non-coincidence between the *now* of publication and the *then* of writing:

> The spirit, as one says, of this chronicle should be that of a freewheeling commentary on current events [*un libre commentaire de l'actualité*], or even a commentary on the mood of the times, as one also says. Experience indicates that the delays in the fabrication and publication of *Futur antérieur* do not allow for staying close enough to the event. (Perhaps that's what the title of the journal is supposed to signify, by the way). . . . If I mention these details, it's not on their own account, you might suspect. It's because I cannot remove the bitter taste [*le goût amer*] left in my mouth by a chronicle I wrote about Bosnia in December 1992 or January 1993, which was only published four or five months later, and which, at the time I'm writing this (for the first time, by hand, in August 1993, then on the computer in September), has lost nothing, absolutely nothing, of a sinister freshness [*une fraîcheur sinistre*].

Monogrammes XIV appeared in *Futur antérieur* 19–20, no. 5–6 (1993); the piece on Bosnia was originally published as *Monogrammes XI* in *Futur antérieur* 16, no. 2 (1993). Reading these remarks some forty years later (as we saw earlier with the *Paragraph* piece, "You ask me what it means today . . ."), one can't help but be struck by the concern about the timeliness or currency of the text, its *actualité* relative to events whose distinctness appears significantly diminished with age, and yet whose "sinister freshness" paradoxically remains stronger than ever. For Nancy, this paradox is observed over a period of mere months rather than years. This anxiety about a six-month delay in publication would seem even more acute were such chronicling to occur in our contemporary social media and Twitter-fed environment, where a statement more than a few hours old may appear already hopelessly outdated—like that other outdated term from antiquity, the monogram. Perhaps the monogram is always already out of date, out of time, anachronistic, unhinged, or disjointed like the traces that make up its contours. This chronic anachronicity of interrupted time should not, however, be understood as a simple state of being always out of date, or as a kind of structural belatedness tarred with all the nostalgia and melancholia of classic romanticism. For Nancy also struggles here with a bizarre, unexpected, and unsolicited kind of *actualité* that makes what was written in either a recent or remote past appear with an unparalleled contemporaneity, a singular "freshness" that is all the more "sinister" for its marking a difference that appears to make no difference at all. The *inactualité* of what was written about Bosnia remains disturbingly more *actuelle* than ever, senselessly making sense. It is this *unheimlich* and multiple, complex, unpredictable untimeliness of the chronicle that draws Nancy's attention.

The specific chronicle that is this installment of *Monogrammes* (number XI) is both in and out of date, even more relevant for its being not, an *inactualité* that is more *"actuelle"* than ever. *Monogrammes* XI is even more peculiar for it being the only one that has ever been republished as such,[9] and yet it is also the only one absent from the *Multitudes* website, where all the other *monogrammes* from the *Futur Antérieur* series are posted. As for the text's "sinister freshness," that uncanny or untimely relation to its own actuality is in fact bolstered by the content of the essay's three sections, one on the relation between the "current" Bosnian crisis and the context of the Yalta conference (itself an historical analysis), a second section responding to media complaints about the lack of involvement of "the intellectuals" in responding to that crisis (which itself emerges as a properly philosophical discussion of the ethics of intellectual involvement), and a final section about Philip Glass's *Einstein on the Beach* (which also phrases the ongoing aesthetic interest of that work, an aesthetic interest, we might add, that has increased rather than diminished over the decades). All three sections, while manifestly rooted in "current" concerns, also speak deliberately and overtly to issues that in one way or another transcend the moment of writing. Why, then, the complaint in *Monogrammes* XIV about a few months' delay in publication when the piece itself is one that so clearly speaks beyond the currency of its context?

In any case, this paradox of an enduring (in)actuality leaves Nancy with a "bitter taste" (*"un goût amer"*): how can the chronicle of a particular event (in this case, that of the war in Bosnia) remain so current? "How can one follow a current situation which has nothing current about it?" [Comment accompagner une actualité qui n'a rien d'actuel], he asks a few lines later. There is a bitterness or a bitter realization here that can only be explained by a much larger set of considerations, one that exceeds the situation in question: "What pertains to Bosnia pertains in an analogous way for most of the former 'Eastern' block countries, but also for Iraq, for Egypt, for Algeria, for India, for Bangladesh, for Somalia, for South Africa and for two-thirds of Africa, for Brazil and Mexico, for Europe." Symptomatically, this list of trouble spots from the nineties seems scarcely different than the one we could make today, in the third decade of the twenty-first century. The last of Nancy's second series of *monogrammes* (and curiously the only one that commences *without* listing various definitions of the word!) comes up against the very concept of a philosophical chronicle that launched his first *monogrammes* to the extent that such a concept would seem to presuppose a certain theory and philosophy of history, and indeed a certain *subject* of history:

> The actuality of these years, which seems stuck in disaster and regression, presents in sum a well-declared Hegelian aspect: the cunning of history [*la ruse de l'histoire*] shows itself bare and crude, but we can no longer call it *the cunning of Reason* without either laughing or crying, or else as a techno-economic reason that would be Marxist-Hegelian but deprived of its supposed rationality. What was once understood as process or as progress shows itself, more than ever, as a sequence of mechanisms, forces, and calculations [*comme enchaînement d'engrenages, de forces et de calculs*], but the process as such no longer has any of the trappings of progression, it has only those of being carried along, of being carried away, and to finish, of explosion and implosion. How can we follow a current situation that has nothing current about it [*Comment accompagner une actualité qui n'a rien d'actuel*], which bears witness only to an enormous, obscure drift [*dérive*]; emerging from the night of time and sliding into another night?

The "inactual actuality" of our times thus points to the collapse of the grand Hegelian narrative (to use Lyotard's well-worn expression), where historical progress would be determined by a certain rationality, whose detours or "cunning" could be recognized and explained as the work of some Reason, whence a certain optimism in historical process as progress reflected in the feeling that "history is on our side." But history appears no longer to be on anyone's "side," if not that of bare "techno-economic" efficiency.[10] The trappings of progress are gone, leaving only the implosive or explosive cycle of brute force and reckoning, the tactical level of cunning, not cunning as a strategy of reason. Or even as a strategy of folly:

> But this aporia is but the flipside of the trust for which it expresses despair. We are haunted by process, and if it does not allow itself to be perceived as progress, we jump to the theme of degeneration. Perhaps it is necessary to arrive at the following understanding: there is no more of a mad cunning than of a rational one. Cunning is a word that presupposes a cunning agent [*un agent rusé*], a clever subject who bets on ends [*un fin sujet qui calcule des fins*]. But what appears to us today as "cunning," or as the overflowing [*débordement*] of history, an

overflowing such that neither history, nor eternity, can be found again, that can only be as follows:

Once history appeared, that is to say a finite destiny, we were quickly overwhelmed [*débordés*] by the absence of a subject of history, that is to say, a support, a henchman, an agent and a guide for it. The ordeal of the totalitarianisms would have been the ordeal of the *subjects* of history, or of subject-histories. Henceforth, it is a matter of understanding that history is essentially without a subject, that *history* or *historicity* means, very precisely: neither destiny, nor subject, but the infinity of an always finite sense [*l'infini d'un sens toujours fini*].

To think history thus without a subject and not as destiny but rather as the infinite of an always finite sense requires another form: "To this, form must be given" [*A cela, il faut donner forme*]. One can no longer write a chronicle in its "chronic" form in the spirit of a "freewheeling commentary on contemporary events" [*un libre commentaire de l'actualité*], since there is no longer anything "actual" in that actuality, nothing rigorously contemporary in what is happening *now*, only the infinity of an always finite sense. Which sense, as Nancy notes elsewhere, is "the only production whose infinity is tolerable."[11]

How to give form or shape, then, to this changing relation to history? Nancy indulges us then with a brief sketch, the monogrammatic contours if one likes, of an intellectual history, the history of the giving shape to history, the history of the making of historical sense, and so the infinity of an ever-finite sense:

> In their time, this is what Montaigne, Cervantes and Shakespeare did. It's what the age of the baroque did or wanted to do: in becoming worldly Christianity gave figure and cadence to the arhythmically unfigurable [*l'infigurable arythmique*]. Still, it was necessary to believe, ultimately, in the birth of man. But during this time, the same Christianity engendered itself as the subject of history: the salvation of the human genus by the generic human being, and vice-versa. This was the subject against man, and the cunning of his reason.

This odd paragraph is not unlike the opening paragraph of *Monogrammes* XIV, where the complaint about publication delays is countered by the persistence of the message's ongoing "freshness." We seem to have gone from the need to invent new forms in the absence of a universalizing history to the very development of that history out of secularized Christianity in the guise of classic, enlightenment humanism. Nancy can't help but comment on the irony of his own historical sketch (*esquisse*):

All of this, this history that I am thus sketching out is too perfect, functions too well through some kind of supreme cunning. This will one day have to be told otherwise, or else no longer told. Cunning and reason will only have been but a time in history. We are at the end. If history shows us its cunning in so ostensible a manner, it is because there isn't any cunning anymore—nor reason either, any more than madness [*déraison*].

The problem is that trying to tell the history of the invention of forms responsive to the ever-finite sense of the historical moment ends up falling into the very form of historical thinking (via the cunning of reason) that is being contested under the current situation where nothing is "current" anymore and where the calculated cunning of techno-economic power is only too obvious (*ostensible*). Nancy concludes, "Another form is to be invented. Cunning is useless, reasoning is useless. So too for spontaneous outbursts (another version of the same cunning, a refreshing one). The only thing to do is to hang on as well as one can, to the invention of forms [tenir bon, sur l'invention des formes]. But to *hang on* as well as one can, up to the point where there is neither support nor resistance [Mais tenir bon jusqu'au point où il n'y a plus d'appui ni de résistance]. To hang on well without knowing why or for what, nor what that *well* might be [Tenir bon sans savoir pourquoi ni pour quoi, ni de quel bon il peut s'agir]. To hang on well because humanity will always give itself a new form." The challenge of finding the right form is not to be underestimated, and we cannot simply rely on previous forms of cunning and reason, nor even upon spontaneous expression, which merely subscribes to the same ruse in another way (since such spontaneity presupposes the validity of a "naïve" response to the moment without thinking that what is in question is precisely how and what we understand by "being in the moment"). But if one does not rise to the challenge of "hanging on well" to the invention of some other form, then some other form will come to us, since "humankind always gives itself a new form."

But *what* that form is matters tremendously. How we think about who we are could not be more consequential, and the last of Nancy's second series of *monogrammes* turns to a singularly devastating critique of the contemporary social sciences (the explicit topic of that entire issue of *Futur antérieur*). In Nancy's view, the social sciences have become organized primarily as an exercise in auto-ethnology driven by surveys and statistics, and thereby have abdicated any responsibility to think beyond the narcissistic self-affirmation of a society complacent in the contemplation of its own image:

> These so-called social sciences hold exactly the place where the worn out or abortive form of this society is made. They are the form of what does not create any form. A society that no longer needs to invent its

> form, that has neither form, nor style, nor rhythm, is a society that can do no more than mirror itself, admire itself and despise itself within an indefinite profusion of reflections of itself, of a *self that is fleeting enough to be merely the stringing along of these reflections themselves. That is what, ordinarily speaking at least, one calls* social sciences: a sociality that is conventional, preprogrammed, with no invention of sociality, of self-knowledge, of a self-image. By indulging in our own ethnology . . . , we project an image of ourselves as a society without history. . . .

The social sciences thus mime the collapse of the historical narrative into mere technique and calculation. In the absence of any utopian or "exonomous" vision or the project of an imagined form,[12] the "science" of society such as it is abdicates any responsibility to (re)invent who we are and thereby abandons all sense of history as sense-making ("the infinity of an always finite sense"), leaving only the narcissism of media-based self-display:

> A society which thereby knows, or *believes it knows*, what it is *qua* society, which knows it and distributes this knowledge, that's what one calls the media, which are nothing other than the self-exhibition and the self-confirmation of the so-called social sciences, relentlessly displaying the anatomy of a social body that is itself defined by its capacity to anatomize itself, and hence by its cadaverous state. This takes place not only in gaudy magazines filled with opinion polls and tests: this also takes place in thick scholarly tomes, filled with surveys and statistics. This society is summed up by the exhibition of its own cunning to invent nothing other than itself. It is for itself and by itself the *absolute social science*: science as sociality and sociality as science, as if, in another register, physics were itself matter, and matter physics. . . .

The social body thus construed is a dead one, incapable of "inventing anything other than itself," and its *science*, social science, consigned to the mere tautology and narcissism of societal self-reflection. Nancy concludes the last of these *monogrammes* with an acerbic and monogrammatic call to arms: "What remains is insurrection, invention of forms" [Le reste est insurrection, invention des formes].

Kantian Schematics

But the end of the second series and the provisional abandonment of Nancy's attempts to write a "philosophical chronicle," as well as the call to invent new "forms," send us right back to the first *monogrammes*. Let's recall the first and third definitions of the term "monogram," which open that entry: "kinds of written monologues" and an ancient, outdated term for "what consists only in lines, in the contours." I neglected to cite the second of the three definitions, something other than either the personal or the institutional (dictionary) definitions that frame and surround this middle definition. This second or middle definition is a philosophically technical one derived from Kant's *Critique of Pure Reason*: "monograms composed of isolated traits and determined by no given rule, forming a wavering design [*dessin flottant*], so to speak, among various experiences." This definition comes from the section on "The Ideal of Pure Reason" in the first *Critique* and rejoins the earlier chapter "On the Schematism of the Pure Concepts of the Understanding," where Kant postulates the necessity of something in-between the understanding and sensibility or perception, something that can mediate between category or concept, on the one hand, and appearance or intuition, on the other, and that "makes possible the application of the former to the latter": "This mediating representation must be pure (without anything empirical) and yet *intellectual* on the one hand and *sensible* on the other."[13] Such a representation is what he then calls a *schema*, whose mediating function he elaborates as follows: "The schema is in itself always only a product of the imagination; but since the synthesis of the latter has as its aim no individual intuition but rather only the unity in the determination of sensibility, the schema is to be distinguished from an image" (273). Kant gives the example, then, of putting five points down in a line as an *image* of the number five, whereas if we "think a number in general," such as the number five, "this thinking is more the representation of a method for representing a multitude . . . in accordance with a certain concept than the image itself." The expression "representation of a method for representing" is quite striking and at the limit of comprehensibility. Given that a "method," as Descartes so famously refined the word (*meta-hodos*, what stands alongside a path, such as guideposts) is already the representation of a *way* of thinking, the schema would seem to be a "thinking" that is a representation *of* a representation *of* a way to make a representation, a tertiary form of representation, then, whose method or procedural thoughtfulness enables it somehow to serve as a pathway between sensibility and the understanding, or between sense and sense: "Now this representation of a general procedure of the imagination for providing a concept with its image is what I call the schema for this concept" (273); moreover, "we will call the procedure of the understanding with these schemata the *schematism* of the pure understanding" (273).

Kant elaborates that "in fact it is not images of objects but schemata that ground our pure sensible concepts," and here he gives another example, the canonical one, also drawn from Descartes, among many others, of the triangle:

No image of a triangle would ever be adequate to the concept of it. For it would not attain the generality of the concept, which makes this valid for all triangles, right or acute, etc., but would always be limited to one part of this sphere. The schema of the triangle can never exist anywhere except in thought, and signifies a rule of the imagination with regard to pure shapes in space. (273)

As such, schemata are "the true and sole conditions for providing [concepts] with a relation to objects, thus with *significance*" (276). But when it comes to differentiating schema from image, Kant demurs: "We can say only this much: the *image* is a product of the empirical faculty of productive imagination, the *schema* of sensible concepts (such as figures in space) is a product and as it were a *monogram* of pure a priori imagination, through which and in accordance with which the images first become possible, but which must be connected with the concept, to which they are themselves never fully congruent, always only by means of the schema we designate" (274).

Remarkably, the schema, which is the very condition of signification in the Kantian critique as what links image and concept, intuition and understanding, the sensible and the intelligible, is "as it were" itself a kind of monogram, which elsewhere is described, in the chapter on "the ideal of pure reason," among "creatures of the imagination, of which no one can give us an explanation or an intelligible concept":

> They are, as it were, *monograms*, individual traits, though not determined through any assignable rule, constituting more a wavering sketch, as it were, which mediates between various appearances, than a determinate image, such as what painters and physiognomists say they have in their heads, and is supposed to be an incommunicable silhouette of their products or even of their critical judgments. (552–53)

If schemata are a kind of monogram or "product of pure a priori imagination," they somehow represent the possibility inherent in the senselessness of the monogram nonetheless to *make* sense; they are the "condition of possibility for signification in general" while themselves remaining unsusceptible of being given "an explanation or an intelligible concept." They "*signify* a rule of the imagination" but are "not determined through any assignable rule"; they are a "*representation* of a method for representing" yet seem to fall below the threshold of a representation: "more a wavering sketch . . . than a determinate image." The monogram is something wavering between what is *given* in sensibility and *thought* in the understanding, an *unum quid* of cognition as the condition of possibility for the difference between sensory sense and intelligible sense, or in Nancean terms, between sense in every sense.

Retraits

The monogrammatic schema thus inhabits a liminal space in Kantian epistemology between the sensible and the intelligible: a space of lines, contours, traces, and *gramma*, not quite an image and not yet a concept. Looking ahead to *Monogrammes XIV*, it is the not yet formed possibility of other forms (invention, insurrection), and as such, it evokes the infinity of an always finite sense. But it is back at the beginning of *Monogrammes II* that Nancy undertakes his most explicit commentary on the Kantian notion of the monogram:

> The monogram is thus something traced before there is sense [*un tracé d'avant le sens*], neither sensible, nor senseless [*ni sensé, ni insensé*]. A wavering trace, not yet a figure, not yet an imprint, and not yet a writing [*Un tracé flottant, pas encore une figure, pas encore une empreinte, et pas encore une écriture*]. Its "wavering" is not for that matter pure and simple chaos; there is tracing [*traçage*], and trace (there is *gramme*), the sketching out of determination, of delineation; there is, not completed and not put together, a pinpointing [*repérage*] of places, orientations, and connections.

The monogram remains at the level of a pre-text, a not yet inscription that is nonetheless a kind of de-lineation of lines; the hint of a determination in an as-yet undetermined, incomplete, and unconnected *pinpointing* of place, direction, and connectivity; a *repérage* or "repair" in the archaic sense of a place one goes back to, a place delineated or pinpointed by the plural singularity of a trace that is always a re-tracing, a *re-trait* that is both withdrawal and emergence, *éclosion et déclosion*. A *retrait* or re-treat that is a "wavering," as in the "wavering sketch" or "*schwebende Zeichnung*," hence a *schweben* in Schlegel's romanticist sense as well.[14] It is not "pure and simple chaos" but rather the lineaments of a schema, a singular de-lineation that is the condition of possibility for sense in general: "This—the schema, schematism—is thus not by itself sense—nor having sense," but "that which, before any sense is articulated (before any object is presented), articulates the possibility of any given sense" ["Cela, le scheme, le schématisme, n'est donc pas par soi-même sens—ni du sens" [mais] "ce qui, avant qu'aucun sens soit articulé (avant qu'aucun objet soit présenté), articule la possibilité d'un sens quelconque"]. The schematism of the monogram in its wavering traits is, "as it were," to the Kantian opposition between the sensible and the intelligible what the "*unum quid*" or the "as if one" is to the Cartesian distinction between mind and body. But only on the condition that this "as if" does not take place as a union of opposites however tenuous, not a dialectical overcoming, but rather as the endless interruption of their differences, i.e., not between *the* sensible and *the* intelligible but as the endless and ineradicable difference between sense and sense, in every sense. Hence, the very condition of sense itself, the possibility of its articulation as the singularity "of any given sense," as well as "the infinity of an always finite sense."

This Bird Has Flown

What is the link, then, between this pre-sense of the monogram and the practice of writing a chronicle? What exactly is the project that unfolds in the series of monogrammes? In *Monogrammes II*, Nancy specifies: "The philosophical chronicle ought to be consecrated, as one says, to this: to what, in the era, in the mood of the moment—and in the mood of people—schematizes philosophy. To that which traces the wavering and fragmentary contours for philosophy" [La chronique philosophique devrait être consacrée, comme on dit, à ça: À ce qui, dans l'époque, dans l'air du temps—et dans l'air des gens—schématise de la philosophie. À ce qui trace des contours, flottants et fragmentaires, pour de la philosophie]. This formulation suggests a different kind of chronicle, one that is neither a simple or "free-wheeling" commentary on current events nor a rigorous decipherment of reason's cunning in the historical moment, but rather an approach to what philosophy should be attending to in the current situation, what "schematizes" philosophy in that singular moment. In other words, those shaky bits of images call for philosophical reflection and the sense-making that is the schematism of the understanding at work in the realm of these disjointed traits that are not yet sense, called monograms. Nancy makes clear that this philosophical *écoute* in the moment is not something "pre-" or "infra"-philosophical, not a "subordination of any kind," and certainly *not* "something like a philosophical potentiality or virtuality that philosophy and its discourse would be charged with actualizing."

Rather, Nancy argues, "The discourse of the philosopher only actualizes that which has effectively already been produced." He adds, "Hegel knew this well: the owl only takes flight at the end of the day" [la chouette ne s'envole qu'à la fin du jour]. But how do we understand the role of this "poor owl?" asks Nancy.[15] It cannot simply be a question of reducing philosophy to the "useless and always belated registering of a history that always precedes it." Rejecting such a "masochistic" view on Hegel's part, Nancy clarifies what Hegel understood by the owl's flight: "Hegel knew (and this might even be exactly what he inaugurated within knowledge) that what is produced does not take place within the instant of its event (or, if you like, that there is no natural history), but only in the repetition of thought." This "repetition of thought," Nancy cautions, does *not* mean that "the event takes place if it is repeated 'in thought' (in the mode of representation, and of discourse), but that which, in it, takes place [*a lieu*]—that which truly *happens* [ce qui *arrive* vraiment]—is what of it is repeated, what of it is thought" [c'est ce qui de lui se répète, ce qui de lui se pense]. It is thus that philosophy, like the owl's evening flight, "actualizes" what happens, because what happens *actually (wirklich)*, or "truly," is what can be repeated in thought, what can be thought. "Thinking," in this sense, adds Nancy, "no longer designates an intellectual faculty, nor the order of discourse (even if it must *pass* that way); 'thinking' signifies that what happens happens" [que ce qui arrive *arrive*]. Thinking (or "being thought" Nancy stipulates) means that what happens actually *happens*, or "truly" happens. Without thought's repetition, the event doesn't truly happen, doesn't matter, or is inconsequential, and an event without consequences cannot, rigorously speaking, be said to be "eventful," is not an event. The task of thinking is therefore not inconsequential at all, but the very consequence of what happens, and it in turn makes what happens consequential. We return to the opening sentence, where we are told that a philosophical chronicle should be consecrated to what "in the era, in the mood [air] of the moment—and in the mood of people—schematizes philosophy" [dans l'époque, dans l'air du temps—et dans l'air des gens—*schématise* de la philosophie]. It's a question of what's in the air (how else might the owl take flight?), or on people's minds, or of the moment (*époque*). "Thought" concludes Nancy, "signifies that what happens really happens."

    A break is introduced into the text at this point, after which Nancy reflects on the preceding discourse: "What I just wrote does not belong to the philosopher." The philosopher cannot take credit for the owl's flight. "A given painter, writer, or musician knows quite well (that is to say, thinks) what is involved. (A given philosopher, on the other hand, knows nothing about it. . . .)" Artists may know what they are making, since it is they who make it (*poein*), but the philosopher cannot speak for others: "I dare not say it: everyone of us knows it, for it is precisely not true, it's not true in a simple and immediate way. 'Everyone' is not without some other form of adjudication, and at every instant, in *truth*. It depends upon what happens (to him/her)." It all depends on what happens, but what happens depends in turn upon "the schema, the monogram, that suspended, wavering trace . . . , through which or along which that happens [*ça arrive*]." This is how philosophy is "schematized," by thinking what happens, by what happens to thought, at the end of the day, so to speak, through whatever it is that "traces wavering and fragmentary contours for philosophy," the monogram.

"Traits of Another Thought"

Another break is introduced, after which we are given an "example" of how this happens, in the explicit form now of a "chronicle of the most minute and most immediate actuality": "For example, and to make a chronicle of the most minute and immediate actuality [pour faire chronique de l'actualité la plus mince et la plus immédiate]—anachronistic by the time you read this— I'm writing these lines in the countryside, in the month of July, towards the end of the day (well, well! [*tiens, tiens!*])." So, the example of how philosophy is schematized turns us back again to the philosopher's "retreat" or repair, his isolated country home far from the urban commotion of the metropolis.[16] It is his "immediate" actuality, because that is where *hic et nunc* he is writing, even if, as if in anticipation of *Monogrammes XIV*, the gap between writing and publication (not to speak of the gap that is the very event of writing) necessarily defers the so-called immediacy of this actuality, made no longer current and in the moment but always already "anachronistic," no longer chronic and thus underscoring the inalterable untimeliness of every chronicle (again in anticipation of *Monogrammes XIV*). Trying to write what is happening now may truly actualize it, may make it really, "truly" happen, but this writing from the outset always comes afterward, at the end of the day. In noting the evening hour when he writes these lines, Nancy exclaims, "*Tiens, tiens!*," as if in surprise before the coincidence that isn't, the moment for the owl to soar.

All chronicles are thus necessarily anachronistic, and never more so than when they seek to be as "actual," as current as possible. Perhaps this suggests Nancy's interesting use of the word "*mince*" to accompany "immediate" as adjectives qualifying "actuality." How can actuality be "thin"? *Mince* is of course related to the word *minute* as a thin or slender slice of time, a "mincing" of time if you will, hence my choice of translation. But it is the "thinness" of the minced moment that strikes me, that recalls the inescapability of the present moment not as presence, being present or present being, but as divided between the marker "now" and what both precedes and succeeds it. The thinness of the actual moment has no depth, being no more than the depthless depth of a line, a mere trace of the difference between "now" and *now*. And in trying to re-mark that trace, to grasp the presence of the "now," we encounter only the re-treat of time, of the finitude that in turn is the condition for what happens to happen, for there even to be something like an actuality to chronicle. For Kant, the monogram that mysteriously takes the shape of a schema, insofar as it is the "apprehension of an intuition" (or more verbosely, "the unity of the synthesis of the manifold of a homogeneous intuition" [274]), is that by which the subject generates time itself as inner sense: "The schemata are therefore nothing but a priori time-determinations in accordance with rules" (276).[17] "*Mince*," we might say! But what about all those other "individual traits not determined through any assignable rule," those "wavering sketches," those monograms, in other words, that do *not* emerge as schemata? What is the determining role "at the end of the day," of apperception, of apprehension, in the actually happening of what happens, in the *schematization* of the monogrammatical, in the flight of philosophy?

And what is it exactly that we get in the guise of this most minute and immediate actuality? The philosopher at home, or more precisely, a prodigiously detailed description of that remote country home in Les Ayes, which we have already encountered twice (once at the break of spring and once at the break of winter). "Now" we have the midsummer heat of July, and the overgrown abundance of an old farmyard left unattended during the year, a vacation retreat where something happens, but what?:

> The old farmyard, deserted during the year, is covered with exuberant vegetation, tall weeds, and grasses dotted with poppies and hairy willow herbs. A young ash tree is already able to bear the weight of the birds on its branches. Has something happened, is something happening? [*Est-il arrivé, arrive-t-il quelque chose?*] In the joyful sovereignty of the vegetation, in the flower-laden wisteria, and farther off, in those nettles as tall as a man, what is happening? Or else, in the flight of the swallows? Or in the secret presence, which only the dogs sense, of some wild animal, maybe a weasel [*belette*]? Does anything happen other than these very images, and this worn-out imagery [*cette imagerie usée*]? Anything other than a romantic or ecologicist sentimentality [*attendrissement*] that takes itself for a meditation on nature stamped with authenticity on account of its having taken place "within" nature? Anything other than the thrill of the philosopher out in the fields, who thinks this is coming cheek by jowl [*qui croit s'aboucher avec*] to the *Physis* (after all, we have on this subject an entire album of photos by Heidegger . . .)?

A beautiful passage indeed, and all the more so since the writer manages to wring out all the possible commonplaces of rustic idyll from what in point of fact appears to be an overgrown, weed-ridden patch of land, concealing and revealing a wildness emblematized by that indeterminate hint of a lurking weasel (a "belette," or "belle petite bête [lovely little beast]," he reminds us, allowing the etymology to convert the specific species into a generic animality). We remember from *Monogrammes III* that "nature likes to hide itself," but what is happening in this stunning *éclosion/déclosion* that is clearly attentive to something else lurking in "worn out imagery" [*imagerie usée*]? The commonplace answers are all ruled out: the paroxysms of romanticist sensibility, the in-situ declaration of ecological "authenticity," the philosophical epiphany of an intimate encounter with the physical world that is nature. It is something other than Rousseau's tears or Heidegger's photos, and certainly something other than a "green" manifesto.

"Something else happens in fact," Nancy rejoins, something coming "through the grasses and fields, fireweed and weasels (and through the words of course . . .)":

> Something wholly other happens, and it takes once again, as if by chance, the voice of Kant: at the end of a Mary McCarthy novel, whose action is situated in Paris during May of '68, Kant appears to the main character to tell him: "Nature is dead, *mein Kind*"—nature is dead, my child.

The contemplation of his unkempt farmyard leads not to the rapture of an immersion in nature but to a literary citation, specifically in the form of a ghostly prosopopoeia spoken by a philosopher, and not just any philosopher but Kant himself, "as if by chance." The citation schematizes the manifold of images into an apperception leading to a conclusion that is different from the simple meaning of the words:

> "Nature is dead," that can be understood and commented upon in many ways, whose tally doesn't interest me. But something happens with "mein Kind," with that slight trembling of the German voice, of the philosophical voice. These two words exceed the variably interpretive abstraction of "nature is dead." They trace a wholly other schema, and that is the schema of a mourning. What thereby happens—and which renders, for us, something in the order of sense and truth—is less the death of nature than the announcement of the mourning which commences, and this news brought out like a child who has lost a mother, along with the pain, the tenderness and the courage that will be needed to accompany the mourning.

What makes this schema wholly other (*tout autre*) is not the content stating the death of nature (a commonplace susceptible to a rather predictable list of interpretations, as Nancy points out and rightly refuses to enumerate) but the *announcement* of the demise of nature spoken in the voice of Kant and addressed to a child listener, who is spoken *to* in English (the child's language) but addressed as such *in* German (the philosopher's language). It is as if the *auditory* dimension unified the visual manifold of images, "that slight trembling of the German voice," with its vocalic "wavering" in place of the sketch's *Schweben*, and the paternal injunction to undertake that "painful, tender, and courageous" work of mourning, whose process Freud described as a conjuring of images, each called up in turn to be let go,[18] like the sequence of images Nancy himself details in describing the farmyard in Les Ayes, evoking one by one the images of nature painfully, tenderly, and courageously: "Through the grasses—and the strange invention of a novelist [l'étrange invention d'une romancière]—comes to me the mourning for a mother, whom one called in effect nature, and along with this mourning, in order to bear it and to follow through with it [pour porter ce deuil et pour l'accomplir], the monogram of a painful, tender, and courageous thought." The mourning comes to him through the plant life and a novelist's "strange invention," comes about (*arrive*) as something that happens and that must be borne by the philosopher, to whom it comes or happens, with a painful, tender, and courageous thinking, a powerful monogram, but one he hastens to add, whose "adjectives are not very suitable, it would seem, for philosophy" [ces adjectifs conviennent assez peu, semble-t-il, à de la philosophie]. That possible "unsuitability," however, and far from being in any simple way "inappropriate" to philosophical reflection, is rather what "schematizes" it, what traces—in whatever wavering or fragmentary way—that to which a "philosophical chronicle," like the *monogrammes* series, should be consecrated. "Here float the traits of another thought" [Il flotte ici les traits d'une autre pensée], writes Nancy in conclusion.

Kind/Kind

If we recall Nancy's later summation from *Monogrammes XIV*: "What remains is insurrection, invention of forms," and the association of such formal inventiveness with the names of Montaigne, Cervantes, Shakespeare, and now Mary McCarthy, then we need to stop and examine the place of literature in the "traits" of that "other thought," in the disjointed monograms that somehow, in this instance, *hic et nunc*, rise to the level of a schema that articulates, *unum quid*, the sensible and the intelligible, that "represents a way of representing" what as yet remains unthought.

The "strange invention" attributed to Mary McCarthy as novelist is a citation from the last line of *Birds of America* (1965), a novel that begins, interestingly enough, with the death of an owl. Curiously, and despite his preceding reflection on Hegel's owl, and on the various birds in his yard, Nancy does not mention the novel by name. Much is at stake everywhere here in the possibilities and conditions of flight, metaphorical and literal, aviary and philosophical, in a kind of pervasive syllepsis. *Birds of America*, as I said, begins with the death of an owl and its emotional impact on a young American about to spend a year in Paris (the year is 1964, not 1968, as Nancy misstates, perhaps by intention). The young man is obsessed with birds and the natural world in general, as well as with Kantian philosophy, and, in particular, with the possible applications of the moral imperative to his daily life. He is also deeply attached to his twice-divorced mother, who is herself associated with nature in general and with birds in particular.[19]

The end of the story is triggered by the protagonist being bitten in the Jardin des Plantes by, of all things, a black swan. Unable to overcome infection and an allergic reaction to penicillin, he ends up delirious in the hospital. First, in flesh and blood, his mother appears from the U.S. and disappears again. Then, in the novel's closing scene, he hallucinates a bedside visit by the philosopher from Königsberg in the guise of a kindly old man with an important message for him. The message is initially misunderstood to be that "God is dead," to which the boy protests, "I *know* that," and "you didn't say that anyway, Nietzsche did." Kant leans forward to specify:

> "No what *I* say to you is something important. You did not hear me correctly. Listen now carefully and remember." Again he looked Peter steadily and searchingly in the eyes. "Perhaps you have guessed it. Nature is dead, *mein kind*." (344; *sic*)

In citing this final line, Nancy corrects the English text by capitalizing "*Kind*" as it should be in German. But the uncapitalized English version generates some different and unexpected outcomes. "Kind" in English refers also to *likeness* (as in the expression, the monograms are "*kinds* of written monologues," or to understand McCarthy's novel as "a *kind* of Bildungsroman"). *Kind*, in this sense, is also a *kind* of schema, a vague likeness or image, the representation of a way of representing. As such, *kind* also recalls the notion of "family resemblance," and indeed the German word for child (*Kind*) is etymologically linked to the English word for likeness of category. My "kind" is also my "kin." Or, as Hamlet says: "A little more than kin, and less than kind."[20]

There is, of course, another meaning to the English word "kind," and that refers to the act of caring and generosity, of being "kind" to someone. Here, we can only evoke in passing both the importance of "care" (*Sorge*) in Heidegger's *Being and Time* and the Kantian moral imperative, which is also the key driver in the behavior of McCarthy's protagonist. He aspires to be kind throughout a series of misadventures, culminating in the swan's bite, all of which, and recalling again the incipit of the dead owl, point to a less than kind image of nature.

The death of nature thus appears more portentous than the misheard and banal death of God, and the weight of that announcement is mitigated by the polysemy of the word *kind*, uttered by the kindly old man who is also the character's philosophical ideal. To be greeted as his child or "kind" softens the blow of the dread announcement and of the task of mourning that must then begin, a mourning that is also a farewell to childhood and the affirmation of the protagonist's incipient maturity and consequent detachment from his mother. The polysemy of the word "kind" also motivates Nancy's characterization of the scene as not only "sorrowful" but also "tender" and "courageous." Alternatively, and a bit more ominously, the philosopher's appearance is also a taking possession of the child—*mein Kind*—correlatively to the mother's suspect disappearance, her vanishing or *retrait* (and this is not the last time we will encounter a problematic retreat of the mother).

The task of mourning the loss of a mother—in this case, what the paternal voice here calls "nature"—is the "strange invention" of a literary text that beckons to philosophy while speaking in the fictive voice of *the* critical philosopher. It is not a question of how to be a philosopher in one's garden or out in the *physis*, but of the philosophical urgency to think beyond the *meta-physis* of some foundational identity, be it God or nature, or history, or nation, or self. Philosophy would *begin* with the awareness of loss, of finitude, of insuperable negativity. The mourning of metaphysics is the dusk that motivates the flight of Minerva's owl through the wavering, disjointed "traits of another thought," the not-yet sense of the monogram that signifies not merely the salutary strangeness of that other thought (that "strange invention," the "insurrection" of forms) but the very estrangement of thought itself, which exceeds any notion of philosophy as merely a technical competency in concepts and discourses.

Stranger Than Thought

In the final pages of *Monogrammes II*, Nancy continues to dwell on the necessary attentiveness to this *"schéma inédit"* or the strangeness of that "other thought." Reflecting on a recent colloquium at his home university of Strasbourg, he points to what is supposed to happen in a *col-loquium* (literally, a speaking together)—namely, the opportunity for thinking to take place in-between the closed idioms of specialized knowledge, on the one hand, and the open communicability of all discourse, on the other: "It is evident that a colloquium cannot take place—if it truly takes place—except in this 'in-between' [*'entre'*]. But how? there again, wouldn't that suppose an unprecedented schema [un *schème inédit*] of pain, tenderness and courage?" The "traits of another thought" are those that float or waver in-between the expressions of clarity and obscurity, universality and singularity, ready comprehensibility and resistant obscurity. *Monogrammes II* closes with a review of a work by his close colleague and friend Philippe Lacoue-Labarthe, for whom Nancy has no higher praise than his pursuing "a constant, obstinate (even obsessive) practice of the *strangeness* of thought [*l'étrangeté de la pensée*]":

> Philosophy, for him, is not the completely localizable [*repérable*], if not wholly familiar, order of concepts and their discourses. Philosophy, for that matter, is not above all the terrain of difficult questions—but of strange questions, barely questions, moreover, and often suspicions, worries, forebodings, always strange.

Qualifying this further, Nancy adds that it is not the strangeness per se of the object studied that matters so much as the concomitant *estrangement* of thought [*l'étrangement de la pensée*]: "It's a thinking that never stops becoming strange to itself, itself losing the very knowledge it acquires. Thereby, it suspends itself, as if by interdiction, at the limit of knowledge, and of the knowledge of self." Can this still be called philosophy, or is it rather the "future of philosophy?"[21] A future not in some progressive or anticipatory sense, much less a developmental one, but rather as what is to come (*à-venir*), what always stands resolutely *in front of* philosophical reflection, the wavering contours and incomprehensible silhouettes that *fore-see* other forms, the "strange inventions" of novelists or artists ("what painters and physiognomists say they have in their heads" [Kant, *Critique of Pure Reason*, 552]).[22]

The monogram signifies that future, that otherness of thought, its very estrangement, the ongoing atmosphere ("*l'air du temps*" or "*l'air des gens*") that is the limit condition of thinking (the "incommunicable silhouette") and where philosophical reflection can only take off owl-like in the twilight of its own mourning. Elsewhere, Nancy describes the "requirement of reason" in the following manner: "that of casting light on its own obscurity, not by bathing it in light, but by acquiring the art, the discipline and the strength to let the obscure emit its own clarity."[23] At the same time, this "demand that carries thought outside of itself"[24] does not suppose a solipsistic figure of the philosopher, on the contrary: "'a philosopher meaning here not a technician of the concept, but first that which is expected, even required, today of common wisdom or conscience."[25] As the practice of such an exemplary *écoute*, Nancy's *monogrammes* remain an interrupted but also interruptive chronicle of philosophy, an interruption of philosophy into the world. They form a philosophical chronicle of interruption, one that anachronistically thinks the air we breathe at any given moment and dares the insurrectional invention of forms, even or especially through the withdrawal (which is always also the emerging) of philosophical thought from the actualities and conditions of the world, be it the estrangement of that "other thought" staged within or without the philosopher's retreat, at les Ayes, in Strasbourg, or elsewhere. . . .

Postscript, Kind of . . .

In 2002, nine years after the last *monogrammes* written in 1993, Nancy returns again to the genre of the "philosophical chronicle" in a series of radio lectures, gathered afterward in a book by that title. There are nine of these short talks delivered over an eleven-month period.[26] The published version indicates the date (but not the place) for each of these texts. The term *monogrammes* seems to be abandoned, despite a certain similarity in the kind of discourse. One major dissimilarity is in the much greater argumentative cohesion of these "chronicles" than the more dispersed and fragmentary style of the *monogrammes* series. Nonetheless, the first of these published lectures discusses what Nancy now means by a "philosophical chronicle." The resulting text can be read as a commentary on the earlier *monogrammes*:

> A chronicle of philosophy. What can this really mean? A chronicle is a rubric indicating something punctual and periodical, whose content has to do either with a particular specialization (gastronomy, gardening, etc.), or with a subjectivity (the world according to the mood of the chronicler). But philosophy, in whatever manner we envisage it, aspires to be removed from specialization as well as from subjectivity. From the beginning and in principle, it demands the universal and the objective.

The "philosophical chronicle" appears as a perilous and insuperable oxymoron. To philosophize is to reject every conditionality, to seek the unconditional, but that would mean an invariant that is utterly at odds with the necessary variability of a chronicle. To engage the form of the chronicle would not only be to abandon this philosophical imperative but also to risk the tendency "today" of a certain "cultural mode of 'philosophy' that endlessly warms up [a] very light broth [of 'values,' 'virtues,' and common sense], while letting the vague promise of an unconditional final truth float about in its vapor." The result is to accept "a cheap ethico-pragmatic consensualist ideology while boosting the market value quoted for 'the philosopher.'" But, as I hope these pages have shown, it is a distinctive *trait* of Jean-Luc Nancy's work to address the singular concerns of the moment while maintaining a philosophically committed approach to the questions involved, to pursue a philosophy that does not eschew but rather fearlessly engages the singular and the particular, the chronic and the anachronic, as a genuine philosophical problem.

> I do not claim that I can avoid the cultural peril without remainder or risk. I have chosen to brush up against this ambiguity because this cultural danger must be confronted on its own territory—by speaking on the radio, for example. This is not just a matter of strategy. It is also because the cultural development of philosophy itself opens up a question of some philosophical importance.

I could begin again by citing the very first of the *monogrammes*, written over forty years ago but under strikingly similar circumstances, during the first manifestations of the media-savvy *"nouveaux philosophes,"* whom Nancy takes to task in those first *monogrammes*. The challenge, then as now, is to engage the new venues and media while "hanging onto" or grasping the invention of forms, while resolutely practicing the insurrectional strangeness of thought itself. Strangely enough, this engagement might not be something new at all but, in effect, a return to a certain "classical" way of philosophizing, as Nancy writes at the beginning of *Monogrammes I*:

> A philosophical chronicle, today, what could that be then? The opportunity having been offered to me, my curiosity piqued, I seized upon it. I don't know if this venue is suitable, nor if I have the physical stamina for the job. . . . I dream of something that philosophy would have lost: an existence that is *chronic*, precisely, following the thread of time, tied to the rhythm of the seasons and reasons, partaking in our history, periodized and syncopated, full of occasions and interventions. I imagine classical philosophy existed like that. . . . Descartes, Leibniz, or Hume circulated in every way.

The "circulation" of classical philosophy and philosophers circles us back, then, to an existence that is demonstrably *chronic*, actualized in the presence or absence of any given *actualité*, "full of occasions and interventions," of interruptions, a syncopated philosophizing that finds its forms, insurrectional or not, in the disjointed traces or wavering designs of the monogram.

Impossible Return

After another long interruption, Nancy relaunched the *monogrammes* series one last time, beginning with the Number 10 issue of *L'Impossible* (February 2013) and continuing with two installments in Numbers 12 (April 2013), and 13 (Summer 2013). Nancy's reiterated reprise of the ever-interrupted *monogrammes* thus casts a rather obvious pall of anachronicity, if not to say inaccuracy, over any remarks regarding the definitive abandonment of the term *monogrammes*. But then it always was within the potential of the "series" to begin anew and unexpectedly after a long hiatus (as happened before in the decade between the contributions to *Digraphe* and to *Futur antérieur*). And I did speak earlier of the "seeming" disappearance of the word *monogrammes* from an experimental form of occasional philosophy that can just as easily take on different names (chronicle, for example) as well as different venues, times, and places. Appearing in the journal *L'Impossible*, the first of these last *monogrammes*, in characteristic Nancy style, redirects the name of the venue itself by taking the word "impossible" to mean something other than what is "not possible" or "unrealizable," but rather as "what is foreign to the economy of the possible and the impossible, to the calculation of what is (un)feasible, *in today's jargon*" [emphasis added]. It is, once again, to pursue the strangeness of philosophy to itself, interrupting itself, to ask the question of sense in the singularity of any given existence: "To think outside the possible is to think the unstated, the unheard—what every existence bears along with itself and which is never given or deposed." But the *sense* of thinking that singularity is never given simply, and never simply given. Rather, it only points the direction (another sense of the word "sense") to an impossible task, to be begun ever anew, "each and every time," as the untimely chronicle, the singularly plural *monogrammes*, of what is always yet to come, of what is an always ever-interrupted horizon of thought.

Monograms to Monographs

It would be an error, though, to limit Nancy's interventionist style of philosophy to only those texts explicitly labeled "monogrammes." That style also comes to take place in the well-recognized form of monographs, books, articles, interviews, and the like. We see this tendency especially in his later works, beginning *inter alia* with *After Fukushima* in 2012 and culminating in three late works whose topicality is underscored by their titles: *The Fragile Skin of the World* (2020), An *All-Too-Human Virus* (2020), and *Mascarons de Macron* (2021).[27] Like the original monograms, dates, times, and places figure prominently in these essayistic writings, which address various contemporary disasters, crises, or challenges. At the same time, every one of these late works argues against the "equivalence of catastrophes" (the subtitle for *After Fukushima*), i.e., their subsumption under capitalism and the "general equivalent" that reduces everything to the money form. Concomitantly, these works also advocate for an "esteem of the singular," or even an "adoration directed at singularity as such" (*After Fukushima*, 39–40). Esteem, specifies Nancy, is to be understood in "the most intense sense of the word: a sense that turns its back on 'valuation' measures," what "goes beyond itself and addresses something inestimable, ... something more precious than any price, something incalculable" (39), something of incommensurable value. As opposed to standard estimation or valuation that brings everything back into an economy of circulation and exchange, esteem "summons the singular and its singular way to come to presence" (39), just as by its very address or adoration it acknowledges the "nonequivalence of all singularities" (38), their fundamental disparity, irreducibility, and plurality.

This esteem for the singular is also political to the extent that democracy, Nancy argues, "should be thought of starting only from the equality of incommensurables: absolute and irreducible singulars that are not individuals or social groups but sudden appearances, arrivals and departures, voices, tones—here and now, every instant" (41). What one calls "common equality" in this democracy of singularities is actually their "common incommensurability" or "a communism of nonequivalence" (41). But this communism or commonality of singularities must also imply their fundamental discontinuity or constitutive finitude, the liminality of what is singular *each and every time, here and now, every instant*, as the instance of its very interval, in-between the interruption of its coming or going, in the discretion of "space-times or takings-place that are also each time outsides-of-time-outsides-of-place" (*Fragile Skin of the World*, 98).

Finitude, writes Nancy, "constitutes the very essence of singularity" (98), an ironic statement to the extent that the singular by dint of its very (incommensurable, nonequivalent) singularity cannot be ascribed an essence, before which it would in any case leave no more than the trace of its retreat. But if finitude is said in turn to be constitutive of singularity, then, specifies Nancy, it is because "finitude thus lends itself to being understood neither as a limitation nor as a lack with respect to an infinitude, but on the contrary as the proper mode of accessing being or sense": "What takes place in singular finitude is the sharing-out [*partage*] of being and sense—of the sense of being, of being as sense—, a sharing-out that does not cross or blur the limits or the *ends* of the singular but that, on the contrary, distributes them and, in doing so, affirms them each time according to their exception" (*Fragile Skin of the World*, 159). This exceptional distribution, or distributive justice, also refigures Nancy's previously indicated concept of democracy as a communism of the nonequivalent, the common sense of a being-together only insofar as what makes us uncommon, singular, in our plurality.

Moreover, it is the recognition of "our knowing ourselves as finite—positively, absolutely, infinitely, and singularly finite and not indefinitely powerful [that] is the sole means of giving sense to our existences" (*An All-Too-Human Virus*, 40). Esteem for the singularity of finite being is thus also the condition for making sense in general, and *a fortiori* for making sense of the senselessness of existence, of the world. That esteem is thus also an exigency to be attentive to the singularity of the present, in its fleeting interruption as unexpected event. *After Fukushima* concludes with such an eloquent call to heed what is singular in the moment:

> The present I mean to evoke is the one that opens to this esteem of the singular and turns away from general equivalence and from its evaluation of past and future times, from the accumulation of antiquities and construction of projects. No culture has lived as our modern culture has in the endless accumulation of archives and expectations. No culture has made present the past and the future to the point of removing the present from its own passage. All other cultures, on the contrary, have known how to care for the approach of singular presence. (40)

Nancy's monograms, as a writing practice at least partially inspired by the Kantian notion of the schemata, does not as with Kant posit the *unum quid* interface between the sensible and the intelligible but rather navigates the ever-unpredictable relation between sense and singularity as what happens here and now, in the vanishing instant that is the passing of "singular presence" or the singularly present, its retreat or the interruption of its approach and withdrawal.

But the monograms do not merely bear witness to the interruption of the moment (be it the "sinister freshness" of a now that becomes even more of a "now" with delays, suspensions, and postponements); they, like Hegel's owl, also serve to actualize what has already happened, even in the moment—that is, to serve as a mode of interruption or intervention into the retreat of a singular presence. Giving a name to that singularity is one way for thought to take flight in the strangeness of the moment, as Nancy does in his late *Mascarons de Macron* (2021). Taking on the administration of France's current president, Nancy launches a series of short satirical sketches (schemata or monograms), actualized image-concepts of various Macronian moments that he names after the ornamental bas-reliefs one finds sculpted onto the facades of buildings, called mascarons, and that typically bear a name to match the face or icon. As opposed to a mask, however, which would hide something other than it shows (the very emblem of metaphysics incarnated in that masked philosopher who steps out either on stage or for God), a mascaron "dissimulates nothing: it is identical to the thought that it figures" (*Mascarons*, 10). But isn't this still another way of describing the schematism by which the understanding thinks what the senses give, or figure? Another term perhaps for the traits of that wavering sketch, "not a ciphered message, it's the Cipher itself, which does not cipher and thus does not decipher anything," to recall *Monogrammes* IV, the mascaron is but the ultimate monogram and *Mascarons de Macron* the final installment of Nancy's *monogrammes*. And in this series, the mascarons chronicle differing moments in a changed political environment—not the mask of power behind closed doors but the monogram that shows nothing beyond itself, like the featureless face of the president himself. It is a politics that is no longer political as it extolls only the value of management, a politics where the political has vanished, where it is in retreat. But this brings us back to an earlier development in Nancy's thinking, a moment when his incipient explorations of the monogram as a mode of interventionist writing, of writing as the very interruption of the singular, also raised the stakes for the political thinking that would ensue under the aegis of the Center for Philosophical Research on the Political, to which we will now turn. There it will be a question of a "singular logic."

3
The "Singular Logic of the Retreat"
Interruptions of the Political

> There where it withdraws, it should come to us.
> [*Là où ça se retire, ça doit nous arriver.*]
> —PHILIPPE LACOUE-LABARTHE AND JEAN-LUC NANCY,
> "LA PANIQUE POLITIQUE"

Interruption has so far defined both finitude and singular plurality as key elements of Nancy's thinking, first in the conceptual dimension of the deconstructed subjectivity he explicates with regard to Descartes and then in the prose practice of the monograms as a singularly plural philosophical practice. In the first case, Cartesian solipsism is convulsed by the *unum quid* of a retrenchment, of an iteration, that disintegrates the oneness that it posits, withdrawing its very sense of self from itself, be it mental or corporeal. The cogito is thus "constitutively unstable," in the unspeakable retreat of its utterance. In the second case, we see this iterative paradox again at work in the "wavering sketch" of the monogram, which is anything but "mono." Like Descartes's *unum quid*, the monogram is not so much the unity of the sensible and intelligible (or body and mind) as their uncommon ground, the gap that makes for sense in every sense. As for the sense of the singular, that is also the latter's vanishing point, the interruption that marks at the end of the day the taking flight of the philosophical, the thinking or making sense of what is sensed or given but only in its retreat. But this paradoxical logic of retreat or withdrawal, of appearance in or as disappearance, while underscoring the absolute finitude of the singular also opens onto the infinity of an ever-finite sense in the structurally in-between, the as-if bringing together, *unum quid*, of what is constitutively apart. Such a paradoxical being "with," channeling Heidegger's notion of *mitsein*, is a frequent theme in Nancy's thought,[1] but especially prominent in the social and political dimensions of his thinking as it emerges after *Ego Sum*[2] and after the first series of *Monogrammes*. This thinking is profoundly marked by his collaboration with Philippe Lacoue-Labarthe on the *Centre de recherches philosophiques sur le politique* from 1981 to 1983, an intellectual being-with that ultimately leads into his groundbreaking works on *The Inoperative Community* and *Being Singular Plural*.[3] At heart in this expansion of Nancy's philosophical project is what he and Lacoue-Labarthe suggestively term the "singular logic of the retreat," and so it would seem propitious to retrace the development of this term from its roots in Derrida's "The *Retrait* of Metaphor,"[4] through its application via the Center to the question of the political, and subsequent aporias in its articulation, or interruption, of the being together of singular beings. Rather than an overview of Nancy's political thinking per se, compelling examples of which can be found elsewhere,[5] this chapter will address the specific itinerary of the term *retrait* as it informs the expansion of his philosophical project to embrace the social and political while further elaborating the guiding relations between sense and singularity as interruption of philosophy.

Lexical Pre-considerations

The deployment of complex neologisms is a salient feature of Nancy's thinking and writing, evident in such terms such as *areality, disenclosure,* and *exscription*. By complex neologisms, I mean that these terms are not merely newly minted words but that they also function as critical operators that name the unforeseen and the unprecedented that appear in the spaces opened up by the adventurous rigor of his thought, by his very practice of philosophical estrangement and interruption. Although not a neologism per se, the French word *retrait*, which we have already encountered a number of times in this study, features among these terms as evidenced by the challenge it raises for English translators who find themselves struggling between its various meanings of withdrawal and retreat, sometimes opting for the neologistical "re-treat" or its even more neologistical verbal counterpart of "re-treating," or even the translator's decision *not* to translate the term, thus neologistically allowing the word to acquire its own semantic resonance, yet running the risk of making strange in English what passes (perhaps all too deceptively) for colloquial in French. In any case, the word *retrait*, including its morphological companions/ derivatives, is striking both for its prominence in Nancy's work—most dramatically, as we shall see, in those early analyses with Philippe Lacoue-Larbarthe of the "retreat of the political [*retrait du politique*]"—and its seemingly irreducible polysemy as applied to the political, but ultimately to other categories of analysis in Nancy's work: community, love, freedom, world, the divine, even thought itself.[6] Yet, at the same time, the word passes for innocuous and is barely perceptible in many of its iterations, thus both prominent and curiously discreet, seemingly simple and yet impenetrably dense. Nonetheless, its reach extends to touch almost every facet of Nancy's thinking. While not a neologism per se, its *use* is neologistical, like the foreignness of the foreign word in Benjamin's theory of translation, bending language to the strangeness of its sense, not just inter- but also intra-linguistically, not just the language of the other, but the very otherness of language itself.[7]

What does it mean for something to be "withdrawn," the most basic sense of the word, *retrait*, from *retraire* as a form of *retirer*, etymologically derived from Latin *retraho, retrahere*, meaning to draw back, withdraw, or pull back but also to divert, bring back, or make known again? At bottom, the prefix *re-* signals a revision of the act of dragging or pulling that *trahere* designates, but that *re-*, the very mark of repetition, leaves the actual sense of the repetition unspecified. It is indeed a renewed dragging or pulling, like the action of a tractor, but not necessarily in the same directional sense. In fact, does not the predominant sense of *retrait* specify the repetition of a renewed pulling, albeit *in the opposite direction*? A reversal rather than a mere repetition, hence also the sense of withdrawal, or that of retreat in the military or strategic sense. (Or, even that of a shrinking back or diminution, as attested by the earliest usage in French, actually Judeo-French, in the twelfth century, according to the *Trésor de la langue française*. And prior to adopting *retrait* as a conceptual operator, Nancy used the word *retrancher*, most notably as we saw in *Ego Sum*, a word that is also similar to this early sense of *retrait*.) The prefix *re-* designates a movement backward rather than a renewed movement forward, an interruption indecidably active and passive, withdrawing oneself as one makes the other withdraw.

Clearly, a *sense* of absence is also evoked but always already a noticeable one, such as when one speaks of someone being "withdrawn," a *socially marked* lack of sociability, as opposed to passing merely unnoticed. Or perhaps, more concretely, we should think of drawing or "withdrawing" money from the bank, the most quotidian meaning of the French word *retrait*. This is, for the withholder, more of a taking than a loss. On the other hand, when your employer withholds a certain amount from your paycheck as an advance deposit to the IRS, that has all the appearance of a theft, albeit one to protect you paternalistically from having to pay more taxes later.

The sense of absence from withdrawal thus always paradoxically presents itself as some kind of re-presencing or re-drawing, where what is removed seemingly reappears somewhere else, such as from your bank account to your billfold, a re-placement concomitant to the re-treat, a repetition and/or as displacement. But would this then lead us into a merely transactional sense of ontology, being withdrawn only to come forth elsewhere, a zero-sum circulation of being as a play of interchanging appearances and disappearances? Does every retraction posit an equal and simultaneous re-traction? "What erasure does not necessarily retrace what it erases?" writes Nancy.[8] But then are we not recaptured within a traditional logic of repetition, of presence and absence, be it a "singular" one?

In one of their earliest iterations of this term, Nancy and Lacoue-Labarthe qualify the logic of retreat as something other than a mere play of presence and absence, no simple alternation like the child's game of *fort/da* described by Sigmund Freud in his elaboration of the death drive as repetition compulsion.[9] Instead, they reject the concept of retreat or withdrawal as a kind of absence, as a mere disappearance: "*Retrait* is the act of appearing disappearing [*apparaître disparaissant*]. Not just of appearing *while* disappearing [*apparaître en disparaissant*], but of appearing as disappearance [*apparaître en tant que disparition*], within disappearance itself [*dans la disparition même*]."[10] As such, *retrait* is claimed to partake in the general Derridean-inspired problematic of "inscription, which traces itself only by withdrawing (within the unfigurable thickness of a material) the very incision that inscribes it." Moreover, "the incision—or excision—on the surface of an ego withdraws into an unfigurable, unidentifiable matter—which one would, nonetheless, have to call social matter." One readily discerns the deconstructive move of this analysis, but how does that approach lead us from the general ontological paradox of retreat as such to the more specific question of the social and political?

The *Retrait* of Metaphor

First stop, Derrida. Or, perhaps, first *step*, since this 1978 essay on "The *Retrait* of Metaphor," as it has been most judiciously translated by Peggy Kamuf, not only launches the term in its critical sense but also ends with Derrida's final definition of *retrait* as "what I have elsewhere tried to name according to the stepping movement of a certain *pas* [referring to his earlier essay on Blanchot's *Le pas au-delà*]"[11]: "Here again, it is a matter of the path, of what passes there, of what passes by it, of what goes on there, or not—*ou pas*."[12] *Retrait* is already the repetition of another term, but also the repetition of a return, the "here again" of a coming back that is also a setting or stepping forth, an effacement or withdrawal (*pas* as negation) that is also re-inscription (*pas* as the tracing of a path or track by one's steps), the (non)movement of a *trans-latio*, the economy of a repetition that brings the same back in/as a different place, here again, inescapably, as the supplementary trait of a *re-trait*, back to a home that is (n)ever more unhomelike or *unheimliche*. But *retrait* also turns out to be already a translation, the repetition or return of another word, a foreign one, into one's mother tongue. *Retrait* is specifically Derrida's rendering of *Entziehung* as it appears in Heidegger, most notably with the fundamental concept of the "withdrawal of Being," *der Entzug des Seins*: "The word *retrait*, which is 'French' up to a certain point, *is not too abusive*, not too much so, I believe, as a translation of the *Entziehung*, the *Sich-Entziehen* of Being, insofar as, suspending, dissimulating, giving way, and veiling itself, and so on, it withdraws into its crypt" (66). The Heideggerian truth of *aletheia* as the unforgetting or deconcealment of Being would then be, as Derrida specifies, the withdrawal of the withdrawal, the *retrait du retrait*. But this *re*-trait of the *retrait* is then necessarily the tracing of another trait, its supplementary reinscription captured in/as an endless play of return and repetition.

Derrida's essay is ostensibly about the dilemma of metaphoricity as per its title of "The *Retrait* of Metaphor"—namely, the dilemma whereby any discourse about metaphor inevitably finds itself caught in ever more metaphor, a situation shown to be not unlike that of metaphysics, where the attempt to leave metaphysics merely entrenches one even more within it. It seems to me, though, that Derrida's major insight here concerns the relation or convergence between "two families, so to speak, of words, nouns, verbs, and syncatagorems": "They are, on the one hand, the 'family' of *Ziehen* (*Zug, Bezug, Gezüge, durchziehen, entziehen*), and, on the other, the 'family' of Reissen (*Riss, Aufriss, Umriss, Grundriss*, etc.). . . . [This crossing] is more or less than a lexicon since it will come to name the trait or differential traction as the possibility of language, of *logos*, of *lexis* in general, of spoken no less than written inscription" (72–73). What Derrida also calls this "quasi-archi-lexicon" (73) articulates the relation between the drawing back and forth of presence and absence (or the play of withdrawal), on the one hand, and the arché-incision of the trait (or of redrawing), on the other, thus effectively reinscribing the Heideggerian question of Being within the Derridean problematic of the trace, or what Lacoue-Labarthe and Nancy call "inscription." In turn, this lexical crossing justifies his "abusive" translation of *entziehung* as *retrait*, "since in French usage *retrait* has never meant *re-tracing* [just as in English usage withdrawal has never implied redrawing]" (77). Derrida alludes to the French word's "rather rich polysemy," which "—at once intact and forced, save/safe in my language, and simultaneously altered—would be the most proper to capture the greatest quantity of energy and information in the Heideggerian text from within the context that is here our own" (62–63). The "abusive" character of the translation—Derrida notes parenthetically that "a 'good' translation must always *abuse*" (67)—arises not from any imprecision in rendering the German into French (or English), but from the necessary havoc such precision makes of each of these mother tongues in turn, or even that there is ever even a question of there being only one language, "for there is always *more than one* language in *the* language" (78): "These translating capacities can at the same time (as will be the case here) violate in the same gesture their proper mother tongue at the moment they import into it and export from it the maximum of energy and information" (63).

But isn't the standard French translation of the *Sich-Entziehen* of Being already *se retirer* and *retrait* the standard translation for *Entzug*? So, where's the "abuse"? Again, the issue is not so much that of the point-to-point accuracy of the word choices made across the divide between different languages but of the potential or "energy" enabled by the word's "rather rich polysemy" to "capture" a complex set of lexical relations from one language into the other. The properly abusive *übersetzung* has to take place as a radical, questioning *auseinandersetzung*, which will disclose not only the difference between languages but the difference within as well. *Retrait* is a perfectly reasonable rendering of *Entzug*, but by abusively unraveling the *re-trait* or re-tracing or re-drawing within the with-drawing that is the *Entzug*, we enter into the associative network of *Ziehen* and *Reissen* already at work in the Heideggerian text but massively disclosed in the course of Derrida's deconstructive reading. *Retrait* tells us that withdrawal entails inscription, *entziehen* is/as *Riss* or *Umriss*.

As such, the abusive translating of *retrait* addresses an even wider set of relations, including the relation between metaphysics and metaphor, between *uberträgung* and *ubersetzung*, between *Dichten* and *Denken*, among others. In each case, there is a play of withdrawal and repetition, or the supplementary reinscription of an erasure.[13] All of which is to think "the withdrawal of Being as a withdrawal/redrawing of metaphor in all the polysemous *and* disseminal potential of the *retrait*" (67), but then this *retrait* requires an altered— Derrida says "catastrophic"—sense of metaphor, or quasi-metaphor. Traditionally, metaphor could be said to be a way of thinking something new or unfamiliar by way of its posited resemblance to something known or familiar. Derrida twice cites Aristotle's example of the "evening of life" as a way to understand old age and the impending end of life (51, 68), but in the case of the "withdrawal" metaphor, the outcome is rather different: "Its aim would be to state something new, still unheard-of about the vehicle and not about the apparent subject of the trope. *Withdrawal-of-Being-or-of-metaphor* would be on the way toward giving us to think less Being or metaphor than the being or the metaphor *of the withdrawal*, on the way toward giving us to think about the way and the vehicle, or their making-way" (68).

Derrida offers a second example of this conundrum in Heidegger's famous dictum of language as the "house of Being," which "transports a familiar predicate (and here nothing is more familiar, familial, known, domestic, and economic, or so it is thought, than the house) toward a less familiar, more remote, *unheimlich* subject, which it would be a question of better appropriating for oneself, knowing, understanding, and which one designates by the indirect detour of what is nearest: the house" (69). But with this "quasi-metaphor" what happens is that "Being, from its very retreat, would give or promise to give one to think the house or the habitat" (69). The "promise" of this quasi-metaphor is not, however, to be construed as a mere transfer (*Übertragung*) or tropical inversion between the terms; it is not that Being has become the near or familiar term and home the distant or *unheimlich* one. Rather, the very relation between near and far, or familiar and strange, is called into question, and all the more so, since the expression "house of Being" refers to language, to cite Derrida citing Heidegger: "*Die Sprache* is the house of Being in which man ek-sists by dwelling."[14] Derrida concludes that "this movement is no longer simply metaphoric," since it bears both on language as itself an "element" of the metaphoric and on Being, "which is nothing," but whose withdrawal "makes possible both metaphoricity and its withdrawal," and thus "this phrasing is neither metaphoric nor literal" (70). The metaphor of Being leads us back to the being of metaphor, and the being of metaphor only entails more metaphor, be it the kind of quasi-metaphor analyzed here: "always one more metaphor when metaphor withdraws/is retraced in opening out its limits" (71). Hence, the "*retrait*" of metaphor in all its senses.

We are not yet done, however, with the sense of the trait itself, what Derrida calls "this plural word" (72). Playing on the double register or double crossing of *ziehen* and *reissen* in the aforementioned "quasi-archi-lexicon," the trait is what both separates and brings together, as in the French word for hyphen, *trait d'union*, which joins two words while marking their difference (another form of the *unum quid*), a "union" in difference, literally hyphenated by the most minimal of diacritical marks, a mere horizontal streak, not even so much as a "dash." Derrida pursues this discussion by revisiting Heidegger's "supposedly metaphoric discourse" in "The Nature of Language" on the relation between *Denken* (thought) and *Dichten* (poetics). In that passage, Heidegger describes the "relation marked by the 'and' between *Dichten* and *Denken*" in terms of a "neighborhood [*Nachbarschaft*]" only to ask "by what right we talk about such a thing" and "what 'neighborhood' is supposed to mean here" (82).[15] Heidegger states, "A neighbor [*Nachbar*], as the word itself tells us, is someone who dwells near to [*in der Nahe*] and with someone else. This someone else thereby becomes in turn the very neighbor of the one. Neighborhood, then, is a *relation* resulting from the fact that the one settles face to face with the other" (82; emphasis added). Derrida concludes that "neighborness is thus a *relation* (*Beziehung*) . . . that results when one draws (*zieht*) the other into one's proximity so that it may settle there" (72). But, once again, this quasi-metaphor of neighborhood seems to tell us less about the relation between *Dichten* and *Denken*, about the nature of the "and" between them, the object of the metaphor, than about what neighborhood and nearness and proximity of settlement might mean in themselves. "Not that neighborhood would be strange to us," continues Derrida, "before this access to what it is between *Denken* and *Dichten*": "Nothing is more familiar to us than this, as Heidegger points out right away. We dwell and move in it. But it is necessary (and this is what is most enigmatic about this circle) to come back to where we are without properly being there" (71).

This enigmatic, improper return brings us back to the track or trace of the trait, and Derrida quickly assimilates "this relation, this trait" to what he calls the *neighboring* or the *approaching* trait—namely, "the proper trait that relates (*bezieht*) *Dichten* . . . and thought (*Denken*) one to the other in their neighboring proximity, the trait that sets them *apart* and of which they both *partake*, this common differential trait that attracts them reciprocally, even while signing their irreducible difference, this trait is the *trait: Riss* . . . And this trait (*Riss*) is a *cut* that the two neighbors, *Denken und Dichten*, make into each other somewhere in infinity" (73). The *Beziehung* or relation seems also to be an *Entziehung*, or withdrawal, as "they cut each other again [*se recoupent*; also they coincide, support, and confirm each other] with/off from their trait and thus with/from their respective withdrawal [re-*trait*]" (73).

As such, "*Dichten* and *Denken* are parallels (*para allelo*), one beside or along the other, but not separate, if separate means 'to be distanced in the without-relation' (*ins Bezuglose abgeschieden*), without the traction of this trait (*Zug*), of the *Bezug* that relates or transports one toward the other" (74). But what then is this "trait," if not that of a "first cut," an *entame*, an *Aufriss*, that breaches and broaches (*er reisst auf*) the relation between *Denken und Dichten*, as an "approaching," as "the *Ereignis* that sends *Dichten* and *Denken* back into the proper (*in das Eigene*) of their essence (*Wesen*)" (74–75)? But this trait neither comes after the two "propers" nor precedes them, as if it or they were priorily constituted entities. Derrida insists that it is not an "autonomous, originary instance": "Being nothing, it does not itself appear, it has no proper and independent phenomenality, and not showing itself, it withdraws; it is structurally in withdrawal, as gap, opening, differentiality, trace, border, traction, effraction, and so on. From the moment that it withdraws in drawing and pulling itself out, the trait is a priori *retrait*, withdrawal, unappearance, and effacement of the mark in its first cut" (75). Thus, "the *re-* of retrait is not an accident occurring to the trait" (75) but implicit in its very tracing. The trait is thus always already *re-*trait, "singularly plural in itself" (80), Derrida concludes, in uncanny anticipation of Nancy's later massive development of this other expression as well, most notably in *Being Singular Plural*. But what for Derrida remains a quasi-metaphor for the ontological difference or for the ontology of metaphor in its very retreat (a figure of figuration itself as the truth of (de)concealment, of (de)concealment as truth, *aletheia*), follows a different path with Nancy. While Derrida's use of and reflection on the term of *retrait* both begins and seems to come to an end with this 1978 essay (although it does make a brief reappearance in his 1983 radio interview "Le retrait de l'apocalypse"),[16] for Nancy, in shall we say, "neighborly" collaboration with Philippe Lacoue-Labarthe, what they will refer to as the "singular logic of the retreat" will open a specific and strategic space for rethinking not just the neighborhood in its relative intimacy, but the *polis* more broadly, understood as the specific withdrawing/redrawing that defines the actuality of being together, the very being of "being with." As such, the neologistic sense of *retrait*, its "singular logic," marks the occasion for a decisively philosophical interruption of and into the political as such.

On the Way to the Political

That expression the "singular logic of the retreat" appears in a circular distributed in 1982 by the Centre de recherches philosophiques sur le politique and published under the title "annexe" in *Le Retrait du politique*, the second and final volume of papers presented at the Center. The full sentence reads, "The entire singular logic of the retreat demands to be articulated *in terms of the political*" (139; emphasis added).[17] By this "entire singular logic of the retreat," Nancy and Lacoue-Labarthe refer directly to the Heideggerian sense of *retrait* or *Entzug* as "the presentation which only takes place as the concealment or the disappearance of what is presented (this is the structure or the movement of *aletheia*)," and specifically to Derrida's reading of that term in Heidegger: "the Derridian value of the 're-treat,' of the 're-tracing' (combining *Zug* and *Riss*) implying in the retreat a 'new' incision or inscription, which cuts out again that which retreats" (138–39). All fine and well, but why does this "logic" (or "structure" or "movement") then also "*demand* to be articulated in terms of the political [*quant au politique*]"? Is there something at bottom political about *retrait* in addition to the ostensible concern with a withdrawal or *retrait* of the political? And isn't the very "demand" to be articulated in terms of the political, insofar as it appears qua demand, always already political?

And is the articulation "in terms of" the political (as not incorrectly translated here by Simon Sparks) the same as an articulation "as for" or "in regard to" the political (to get closer to the actual French preposition *quant*), trading the latter's indeterminate relationality for the former's more specific sense of translation (articulating the one "in terms of" the other)? What, in short, is the *relation* between *retrait* and the political? This relation bespeaks something other than the neighborly parallelism between *Denken* and *Dichten* and a "demand" irreducible to the infinite regress of metaphoricity.

To be sure, the recourse to the Heideggerian-Derridean version of *retrait* only emerges in this text as the third of ("at least") three possible understandings of the expression, "the retreat of the political," the clarification of whose "definition" and "stakes" is the self-declared aim of this circular "annexe," put out by Lacoue-Labarthe and Nancy. The urgency of the missive is occasioned, they say, by the preceding discussion, on February 15, 1982, of a paper by Jacques Rancière, "The Representation of the Worker, or the Class That Can't Be Found."[18] Now, nothing in that paper or in the published discussion following its delivery suggests any specific problem or controversy with the expression "retreat of the political," yet the specificity of the expression itself appears to have been subject to ongoing discussion and repeated questioning throughout the Center's existence, and Nancy and Lacoue-Labarthe intervene on a number of occasions to try and nail down the meaning of this in fact rather slippery phrase, from their "Opening Address" for the Center on December 8, 1980, to their summative "The 'Retreat' of the Political," dated June 21, 1982, to this curious "Annexe." As they admit, "the expression plays a major role in the determination of the Center's work. Which means that it needs more work" (138). More "work" is needed, then, to determine the expression that determines the work of the Center for Philosophical Research on the Political.

Three possible meanings are proposed, the first two deriving from the clearly political philosophical work of Hegel and Marx, before being summarily rejected. In the first case, withdrawing/retreat is assimilated to the work of the dialectic, the *Aufhebung* transliterating *"retrait du politique"* as *"relève du politique."* This can only be the case, they say, "if it is admitted that the Hegelian State *aufhebt* [*relève*, dialectically supersedes] the political itself" (138), but then it follows not only that the state's negation of the (civil society's) negation of the political is in turn political, but also that the dialectic as such is in and of itself "fundamentally political" (138).[19] The dialectical model is, however, not quite what Lacoue-Labarthe and Nancy have in mind by the retreat of the political. Nor is it what could be viewed in Marx as a "secondarisation" of the political, the second of the three proposed meanings. And here there seems to be two variants. One would be "Marx's gesture of reducing the political to bourgeois political illusion," but this would seem to be misconstruing the admittedly "bourgeois" illusion of what passes for politics [*la politique*] with the fundamentally political [*le politique*] that drives the class struggle. The second variant would detect in Marx a "radically infra-political 'ontology of the individual'" (138). Referring to the work of Michel Henry,[20] the two philosophers decide as they did with Hegel that the answer to this question would require an extensive rereading of the Marxian (or Hegelian) corpus. Thus, a rejection that takes the form of an indefinite deferral of analysis.

It is here that we come, as in Freud's folktales,[21] to the third or preferred option, the aforementioned one of Heidegger reread through Derrida, which they champion without explanation as "the only one which justifies a philosophical use of the term" (139), and which, as previously noted, is the one that also "demands" its articulation with/as the political. They further specify, however, that this articulation "can be initiated with at least two 'hypotheses'" (389), once again splitting what they call the "structure or movement" of retreat from itself. It is to be assumed that this generation of multiple hypotheses is behind the justification of the expression's "philosophical use," as opposed to making it synonymous with the dialectic's "magical power" of the negative or marking the mere devaluation or becoming secondary of the political, or in more classical Marxist terms, its merely superstructural status relative to the fundamental determinism of the economic base. On the contrary, the philosophical justification of *retrait* as withdrawing/redrawing implies, according to Nancy and Lacoue-Labarthe, a distinct primacy of the political, whose articulation it demands, as if the articulation of a demand does not in and of itself describe the ground of the political and, *a fortiori*, the demand for articulation.

The *demand* of the political is what governs the two subsequent "hypotheses" regarding the retreat of the political as understood within the Heideggerian-Derridean reading, which means the articulation/translation of an ontological, aesthetic, and scriptural category into an actual "logic" of the political, no matter how "singular." Inspired by the work of Hannah Arendt, the first of these two hypotheses explicates the meaning of "retreat" as what, in subjective genitive terms, "accompanies, in reality, a retreat of the political *itself* within and from the epoch of its world domination": "that is to say that the 'everything is political' conceals an effacement of the specificity of the political" (139).[22] In other words, the politicization of everything concomitantly implies a universal depoliticization and the loss or withdrawal of whatever meaning or specificity the political might still have had, its disappearance in sum as a *meaningful* category, "separate and distinct from the other components of the social whole." But if the philosophical category of the retreat thus "accompanies" the actual retreat of the political (subjective genitive) and the loss of the latter's specificity, the philosophical objective would then be to "retrace the contours of this specificity, whose actual conditions would need to be reinvented." Such a project of withdrawing/redrawing and reinvention is said to be embodied by Hannah Arendt, at least as "one aspect" of her thinking. In this case, then, the "retreat" of the political is tantamount to treating it differently or anew, to "re-treating" it, as in translator Simon Sparks's felicitous turn of phrase. It is also the overt sense of the Center's first publication of essays, *Rejouer le politique*, to re-play the political, or to play it again, to put it back into play.

Alternatively, though, according to the second of the two hypotheses, "retreat operates in relation to the political in general and absolutely," but "what retraces itself, then, would be a space *other* than the political." That space, though, of "this 'other' would remain to be named." Here, the intellectual model for elaborating such an "other-than-the-political" would be that pursued by Georges Bataille (and possibly the late Heidegger).[23] It is also the kind of inquiry we find in Lyotard, and most especially with his concept of the "intraitable" (clearly, the negative corollary of *re-trait* would be a kind of unnamable *in-trait*) as what cannot be managed, politically or otherwise, what resists its being retraced, but that nonetheless shapes and inhabits our political existence.[24] We might, in this regard, see Derrida following more closely in the pathway of Arendt, and as per the previous hypothesis, by reshaping, retracing, replaying what we mean by the political as such. So we seem to be left with the question of whether the philosophical work of *retrait* is the "reinvention" of *another kind* of political, or else that of excavating *something other than* the political, which nonetheless would still lie at the very heart of the political? Do we follow Derrida and Arendt or Lyotard and Bataille?

Nancy and Lacoue-Labarthe caution, however, that it "is not certain that it is a matter of discerning [or deciding (*trancher*)] between the two hypotheses": "But what is certain is that hypotheses of this sort are implicit in all critical, interrogative or deconstructive discourses (for example, those which came out of the Center) on the political, and that such hypotheses demand to be brought to light and analyzed" (139). It is less an issue of deciding between the two hypotheses in question than of recognizing a potentially indeterminate number of such hypotheses, each of which in turn would demand (more demand!) its being "brought to light and analyzed." Furthermore, such hypotheses are to be found "in *all* critical, interrogative or deconstructive discourses on the political," and exemplarily so in the discourses emanating from an aptly named Center for Philosophical Research on the Political. But what exactly are these "hypotheses of this sort," if not precisely those where the singular logic of the retreat is at work and that in turn each demand the articulation of their relation to the political (without necessarily predetermining what that relation might be)—that is, the singular articulation of relations that are in themselves singular?

Articulation and Dissociation

Nancy and Lacoue-Labarthe try to generalize this predicament as "involv[ing] the thought of 'dis-sociation,'" but that effort cannot help but return to the retreat by way of the specific work conducted by the Center: "All the contributions to the Center's work have indeed implied, more or less directly, or more or less thematically, a thought of 'relation' (or the 'social bond') as constitutive of a break or of an 'unravelling' [*déliaison*] whose nature or structure has, until now, been formulated only in opposition—let us say—to self-relation (to the Subject as self-present)" (140). Whatever the other differences between the Center's contributors, they share a common suspicion or opposition toward a political thinking that would proceed from the point of view of a selfsame subject whose self-presencing would then be merely expanded to encompass a society of individuals as some sort of collective subject. The task at hand for the Center—one fully realized with the publication of Nancy's *The Inoperative Community* in 1983—is not merely to oppose or deconstruct this reduction of relation to self-relation, of *mitsein* to *ipseity*, but to think through the social bond as a relation built in alterity: it is relation as the commonality of difference, and thus a break or disconnection in the very gesture of joining or connecting its constituents; it is the simultaneity of their being *destituted* in their being *constituted*, an association in dissociation, *unum quid*. We already saw this conundrum at work in Derrida's analysis of Heidegger's "neighborhood," which we can now read as a society in miniature, perhaps down to a community of only two. That neighborly relation, *Beziehung*, is the partaking of a trait that both unifies and separates: "the trait that sets them *apart* and of which they both *partake*, this common differential trait that attracts them reciprocally, even while signing their irreducible difference" (Derrida, "*Retrait*," 73). That trait, as we remember, is always already a *re-trait*, and thus it is no surprise to see Nancy and Lacoue-Labarthe conclude in regard to the relation of dissociation that "it could be that the retreat is the—theoretical and practical—gesture of relation itself" (140), thus charting the intersection of dissociation and retreat [*Entziehung*]. That said, it still remains unclear whether this "gesture" should be "attributed to a retraced politics or to something 'other'—or otherwise—than the political." Concomitant to this dilemma is a questioning of the relation between theory and practice, with the conclusion that a Center for the Philosophical Research of the Political cannot be "theoretical alone": "It should be allowed to set out, for example, a work such as that of the Centre according to an actuality which is neither that of a disengagement, nor that of a militant action. An actuality which is, consequently, consonant with the retreat" (140). The intervention of philosophy thus occurs as an interruption of these very categories, perhaps as the kind of monogrammatic intervention we have already seen.

Retreat appears to be a rather shifty movement, with its terms sliding unpredictably into and out of each other. A most "singular" logic indeed. In the case of the "actuality" of the Center, it is the logic of a *neither . . . nor . . .* (neither disengagement nor militancy) but also and at the same time that of a *both . . . and . . .* (theory *and* practice). In the world of (or in?) retreat, things are never as they seem. Perhaps a *feigned* retreat is as good as an actual one, since the retreat is always the feint of a withdrawal that redraws itself elsewhere, disappearing only to show up in another place, an "act of appearing disappearing." But then retreat itself, like the political in the high tide of its ubiquity, would also lose any *sense* of specificity and meaning. Then, to continue the movement of this singular logic, would we be faced again with the dilemma between retracing or re-treating the retreat, on the one hand, and revealing something other than the retreat, on the other? In either case, however, we come back to the very "structure or movement" or "logic" of the retreat, either as its incessant re-tracing and re-drawing or as the iterative recurrence as what it in fact is (not), a logic, if we can say so, of interruption.

From Cerisy to Center

Moreover, we still don't have an answer as to why specifically the figuration of such a generalized tracing/tracking should demand its articulation in terms of the political. Or, would it not be the political that demands its articulation in terms of the retreat? Can we speak of a retreat of the political without also unpacking the politics of the retreat? "Annexe" signifies a rather late formulation of the question (it is in fact the very last item in the last of the two volumes issued by the Center for Philosophical Research on the Political and thus in a sense the Center's final word on the retreat of the political), but the development of Nancy and Lacoue-Labarthe's thinking, especially their political thinking, after Derrida's 1978 essay and leading up to the circular of 1982 might give us some other clues. A key moment occurs at the 1980 Cerisy conference on Derrida, "Les fins de l'homme," during and after the breakout session billed as the "political seminar."

There, Christopher Fynsk first raises the question of the political, not in relation to its general understanding, but limited to the specific question of Derrida's politics, which he describes as a certain "retreat"—that is, "legible, firstly, in a certain silence or hesitation" (488).[25] But rather than the complex dynamics of withdrawing/redrawing we have been explicating, what Fynsk describes appears more like a simple reserve or cautiousness in how Derrida responds to the question of a deconstructive politics, a reserve that ranges from the brief allusions he makes to various "lacunas" in his texts to "the multiplication of the precautions which spring up the moment a political question is broached." There is also a certain skepticism evinced with regard to a "theoretical elaboration" and "conjunction" of deconstruction with Marxism that is "still to come," with Fynsk wondering aloud about the status of this "still to come" and seeming to suggest that this eventuality may be a perpetual deferral. What Fynsk channels is the broader set of queries and concerns at that time regarding if there could even be a politics of deconstruction, and, if so, what it would look like, as well as curiosity about Derrida's own politics (that inescapable weathervane by which "intellectuals" are summarily judged). It would be well over a decade before Derrida would publish *Specters of Marx* (1993) and the arguably more overt political writings and activism of his later years, but in 1980, at the time of the Cerisy colloquium, suspicions of apoliticism shadowed the early development of deconstruction.[26] But, even at that time, as Fynsk duly notes, Derrida's writings made frequent allusion to the potentially political dimensions of his work: "Now, if Derrida thus hesitates to engage in immediately political questions (if he does not *politicize* his thinking), he nonetheless still affirms that his practice *is* political, that all philosophical activity is, in general, a political practice" (488/88). It is legitimate to ask then to what extent the organization of the Cerisy conference itself was motivated by Nancy and Lacoue-Labarthe in an attempt to engage overtly the discussion of a deconstructive politics, and notably by titling the conference after one of the early Derrida's more pointedly political essays, "The Ends of Man."[27]

In a rejoinder to Fynsk's remarks, Lacoue-Labarthe reformulates the issue somewhat otherwise, retracing the retreat into the more familiar or "singular" form we have been tracking while offering some precious clarifications. For him, it is less a question of Derrida's allusive political rhetoric or to what extent his "philosophical activity" is to be understood or not as a specifically political practice than the general "necessity" of the retreat of the political in a world defined (following Arendt) by the total domination of the political—in other words, the previously discussed conundrum of the "everything is political" devolving into nothing being specifically political (which it should be noted is very different from the more outlandish claim that "nothing" at all would be political).[28] Nonetheless, he continues, "the gesture of the 'retreat' cannot be a simple one. It is not a matter of turning away from the political and of 'moving on to something else'—assuming that there could still be, today, something other than the political. No 'retreat,' no *safe haven*, if you like, could accommodate the one who 'retreats'" (96–97). It is not a question of retreating *from* the political when the political itself is in retreat, when it has withdrawn from a world it has saturated absolutely and totally. This saturation, Lacoue-Labarthe adds, "represents, in every instance and in all its forms, the completion of a philosophical program" (96), if not the "completion of philosophy itself as a political program": "Historiographically—and that is to say, historically—a limit has been reached, and this is the *totalitarian* fact as it accompanies the movement of philosophy to a close. Which does not mean that the gulag is in Hegel or Birkenau is in Nietzsche, but that we have to cease denying the actuality of the various modes of the completion of the philosophical: from the Party-State to psychological dictatorship" (96).

The questioning of this co-implication or "co-belonging" of the philosophical with the political, from the grounds of the Greek *polis* to the "completion" of Western metaphysics in the actuality of modern totalitarianism, will become a driving concern of the Center for Philosophical Research on the Political, which Nancy and Lacoue-Labarthe will found in the immediate aftermath of the Cerisy Conference with the acknowledged help and support of Jacques Derrida himself.[29] Within this concern, the themes of dissociation and of totalitarianism emerge as corollaries to the question of the retreat of the political. Lacoue-Labarthe already signals this direction when he follows up the previous quotation about the "totalitarian fact" with the following general remark: "Any gesture of dissociation with regard to the philosophical can only take the form of a 'retreat' of the political" (96). Such a statement can only have meaning, though, if dissociation in turn beckons both the philosophical question of the political *and* the political question of the philosophical: "The essence of the political, in other words, is by itself not political."[30] To think through the political in dissociative terms rather than simply the familiar modes of association that organize human beings into groups or societies (democracy, oligarchy, monarchy) seems nothing less than to upend or interrupt the very concept and deep traditions of political philosophy itself.

The Political and the Philosophical

Right from the beginning, the Center's very name—"for Philosophical Research on the Political"—questions the relation between the political and the philosophical, in particular by the double strategy of the "philosophical questioning of the political," on the one hand, and the "questioning of the philosophical itself as to the political," on the other. Together, the aim is to probe the "essence of the political," which we have already understood as "by itself not political" (108). Alternatively stated, the Center would embrace both the philosophical interruption of the political and the political interruption of the philosophical, the one cutting or intersecting the other at some point by a trait that is also a *re-trait*, a mutual withdrawing/redrawing.[31]

Most relevantly, the philosophical is said to be not just historically coterminous with the *polis*, but what has most desired is its own "practical realization" in/as the political (96), which thus paradoxically emerges "as the effect of a certain retreat of the philosophical, and that is equally to say of a certain completion of the philosophical" (125). The ultimate end or completion of this program is said to be accomplished in the advent of modern totalitarianism. Given this programmatic eventuality, Nancy and Lacoue-Labarthe rewrite Sartre's dictum about Marxism to declare *totalitarianism* instead to be the new "unsurpassable horizon of our times" (126).[32] They turn to the classic work of Hannah Arendt, for whom the conditions for totalitarianism are met, first, when the human is defined solely as worker or *"animal laborans,"* second, when the (properly political) space of the public is reduced to the social as mere biopolitics—"that is to say by a common-life or an interdependence regulated according to life or subsistence, and not according to a public or political end in itself," and third or finally when there is a loss of authority "as the distinct element of power," accompanied by a concomitant loss of freedoms.[33] For Nancy and Lacoue-Labarthe, these conditions apply not only to the "classic" forms of totalitarianism, such as fascism, Nazism, and Stalinism (which they further view as invested in a structure of societal immanence to itself as figured in nation, leader, or reason of history), but "lurk" more "cleverly" or "subtly" within modern democracies themselves, where civic participation is reduced to the spectacularization of elections as an "absent public space" and where power is concealed by the banality of managerial dicta and the rule of technical efficiencies (126–27).[34]

It is in the context of this apparent ubiquity, or dare we say, "globalization," of totalitarianism in its various contemporary versions that the so-called retreat of the political takes on its sense of urgency: "In the totalitarian phenomena thus understood, nowhere do even the least of specifically political questions come to be asked, do new political questions (corresponding to transformations of the world) have the chance to emerge" (127). It is not inappropriate to understand these remarks and concerns within the context of the Center's emergence during the French electoral season that would lead to socialist François Mitterand's election in May 1981. While an end to the anti-university regime of Giscard d'Estaing provided a distinct sense of relief, there was also the incipient expression of a certain skepticism toward what a "socialist" program under Mitterand would actually mean, especially in the context of the contemporary implosion of the French Communist Party and the concomitant disappearance, or withdrawal-retreat, of the alternative it would have marked. While the end of the Cold War and the triumphalist American assertion of a "new world order" would still be almost a decade a way, the kinds of concerns raised by the Center's participants already reflect a certain decline of traditional Marxism as an unsurpassable horizon (or now "lost horizon") and the development of various neo-Left strands of thinking that would earn the label of "post-Marxism" in response to the contemporaneous right-wing resurgence evidenced by the electoral victories of Thatcher and Reagan, in 1979 and 1980, respectively. The latters' policies indeed applied a specific "philosophical" program, neoliberalism, associated with the works of F. A. Hayek and Milton Friedman, among others. Their success would eventually cross over to subsequent left-liberal governments as well as right-wing ones, emerging as the dominant political ideology of the post–Cold War era, shaping the very constitution of various post-communist regimes throughout Eastern Europe, Central Asia, and elsewhere. The salient features of neoliberalism map well onto those phenomena presciently described by Nancy and Lacoue-Labarthe as the "retreat of the political," in particular "the fact of the political ceaselessly merging with all sorts of authoritative discourses (in the first place, socioeconomic, but also technological, cultural, psychological, etc.) and, despite the 'media' circus or the 'spectacularization' of an absent public space, everywhere converting itself into a form of banal management or organization" (126–27). Now, some forty years later, we are witnessing the extreme repercussions of these policies in the rise of ever more right-wing populisms, which "complete" the philosophical program of neoliberalism not only in or as a "softer" version of totalitarianism but even as explicitly calling forth a return to the classic, "historical (but not entirely 'past') figures of totalitarianism" (128). While the latter evoke an "initial and pure figure of totalitarianism in all its radicality and brutality" (128), Nancy and Lacoue-Labarthe dare in 1982 to ask the question whether "a more insidious and (as one says of some technologies) 'softer' form of totalitarianism has not been installed, more or less without our knowledge or through the unappearance of which we have spoken," specifically in the guise of the retreat of the political as the "absolute paradox" of the total domination of the political: "under such a domination, the political becomes *unapparent* (it has the obviousness of an 'it goes without saying') and that its unappearance is proportionate to its all-powerfulness" (126).

And so, the question of totalitarianism following upon that of the relation between the philosophical and the political bring us back again to the question of the "retreat" as "the act of appearing disappearing." And it is this retreat of the political that marks the "new" totalitarianism, which Nancy and Lacoue-Labarthe want nonetheless to distinguish from the old or classic version while questioning the "ready-made and much circulated opposition between totalitarianism and democracy" as "a little too simple." As they admit, "We do not have camps and our police, however 'technologically advanced,' are not the omnipresent political police. But this does not mean that our democracy is that of Tocqueville. And if Tocqueville's democracy contained the germ of classical totalitarianism, nothing guarantees that ours is not in the process of secreting something else, a new form of totalitarianism" (128). Nancy and Lacoue-Labarthe, citing generally the work of Jean-François Lyotard and Claude Lefort, do make a crucial distinction between classical totalitarianism, which "proceeds from the incorporation and the presentation of transcendence (as the work of art in Nazism and the reason of history in Stalinism), and new totalitarianism [which] would itself proceed from the dissolution of transcendence, and henceforth, come to penetrate all spheres of life now devoid of any alterity" (129). The latter part of this sentence is drawn explicitly from Marx's early "Critique of Hegel's Doctrine of the State" (1843), where he defines democracy as "materially penetrating the content of all the non-political spheres," a formulation that already anticipates Arendt's total domination of the political and that also presents that "absolute paradox" of the *retreat* of the political, its "unappearance."[35]

What is different about the "new" totalitarianism that takes democratic form is the very retreat of the transcendence that defined "classic" totalitarianism, but so they add importantly, this "clearly does not mean that it is for us a matter of repeating the appeal to a transcendence, whether it be that of God, Man or History: these are the transcendences which have installed totalitarianism or those in which it has installed itself, converting them into the total immanence of life-in-common." Readers of *The Inoperative Community* will recognize an early formulation here of Nancy's critique of communal "immanence," whether it be that of a transcendental unity that subsumes all differential identities within it or that of the agglomeration of supposedly already existing individuals. In both cases, we confront "the total immanence of life-in-common" as a dominating myth that founds community (or society) as completed work. Alternatively, one can read in this difference that adumbrated by Lyotard in *The Postmodern Condition* between the so-called "grand narratives" that defined modernity (and "classic" totalitarianism) and the postmodern predicament of extracting ever more performativity and efficiency in all human activities (the "new" totalitarianism).[36] In addressing then the retreat of transcendence "or of alterity" in the "new" totalitarianism, Nancy and Lacoue-Labarthe insist that "the question of the retreat is not one of 'regaining' a remote transcendence, but of wondering how the retreat compels us to displace, re-elaborate and replay the concept of 'political transcendence.'"

We return then to the underlying concept of retreat as a retracing or "retreating," which also means the reinscription of a certain alterity, which is not necessarily transcendent. What is withdrawn or what withdraws itself in the retreat of the political (qua subjective genitive) is "the political itself as a specific dimension or as the dimension of a specific alterity" (130). This specificity or this alterity is also what is called "sovereignty" in the exact way that term is elaborated by Georges Bataille, such that "the retreat of the political is nothing other than a retreat of sovereignty" (131).[37] Nancy and Lacoue-Labarthe conclude, "Such a retreat makes something appear or sets something free. At the very least, we sought to question ourselves not according to the rule of a nostalgic lamentation for what would have drawn back . . . , but according to the hypothesis that this retreat must allow, or even impose, the tracing anew of the stakes of the political" (131). There is an event in the retreat of the political, where "something appears" in the very gesture of a disappearance, something that shows itself under the very guise of its unappearance (not an absence but the "act of appearing disappearing"). The withdrawal is once again a redrawing, as per Derrida, but it is Lyotard who frames the final step in explicating "the basic *traits* presented by this 'something'" that emerges from the retreat, something that circumscribes the "essence" of the political itself, if as Nancy and Lacoue-Labarthe further claim, "it is indeed *from* the retreat of the political that the political 'itself,' its question or its exigency, arises" (131). In other words, the withdrawal of the political by dint of its very penetration into every sphere of life and the resulting loss of its meaning and specificity, its structure of alterity, for that matter, raises the very question of the political and—to speak Bataille—the urgency of its sovereign task, of sovereignty as its task. When under totalitarian conditions—be they "classic" or in democratic form—, "nowhere do even the least of specifically political questions come to be asked, do new political questions (corresponding to transformations of the world) have the chance to emerge" (127), then the political itself becomes a question, if not *the* question. Such a *question* is "ineluctably philosophical" to the extent that it is the very question of the *polis* or the *res publica*, of the "civility" of the city, of the public "thing," or, to cite Claude Lefort cited by Nancy and Lacoue-Labarthe, the political as "the manifestation of the social to itself" (130).[38] We thus come to an "essence of the political" that is nonetheless "by itself not political."

Why is this a *philosophical* question, though, rather than, say, a question of political science, of sociology, of history, or of literature even? One might have expected the answer to be that such regional sciences or practices of knowledge remain merely ontic when an ontological approach is required— that is, the question of the very being of the political whose essence cannot be presupposed in advance, all the more so if the retreat, to recall Derrida, is itself an interruptive movement that "breaches/broaches the ontic/ontological difference itself" ("*Retrait* of Metaphor," 80). Instead, a certain "lexical difference" is introduced by way of a long citation from Lyotard that defines the "preferential suitability" of philosophy for the question of the political insofar as philosophy is defined not as a regional knowledge but as "that discourse which has as its end the discovery of its rule" (132).[39] To the extent that "the political does not give itself (or no longer gives itself) to be phrased as something given that can be presented according to the rules by which phrases regulate themselves" (132; translation modified) it is not what Lyotard would call a "genre of discourse" with an already given "regimen of phrases."[40] At the same time, and "nonetheless," the political "'hands itself over' to being phrased, all the same" (132), whence the necessity of a specifically philosophical questioning, of the questioning that *is* philosophy.

Nancy and Lacoue-Labarthe then translate Lyotard's "lexicon" back into their own, as follows:

> The political withdraws its determinable and presentable specificity; but in this indetermination, which simultaneously corresponds to its dilution or to its general impregnation, it unburdens itself anew, and delivers a question or the outline of a question. If you prefer: the retreat of the political corresponds to its *closure*—and, by the same stroke, to the opening of the following question: on the basis of what, against what, or along what, does this discourse trace itself. It does not simply trace itself "against" the non-political. (132; translation modified)

That "singular logic" of the retreat bespeaks a closure, the completion of the political in the dominance of its ubiquity—that is, in its utter "dilution" and general withdrawal, whence concomitantly the urgency of its renewed questioning. But if the retreat is therefore the demarcation of a closure, the tracing of a limit, then what does it draw the line for or against? The answer cannot be what is "non-political," since the closure of the retreat is obtained precisely by the "general impregnation" of the political into *all* spheres of human activity, and in particular, everything that can be named under the rubric of society or the social. "On the contrary," state Lacoue-Labarthe and Nancy, citing again Lyotard, "the closure opens onto 'something,' as Lyotard says, something which would be 'the political'—or the essence of the political—drawn back from the total completion of the political in the techno-social" (132). In his later work, Lyotard would indeed attempt to define this political "something" as the *intraitable*, the thing, or even childhood (as an existence prior to any subjectivity). For him, this something is precisely what cannot be treated or re-treated; it is the irresistible essence of the political that politics would ceaselessly aim to repress, but that at unpredictable moments and in unforeseen places interrupts whatever passes for the political as usual.[41] Translated back into Nancy and Lacoue-Labarthe's terms, this means that there is no "getting out" of the retreat (131), there is no "outside" of the political from which to save it or to found it. This is why the political is never settled, never done, endlessly opened to and interrupted by new antagonisms and a sovereignty always ever to come.[42]

The Five Traits

But what about this "essence" of the political that is said to be "by itself not political"? Nancy and Lacoue-Labarthe end their summative essay on "The 'Retreat' of the Political," which, aside from the "annexe" and the discussion summaries, closes their collective volume, also titled *The Retreat of the Political*, by "quickly listing" what they see as the five "basic traits" presented by the something "which would be 'the political.'" These *traits* are presented in order of increasing complexity with the earlier traits quickly folding into the latter ones. Specifically, the first trait, the predictable "exigency of getting away from the metaphysical *ground* of the political, from a transcendent or transcendental ground, for example, in a subject," finds its answer in the second trait—namely, the very Nancean "motif of finitude," which itself implies as a third trait "the true place of its determination, the question of relation" (133). This question is then said to be "*the* central question; as such, it is even, perhaps, the question of the essence of the political." So central a question is this third of the five traits that the authors note that it "shows up almost everywhere in the Center's work," and "with the insistence of a theme—in truth, still not particularly thematized, if it ever could entirely be so—the theme of *desertion* or of *dissociation*" (133).[43]

Before considering the final two traits, let us resume what we can glean from the first three. The *essence* of the political, which is "by itself not political," is to be found in the question of relation, specifically that of the social bond, but as a relation of finitude, of a *mitsein* or of a being-in-common where difference is what is "in common"—that is, as a relation of difference between finite singularities, not unlike the "neighboring trait" described by Derrida, a *trait d'union*, both uniting and separating, where the terms cut or trace into each other "somewhere in infinity," or again, as another case of *unum quid*. The trait that is the relation of finitude is not a thing, or "nothing," and certainly nothing that can serve as a ground or foundation. Likewise, the *polis* is not a founding ground based upon a civic entity, but an ever-shifting web of relations among finite singularities in retreat, "as a network of paths and directions rather than as a circumference already in place."[44]

Dissociation, though, is the term that keeps appearing to designate the malleability or precariousness of what constitutes relation, not the negation of relation as association, not dis-association, but as Derrida explains in the discussion following the reading of "annexe," dissociation plays a determining role in the "ontological structure of *Dasein*": "There is a whole series of dissociative terms at play: *Zerstreuung, Zersplitterung*, etc., which, in spite of their negative resonance, are not to be taken negatively. The prefix *zer* is to be understood, rather, on the model of the English "dis": there is something like an originary dis-tension of *Dasein*: *Dasein* is originally dis-tended, and it is in such a distension that history and spatiality originate" (141). This ontological structure of an originary dis-tension also explains dissociation as relation, and this despite the ensuing remark by Philippe Soulez about the "phantom of unity" whereby "the social bond itself already consists in acting as if there were no dissociation" (141). Dissociation is presupposed as the very condition of association, of relationality itself. If the distension of *Dasein* is at the origin of "history and spatiality," of, if one prefers, those very Kantian a prioris of space and time, then dissociation is not unlike the structure of the *trait d'union*, or *unum quid*, whereby relation is both gap and connection. On the other hand, dissociation appears capable of tracing all kinds of "relations," not just the rigid case of parallelism (*para allelo*), as in Derrida's rendition of Heidegger's neighborhood. The social bond, in particular and in its finitude, is capable of an infinite variety of inflections, not just in terms of spatiotemporal coordinates and limits but also in terms of varying differentials and stratifications of power, (in)equality, injunctions, prohibitions, and expectations.[45]

Identity itself, as we will see, is implicated in the dissociative basis of social relations, and all the more so if, also following an additional remark by Soulez, we recall the clinical origin of the concept of dissociation. First theorized by Pierre Janet in the late nineteenth century, the psychological condition known as "dissociation," or "dissociative disorder," is not so easily defined and remains one of the most debated and contested terms among psychiatrists and psychotherapists. It appears to cover everything from daydreaming and absorption/contemplation to what has been called "multiple personality disorder." Moreover, the boundary between the "normal" and the pathological seems especially fraught with regard to dissociative behavior, whose broadest parameters are consistent with the notion of a split consciousness.[46] The problem, though, is that there really can be no concept of consciousness without the possibility, nay the necessity, of there being a split. Indeed, some kind of split in consciousness, be it interruption or dissociation, has to be constitutive of consciousness itself, as we know not only from Freud, and before him, Hegel, but also from Descartes himself, whose iterative cogito we have seen as analyzed by Nancy in *Ego Sum*. And if we remember Lacoue-Labarthe's comment with respect to Derrida that "any gesture of dissociation with regard to the philosophical can only take the form of a 'retreat' of the political" (96), does not the case of Descartes emblematize that particular (objective genitive) "form of a 'retreat' of the political," to the extent that his philosophically (but perhaps also clinically) dissociative gestures with regard to the philosophical are accompanied by a dramatic, perhaps all too dramatic, retreat not only from the political but also from any kind of social bond? Whence the masked philosopher's exuberant declaration at the very midpoint of the *Discourse on Method* that he has found refuge in Holland as an asocial if not downright misanthropic utopia: "Living here, amidst this great mass of busy people who are more concerned with their own affairs than curious about those of others, I have been able to lead a life as solitary and withdrawn [*retiré*] as if I were in the most remote desert [*dans les déserts les plus écartés*], while lacking none of the comforts found in the most populous cities" (I:126). The founding gesture of the *larvatus prodeo* thus also follows the strange logic of the retreat, albeit in the most literal of ways, appearance as disappearance and vice versa, withdrawing and/as redrawing, iterative dissociation, interruption, and finitude at all levels.

"The Mother"

We can now consider the last two of the five "traits" that determine the "something" that would be "the essence of the political." In a sudden and unexpected move, Nancy and Lacoue-Labarthe refer the entire question of "relation" and of dissociation "consequently," so they say, to the seemingly unrelated *question* of "the mother," or more precisely to the mother "as the index of a question." This "index" of a question, which they claim "comes to us from Freud," is in fact, the "question of identification" (or the question, if one likes, of a certain index or indication), which is in and of itself, according to their citation of Freud, "the earliest *Stellungnahme* toward the Other" (133). A lot of questions all of a sudden converge under this rubric of "the mother" with regard to the "essence" of the political in terms of relation, dissociation, interruption, and identification.

The Freud passage in question is from Chapter VII of his 1921 *Group Psychology and the Analysis of the Ego*. That chapter bears the title "Identification" and appears to begin with the line quoted by Nancy and Lacoue Labarthe: "the earliest *Stellungnahme* toward the Other" (133), which corresponds to what the Standard Edition English states as "the earliest expression of an emotional tie with another person."[47] The problem, though, is that the German word *Stellungnahme*, or the taking of a position, despite their highlighting it, does not actually appear in the German text here, which reads, "als früheste Äusserung einer Gefülsbindung an eine andere Person" (XIII:115), correctly translated in the Standard Edition as indicated earlier. *Gefülsbindung*, an "emotional tie" or a bond of feeling, is not exactly *Stellungnahme*, often translated as "attitude" or opinion. *Stellungnahme* does appear, however, in a long footnote at the very end of the chapter in a passage that represents a kind of summation and self-critique of Freud's thinking at this point that is nonetheless relevant to the concern about originary identification, the mother, and the political:

> We are well aware that we have not exhausted the nature of identification with these examples from pathology, and that we have consequently left part of the riddle of group formation untouched. A far more fundamental and comprehensive psychological analysis would have to intervene at this point. A path leads from identification by way of imitation to empathy, that is, to the comprehension of the mechanism by means of which we are enabled to take up any attitude at all towards another mental life [Von des Identifizierung fürht ein Weg über die Nachahmung zur Einfühlung, das heisst zum Verständnis des Mechanismus, durch den uns überhaupt eine Stellungnahme zu einem anderen Seelenleben ermöglicht wird]. (SE XVIII:110n2; GS XIII:121n2)

Rather than focus on Lacoue-Labarthe and Nancy's apparent citational misprision, the unclear relation between *Gefülsbindung* and *Stellungnahme* points to the difficulty of understanding the psychic "mechanism" behind our ability to relate "at all" to others, even prior to the question of the "essence" of the political. As Freud notes, "The riddle of group formation" remains "untouched," even though certain signposts along the way have been clearly staked out. There is a "path" from identification to imitation to empathy, which, according to Lacoue-Labarthe and Nancy, "one can and must refer to a general problematic of mimesis" (133), but whether emotional attachment or mere attitude, what remains to be understood then is exactly "how and according to what *relation* does the identification take place" and "what might this relation—in its relation to language, art, death, and eroticism—reveal about the subject of the political" (133).[48] Out of this, Nancy and Lacoue-Labarthe claim to be "only indicating one category of question here": "the question, for example, of identification as the social constitution of identity (and as the constitution of social 'identity'); or that of an 'originary' or arche-originary sociality, or again of an arche-sociality, in which or according to which the entire retreat of the political is played out" (133–34).

The "entire" retreat of the political thus comes down to a question of identification as fundamental to, as the "arche," or essence, of the political, which cannot be political itself, but that out of which the political arises and presumably "withdraws" back into. This is not a simple question, and Lacoue-Labarthe and Nancy go so far as to describe that question as "the great worry [*la grande hantise*] and the stumbling block for practically the whole of contemporary thought," which they take to include a broad sweep of thinkers "from Bergson to Heidegger to Levinas, through Freud, Husserl, Bataille, and probably many others" (134). The claim is less grandiose than it initially appears to the extent that these are the thinkers upon which much of the Center's output is explicitly based and they are repeatedly referenced, although one notes the absence of a more Marxist-inspired current (Gramsci, H. de Man, Benjamin, Adorno, Althusser)[49] that also struggles with the ways in which the "question" of identification and "identity" underpins the *essence* of the political. That most troubling and difficult question is what Lacoue-Labarthe and Nancy then link back again to "the so-called question of the mother," which they assert is "first of all, the question of a *maternal retreat*, of the mother as retreat, and of the retreat of the mother" (134).

So, what does the "mother" or the *retreat* of the "mother" have to do with identification, retreat, and the essence of the political? Why "the mother"? The question is a vexed one, even among the Center's participants, and understandable given Nancy and Lacoue-Labarthe's relatively restrained, scattered, and even cryptic mentions of the matter, starting with the Center's "Opening Address" (although fuller discussions appear in other essays penned by them around the same time).[50] The best account of this confusion, even dismay, occurs during the discussion in response to the last published contribution to the Center, Philippe Soulez's directly provocative "La mère est-elle hors-jeu de l'essence du politique?" [Is the mother sidelined in the essence of the political?]. Soulez's essay relies on a reading of Lacan's critique of Bergson's remarks regarding the reputed violence and cruelty of matriarchal societies, and thus his essay serves as an overt provocation to Lacoue-Labarthe and Nancy that ends with his asking them directly "what they meant to say in speaking about 'the mother,'" and reminding them that among the audience "this mention had already appeared surprising or worrisome right from the opening session" of the Center (181). Lyotard, while not cited directly, is alleged to have expressed concerns about the designation (133), and Derrida raises the question of the phallic mother, while others bring up Julia Kristeva's notion of the mother as "fusion."[51] Nancy and Lacoue-Labarthe strenuously reject all of these possible understandings: "Neither fusion nor phallic, the 'mother' seems to us to be part of the problem of *identification* as Freud leaves it in suspense. . . . Freud indicates in several ways a specific problematic with regard to the 'mother,' that of an identification in a priorly accomplished identity . . . , recalling in effect identification as a 'first taking of position (*Stellungnahme*)' in relation to another psychic existence" (181). We circle back once again to the Freudian question of identification as primordial relation, a question with regard to which the "mother" (and it is worth noting Nancy and Lacoue-Labarthe's consistent designation of the term in scare quotes) is said to be "part of the problem." At this point, it would be helpful to recall the initial evocation of the "mother" in the Center's Opening Address, which follows upon the more general "question of the relation," which in turn is both "the question of the passage *to* community" and "the question of the passage to the subject" (118), the latter passage being for Freud the well-known Oedipal scenario, while the former's "problematic of originary sociality" is described as a "limit question" for the science of psychoanalysis:

> . . . if the "social bond" is a *genuine* question—and is, by the same stroke, a *limit* question—for Freud, it is in that the *given* relation . . . , this relation of a subject to subjectivity itself in the figure of a father, implies, in the origin or in the guise of an origin, the *birth* (or the *gift*, precisely) of this relation. And a similar birth implies the *retreat* of what is neither subject, nor object, nor figure, and which one can, provisionally and simplistically, call "the mother." (188–19)

The difficulty here would be in distinguishing between the "mother" as a kind of primordial or arche-identification, an identification that precedes identification, on the one hand, and the "mother" as the retreated origin, the "birth," of relation itself *as* relation and thus as prior to and as the very condition of any conceivable identification. One might try to capture this distinction in the difference between the previously discussed German terms of *Gefülsbindung* and *Stellungnahme*. Or, one could more closely follow Freud's lead by distinguishing between identification (with the father) and anaclisis or object choice (toward the mother), an unfortunately gender-determined distinction that presupposes only male identity but whose resolution charts the space of group psychology. For Freud, this psychology of the (male) group is consequently defined by a mutually reinforcing relation or "double kind of tie" (130) by which "a number of individuals who have put one and the same object in the place of their ego ideal and have consequently identified themselves with one another in their ego" (116). Group cohesion emerges as a potent compromise between identification with other members of the group and anaclitic object choice toward the leader, expressed as "an extreme case of being in love" (114) whereby the love object is overestimated to the point of supplanting the lover's ego ideal. As such, Freud says the situation resembles that of hypnosis, which while limited to only two people (as in the case of love) is also "based entirely on sexual impulsions that are inhibited in their aims and puts the object in the place of the ego ideal" (143), whence the power of the hypnotist, and in terms of group psychology, the emotional and uncritical fascination with the leader. To this is added "identification with other individuals, which was perhaps originally made possible by their having the same relation to the object" (143).[52] The power of the double emotional tie—horizontal identification with the cohort of members and vertical object cathexis with the leader—that thus energizes the passionate extremism and potential violence of groups depends on some particular psychic transformations that can in turn help illuminate the retreat of the "mother" as the reputed essence of the political. On the one hand, and retracing Freud's demonstrably masculinist narrative, what was originally an identification with the father shifts into a mimetic bond with a group of others, an empathy based in imitation, which Freud suggestively calls *Einfühlung* or a feeling "as one" with what are the equivalent of the brothers in the primal horde. And, on the other hand, what was the anaclitic desire for the mother morphs into the expression of passionate and undying loyalty to the leader as displaced figure of the father. The key to the full development of this "double tie," though, is the existence of a constitutive split between an ego that can identify with similar others and an ego ideal that can take the love object into and as itself. Finessing the slippery reversal between mother and father (and leader), Freud concludes that the origin of the ego ideal, as division of the ego, is "revealed in the influence of superior powers, and above all of parents" (110). But it might be more accurate to say that the *Stellungnahme* that inaugurates the split between ego and ego ideal implies both a *figuration* of the father in/as the ego ideal and a withdrawal or retreat of the mother from any position of authority. Such a schema follows, of course, the classic pattern of the Oedipus complex, where the young boy identifies with the authoritarian figure of the father, while the mother withdraws from the field of object choice only to be replaced or "redrawn" by an exogamous substitute object for the boy's love affection. On the other hand, this double bond of group psychology, which serves to analyze the formation and dynamic of "groups" (masses, crowds, mobs) cannot represent the totality of the political, or even that of all groups, considering Freud's admitted emphasis on organized groups with leaders (or even those with obvious leader substitutes by way of abstract ideas and aspirations).[53] Nothing is said, for example, regarding the soft leadership of groups with rotating processes whereby different members take on the provisional role of leader with defined temporal and procedural limitations on how they can lead the group (a form of "leadership" we readily identify as democratic). Or regarding frankly leaderless groups of various kinds, such as we see in spontaneous demonstrations, wildcat strikes, popular boycotts, occupations, and other self-organizing actions.[54]

Moreover, in considering this vast terrain of social or group psychology, one cannot simply ascribe the ways of being with others as an external limit to psychoanalysis without also conceding the very birth of something like a self as its correspondingly "internal" limit. Viewing the social bond as "external" to some pre-existing subjectivity fails to grasp the necessity of the social bond in the very constitution of subjectivity itself. What one could call the primordial status of the Symbolic in Lacanian terms, or what Nancy and Lacoue-Labarthe refer to as the concept of arche-sociality that "haunts the entirety of contemporary thought," breaches the border between any so-called "inter-" subjectivity and some corresponding "infra-" subjectivity. Rather, it is the very tracing of those distinctions, inter- as well as infra-, that defines the retreat of the "mother," understood here as the very inscription of the difference between self and other. As such, the "mother" stands as neither "subject, nor object, nor figure" but as what gives *birth* to, what gives the gift of, the relation that defines "originary sociality" as *at one and the same time* "passage to community" and "passage to the subject." This is what Lacoue-Labarthe and Nancy mean by the "maternal retreat, of the mother as retreat, and of the retreat of the mother," which is also where "the entire retreat of the political is played out."

We can better understand this by returning one more time to the theme of relation as dissociation, which initially triggered the two philosophers' pivot to the "mother." All the various psychic mechanisms and manipulations we have described earlier in Freud's *Group Psychology* readily demonstrate forms of dissociation, from the hypnotic sway of the group leader as introjected ego ideal to the implicit othering of identification insofar as it "endeavors to mold a person's ego after the fashion of the one that has been taken as a model" (106). This recalls what Nancy and Lacoue-Labarthe refer to as "the incision—or excision—on the surface of an ego [that] withdraws into an unfigurable, unidentifiable matter—which one would, nonetheless, have to call social matter" (*Panique politique*, 72). But these forms of dissociation, or distension, or distraction, work only to the extent that they constitute self and other in the arche-sociality of identification as originary dissociation, as a split or interruption in consciousness that is nonetheless constitutive of the self as *zoon politikon*, as the very "exscription" of being-in-common, to use the language Nancy will subsequently develop. Even the physicality of birth itself can be seen as a manifestly dissociative process between mother and child, a mutual retreat or withdrawal that is also a (r)ejection and a reinscription of relation as a literal dissociation or inter-ruption, an incision/excision physically distended down the length of an (n)ever to be severed umbilical cord, of a separation (n)ever to come. At stake in this process of association/dissociation is "a retreat of identity in the accession of an identity": "Or again, it involves the stakes of a dependency in the accession of autonomy: the dependency of birth, the dependency of prematurity, and finally the dependency that lasts all through life" (*Panique politique*, 71).[55] The retreat is not a process leading to total separation or absence of bond but to an asymptotic "appearing disappearing" that defines our lifelong relation, not only to our mothers but by analogy to all others as well, and to our very sense of identity through the dissociative, distending process of identification as *Stellungnahme*. The retreat of "the mother," in both subjective and objective senses of the genitive, is the birth of the relation to otherness—that is, of birth *as* relation to others, or relation itself as arche-sociality, the interruption of bodies that is their being together.

While birth will emerge, of course, as an important category of analysis in Nancy's subsequent work, in, for example, *The Birth to Presence*, in *The Inoperative Community*, in *Corpus*, and in *Being Singular Plural*, where birth appears along with death as the finitude that marks our being in common, neither he nor Lacoue-Labarthe seems to pursue such radical insights beyond these early essays into the "mother" as where "the entire retreat of the political is played out," despite the fact that the curious relation between mother and child would seem to bear out some of their most radical conclusions regarding the arche-sociality that they also view as the essence of the political. While the relation between two lovers, following Bataille, serves justifiably as a compelling model of minimal community and of bare *mitsein* at the basis of Nancy's *The Inoperative Community*, the equally compelling but less clear model of mother *with* child does not get much attention going forward, bespeaking a disappointing blindness to gender difference reflected in the exclusively male composition of the Center's active contributors.[56]

Conversely, one is struck by the model of (male) friendship and collaboration that marks the personal and professional relationship between Nancy and Lacoue-Labarthe themselves. That friendship performs its own minimal arche-social bond across these early works while complicating the attribution of authorial subjectivity—they cannot be said to speak "as one" but not necessarily even as only two. It also finds its theoretical expression in Derrida's later *Politics of Friendship*, a work inspired by the energy of Lacoue-Labarthe and Nancy's Center, whose meetings Derrida assiduously attended and participated in, although without his ever giving a dedicated presentation.[57]

Perhaps this is because an analysis of the mother-child relation, call it the problematic of birth, needs to work against the full weight of long iconographical and ideological traditions that idealize motherhood and the joys of parturition despite (or even because of) its pains and sorrows, which define women almost exclusively in terms of their "maternity," which police women's bodies according to correlating patriarchal norms and expectations, while simultaneously proclaiming the virtue of motherhood as the core value of nation, religion, and race. But a closer look also reveals an insuperable stumbling block for any ethics based on the selfsameness of the subject. What exactly is the relation between mother and child? To what extent are they one, and to what extent are they more than one?[58] Rather than the image of Kristeva's "fusion" mother, ready to extinguish any daylight between her and child, one might consider the entire process of gestation, of "being with" child, as an iterative pattern of dissociation, interruption, rejection, and retreat. Birth can be a joy, of course, but also a relief after the rigors of pregnancy, and that physical ejection or rejection of the child is mirrored in the post-partum practice of weaning, as observed so manifestly in the animal world, where the offspring is progressively denied the mother's milk, protection, and even presence. Phrased in perhaps a less heartless way, the ultimate expectation of motherhood (and fatherhood, for that matter) is that at some point the child "grows up," leaves the nest, and strikes out on its own. That modern human families exhibit not just love and tenderness for children but even at times clinging possessiveness, stifling overprotectiveness, and protracted infantilization does not for that matter exclude the fundamentally rejecting or dissociating end of weaning (the repression of which can and does create all manner of conflict for parents and children alike). As Lacoue-Labarthe and Nancy elaborate in *La panique politique* with regard to the interruption of the "clinging/un-clinging" that defines the mother-child relation, "The clinging is the tie without tie, the un-tying in which originates (and the origin thus remains unassignable and only repeats itself, and detaches from itself) the one who is neither a subject nor a nonsubject, neither mass nor individual, but the incised Narcissus: that which incises him is the mother who expels and retains him" (*Panique politique*, 28).

An alternative model might be found in Nancy's concept of the "intruder," developed in his own self-analysis of what it means to live with the transplanted heart of another (perhaps that of a woman to boot, as if to replace "the mother" within).[59] To what extent can we understand the child as the stranger within the mother, one whose destiny is only to be more and more estranged? Less an intruder, then, than an *extruder*? And especially if the intruder that is the transplanted heart is in fact but the harbinger of all sorts of other intrusions (pharmaceutical, technological, dietary, physiological, metrical), each one triggering other intrusions, ultimately bringing about "a certain continuity in the intrusions, a permanent regime of intrusion," such that "I become inseparable [*indissociable*] from a polymorphous dissociation" (40–41)? The latter phrase recalls, of course, the Freudian concept of polymorphous perversity notable in small children prior to the socialization of sexual pleasure becoming restricted to those zones of the body specifically designated as erogenous.[60] But this infantile polymorphism is just as "dissociative" in relation to the maternal body (which is simultaneously dissociating from the child as the bond between mother and child transitions from the pre-partum physicality of a condominial relation *within* the body to the post-partum psychological relation *between* two different and differing bodies) as is that of the ill body suffering from the relentless exteriority of ever more intrusive foreign bodies, which make one "a stranger to oneself" (31). In either case, such dissociation exscribes the very line between life and death, which can no longer be "isolated" from each other, but which are "intimately woven each one into the other, each one intruding into the heart of the other" (23). And what thus gives the "gift" of life, tracing the very possibility of the dissociation that opens up every relation, is what one would inevitably have to call "the mother," and that gift in turn follows the "singular logic" of the retreat, a withdrawal that is a redrawing. Thus, the maternal retreat that is at once "the retreat of the mother" and "the mother as retreat." At its most abstract, and looking ahead to Nancy's later work, the "mother" would be inextricably linked to the birth to presence, to the advent of singularity itself.[61]

The relation between the "mother" and retreat—that is, the metaphorical "birth" of interruption and dissociation *as* relation, also recalls the conundrum in Derrida's "*Retrait* of Metaphor," where considering the question of the "mother tongue," he unpacks a telling remark by Heidegger regarding the rooting of language in local dialect—namely, that "the idiom is not only the language of the mother, but is at the same time and above all the mother of language" (62). But, again as elsewhere in that article, the metaphor retreats upon itself, so that an understanding of what language is in terms of the mother does not tell us about language as the object of the metaphor but only leads to a further questioning of its vehicle, in this case, about what motherhood is. As Derrida notes, "A mother tongue would not be a metaphor for determining the sense of language, but the essential turn that must be taken to understand what 'mother' means" (62). Later queried on this point by Nancy at the end of the discussion of Philippe Soulez's contribution to the Center's second volume, Derrida further adds that "the expression 'mother tongue' presupposes language": "But one needs to think language first before being able to think its epithet as 'mother.' Only then could one posit a mother as other than childbearing [*génitrice*], as a first linguistic relation" (182). In response, Nancy wonders whether such an approach "does not arbitrarily presuppose language as coming first, and therefore as maternal," to which Derrida answers that "one must look into language first, but that does not mean the first language will be maternal" (182). It would seem that what matters here is less what motherhood has to say about language (as in the expression "mother tongue") but what language as "first" or primordial *relation* has to say about motherhood, which is itself a specific birth of relation, the gift of arche-sociality, a retreat/withdrawal that is the advent of being in common and of identification as dissociation. Elsewhere, Nancy (in collaboration with Lacoue-Labarthe) writes, "The structure of language is a structure, in the strict sense, of general identification. On the other hand, the process of what makes language possible, the *incisive* process of Freudian identification, as has been recognized, is but a process of *alteration*" (*Panique politique*, 59).

"Something More..."

All of which brings us to the fifth and final "trait" in Lacoue-Labarthe and Nancy's "quick listing" of what would be presented by that "something which would be 'the political'" (132). Each of these traits, they remind us at this point, "refers us to a specificity of the political," implicitly in the wider context of the retreat of the political in the Arendtian sense as the totalitarian dominance of the political across every sphere of life and thus the loss of any specificity to the political, its consequent paralysis, unless, of course, what is understood by the political is retraced or "retreated" elsewhere or in some other way. Nancy and Lacoue-Labarthe are insistent (against the objections of Denis Kambouchner) that the specificity in question "by which the political would be signaled" is *not* of the order of the empirical. Rather, it is a question of a "philosophical fact" or "a sort of *factum rationis* of philosophico-political reason," which they explain as follows:

> ... at least since Aristotle, the being-together of human beings, the *zoon politikon*, does not stem from the factual given of needs and vital necessities, but from this other factual given of the sharing [*partage*] of ethical and "evaluative" speech [*parole*] in general: this "fact" defies all assignation in empirical factuality, to the extent that such a factuality actually exists. What occupies us, in other words, is the *surplus* [*l'excédent*] of this "fact," this excess over mere "living"—and over a simply social "living together"—of "living well" [*du vivre bien*] which alone determines the *zoe* of the *zoon politikon*. It is, in short, such a "good" [*bien*]—this "more than" [*en plus*] of every organization of needs and every regulation of forces—it is such a "good," which we are certainly not burdening with any moral weight, it is such a "good," indeterminate today, which resides

in the retreat and whose question the retreat unburdens and delivers [*livre ou délivre*]. (134; translation modified)

The political, or political life, whatever it might be, represents *something beyond* mere existence, something beyond the biopolitics of what Giorgio Agamben has termed "bare life,"[62] something that is not just living but living *well*. The animate life (*zoe*), as opposed to the mode of survival (*bios*) of the animate creature (*zoon*), is "alone determined" by that excess of mere living that qualifies as living "well" or the "good life," understood *neither* in individual nor in moral terms but as the *common good of a living in common* (as members of the *polis*).

That commonality or communality is not a common ideal per se but the "fact" of one's participation or partaking in "ethical and 'evaluative' speech." The French here specifically states speech as *parole*, or the *use* of language rather than simply the existence of its general structure (*langue*). This makes it, according to Lacoue-Labarthe and Nancy, a philosophico-political fact but not an "empirical" one. Rather, access to speech is what defines being in the *polis*, not so much the partaking in a fact as the very fact or *factum* of partaking. Aristotle specifies that "the power of speech is intended to set forth the expedient and the inexpedient, and therefore likewise the just and the unjust" (*Politics* 1253a, 14–15). More to the point, it is not just any *prise de parole* that matters but what takes place specifically in an "ethical or evaluative" register—namely, a genre of discourse where what is at stake is the well-being of the *polis* itself—that is, the political common good, or if one prefers, the political *tout court*. To rephrase Aristotle slightly, the political is nothing other than the *zoe* of the *zoon politikon*, the irrepressible claim or *demand* for "something more" than the actuality of mere subsistence or survival, whether one calls that something more liberty or equality or justice or something utterly and even incomprehensibly other. That something more is always shared, partaken in the very fact of political life, in a participation that is also a partition, a parturition or birth in the very throes of the separation that sharing also implies. That shared separation [*partage*] defines the identification with one's fellow participants, a dissociative identification that is also the retreat of identity to the extent that identification requires the taking of the other into oneself as the very condition for the *zoon politikon* to have anything like an identity, necessarily constituted, we remember, "as social," as "arche-sociality," the "dis-sociation paradoxically constitutive of human sociality" (*Panique politique*, 104), which is also where "or according to which the entire retreat of the political is played out." That is also where the aspiration for "something more" than the biopolitics of mere subsistence remains or resides, where a response to the question of that common good is "unburdened and delivered."[63]

The metaphor of the mother (but is it a mere metaphor?) returns in the final line from Nancy and Lacoue-Labarthe's eponymous essay, "The Retreat of the Political," to underscore the very birth or parturition of the *polis*. The collective aspiration or demand for "something more" is the core of the retreat, what resides in its core, at its very heart, as the essence and *sense* of the political but that is not in and of itself political—namely, the *interruption* of desire for a beyond of mere survival, which is the question that the retreat answers, so that even with the totalitarian saturation of everything being political, that very closure of the political announces or traces a border for a new specificity of the political (the retreating and retracing of what nonetheless escapes the trait itself, or what Lyotard terms the *intraitable*),[64] always occurring and always to come (like the jurisdiction of the Hegelian monarch, of the sovereign). Whence, at last, the answer to our initial question of why the retreat "demands" its articulation in terms of the political.

Oddly then, the retreat is not just a "singular logic" but something like a logic of the singular, as what both emerges and hides itself in what is "delivered" in the being-together that is the partaking or participation, in the speaking of or for the "good life." The birth of the singular is what is revealed in the "maternal" retreat of the political (subjective *and* objective genitive), in the "mother" as retreat and in the retreat of the "mother" as the political. It is worth considering how not only the mother but the child too as well as all those institutionally rendered as children, as the literal *in-fans* who have no right to speak (women, slaves, foreigners) are withdrawn from the political even as they redraw its contours elsewhere, even while the approved men of the *polis* fully engage in its official politics (*la politique*), and the deliberation of its policies if not the full actualization of its polity. And in the early twenty-first century, no issue has become as political as the place and role of those at risk of withdrawal from the scene of a politics threatened by the storm clouds of budding forms of authoritarian neoliberalism (the current not-so-"subtle" or "soft" mode of totalitarianism). The apparent retreat of the political in the current context of brutal power politics masquerading as spectacular buffoonery is corroborated, at the risk of engaging in rank empiricism, by the impossibility of engaging in any actual political "debate" or dialogue with the likes of Trump, or Putin, or Bolsonaro, or Erdogan, among the many others. Instead, we see the actuality of retreat as again *demanding* a rearticulation in terms of the political, as the redrawing of new political lines of contestation that form each and every time as the singularity of a resistance, of resistance as singular event. The sense of this singularity thus becomes the question of our times, the new horizon for our contemporary creation of world.

Return to Cerisy and a Singular Conclusion

A sense of singularity as well as an "ethos of retreat" haunt the concluding remarks delivered by Nancy and Lacoue-Labarthe at the close of the 1980 Cerisy conference on Derrida, with the words "singular" or "singularity" appearing over a dozen times within the four-and-a-half pages of this closing address. While at first a mere indication of what the conference would have "produced," or "opened up," as less a formal "result" than the event of its collective gathering/dispersion, "neither homogeneous nor heterogeneous," its actualization as a *singular* "configuration" or "constellation," the conference organizers quickly pivot to the notion that "singularity would have precisely been the dominant motif of the colloquium" (690). Thus, not just the singularity of the event itself but singularity itself as the theme that emerges from the event's "singular constellation." Singularity emerges as the dominant motif, whether in reference to the "singularity of a discipline, a writing, a thought, an event" or to "that singular 'singular' we call an 'individual,' that is, an *atom*" (690).

At stake would be the "question of the inseparable [*insécable*]" or what "resists division, in a general regime of division, dispersion, and dissociation." With regard to this individual, this "singular 'singular'" that is the human being in its atomization, what remains or resists under the dissociative regime in question is "a *singularity* beyond individuality and collectivity" (691)—that is, what remains of the human after the "end of man," which is concomitantly "the end of *the* end, its dislocation, its pulverization into multiple, heterogeneous ends, impossible to dominate and to center." What remains, "once this division of ends has been realized, irreversibly," is no longer a subject as substance (or *subjectum*) nor even as "absent or split," but something to be "thought in terms of the *retreat of the subject*" (691), or, if one likes, its "appearing disappearing." To address the status of this post-apocalyptic subject in retreat requires an "*ethos of the retreat*," which is not to be understood as an "'ethics' or edification" but in terms of an "*Unheimlichkeit* to face [*à affronter*]" (691). While the term readily conjures up Freud's concept of the "uncanny" as what is strangely familiar, both homely and "un-homely" by dint of repetition and repression, Nancy and Lacoue-Labarthe, in both their contributions to the Cerisy conference, refer us instead to Heidegger's use of the word, following upon his reading of the famous first choral ode in Sophocles's *Antigone*, as indicating the "basic trait of the human essence": "Manifold is the uncanny [*polla ta deina*; Vielfältig das Unheimliche], yet nothing/uncannier [*to deinotaton*; Unheimlicheres] than man bestirs itself, rising up beyond him."[65] The essential uncanniness of the human being means that s/he is never at home, always other, or as Lacoue-Labarthe specifies, the essence of the human is nothing less than the "in-human" (434), or that "'singular' singular" that remains or resists under the apocalyptic regime of interruption and dissociation. As the "conclusion" to the Cerisy Colloquium states, "all this, in sum, implies a singular *being*, that is, a singular being-for-Being" that is also a "being-in-community" not "as subsumed in a grand Subject, but as the *inter-pellation*, that is, the call of the singular to the singular: the demand, the order" (691). The subject in retreat, or the subject of withdrawal, is the singularity in touch with other singularities (there is never but one singularity, but always irremediably plural, as Nancy often reiterates), the sovereign *demand* for that "something more" than the home, or the *polis*, thus figuring the political as the uncanny, always strange and always familiar, the "traits of another thought," always in retreat and always to come: the singular *there* of a being that is (n)ever just "there."

4
Corpus interruptus
Uncommon Sense and the Singular Crossings
of Eros, Logos, and Tekhnè

To the extent that the retreat of the mother traces a given limit of the political, an "essence" of the political that is not itself political, it also raises the question of the body, or rather of the relation between bodies that define our being together. Whether the insuperableness of that *mitsein* arises to the level of a polis or a community, operative or not, the *unum quid* of the body (or bodies) of mother with child suggests that the moment we call a "birth" is less an actual "beginning" than a singular irruption, disruption, or interruption within and between bodies. Bodies thus first appear as within bodies before emerging as distinct. At the same time, the body is where sense can take place, where it is literally embodied. After the iterative cogito and the Cartesian *unum quid*, after the monogrammatic traits of another thought as creative intervention and the retreat of the political in its singular logic, the question of the relations between sense and singularity urges reflection on the body as the locus of their interface. This chapter will thus focus on Nancy's subsequent writings on sense and corporeality, from the multiple iterations of *Corpus* through related texts on the senses, sexuality, aesthetics, the arts, and technology.[1] We will see how this only apparently disparate series of texts questions the classic philosophical distinction between the sensible and the intelligible, interrupting the seemingly commonsensical categories that derive from that divide and proposing the very sense of sense as what reveals the singular "patency" of the world, rather than metaphysically positing some lurking latency to be uncovered. We will begin and conclude by discussing the multiple senses of sense as the frame for analyzing its embodiment in and between bodies, how the body as locus of multiple senses interrupts any concept of a common sense, how the relation between bodies occasions the singular crossings between sexuality, language, and technology, and their synesthetic interruptions in art and poetry as sense of the world. And finally, how does this play of sense and singularity bring us back to the question of the retreat of the mother as the very interruption of existence that we call life?

Sense in Every Possible Sense

So, then, what do we mean by "sense"? Or, in what *sense* do we mean the word "sense"? It could refer, for example, to mere sensation or "the senses" in the plural, as the various visual, auditory, olfactory, gustatory, or tactile ways we perceive or believe we perceive the world of existence. Or, the word "sense" could refer, in the singular this time, to whatever we mean by "meaning," the sense or signification of any given thing or event, or even of what we sense. Sense could also refer to directional sense, as in that wonderful French expression for a one-way street, *sens unique*. Hence, motion as well as emotion, being sensible as well as sensitive. More germane to this study, how do we understand what Jean-Luc Nancy means by sense, especially within a finite thinking framed by the perpetually receding horizons of retreat, iteration, and monogrammatic "traits of another thought" and a radical sense of the world as defined by the very singularity of existence, if not existence as infinity of singularities, as singularly sublime, if one wishes. What might we come to understand, then, as the *sense* of singularity, or the singularity of sense?

Sens en tout sens [Sense in Every Sense] is the felicitous title of a collection published by Galilée in 2004, edited by Francis Guibal and Jean-Clet Martin, and based on a colloquium held at the Collège international de Philosophie in 2002. The volume is subtitled in reference and homage to the famous 1980 Derrida colloquium at Cerisy, "Autour des travaux de Jean-Luc Nancy," not quite the "à partir du travail de Jacques Derrida," "around his works" (in the plural) rather than "based on his work" (in the singular). A more *circumspect* approach, perhaps, as if to leave Nancy at or as the absent center of this *conferring* or *conferencing* "around" the multiplicity of his works rather than pursuing the line of a consistent opus. This circumspection is corroborated by a remark in Guibal's preface: that Nancy "strongly resisted the very mention of his name" in association with the conference and volume: "This thinker of the singular wished to efface himself as much as possible before the only essential, the '*Matter*' of thought, of what there is to think" [la "Sache" de la pensée, de ce qui est à-penser].[2] Contributors to this circumspect volume include Jacques Derrida, Alain Badiou, Catherine Malabou, and Werner Hamacher, among others. But despite the brilliance of the contributions to the question of "sense," the essays included in the volume tend to limit their sense of the word "sense" to that of meaning, and the expression "sense in every sense" seems to serve primarily to question the meaning of the proliferation of meaning. There are occasional exceptions, of course, as when Badiou casually invokes "another" Nancy, "for whom the enigma of sense is that of our five senses," or Malabou's probing evocation of the "fantasmatic *areality*" of existence in Nancy's thinking,[3] but on the whole, a semantic understanding of the question predominates, along with an odd respect for the traditional philosophical divide between the intelligible and the sensible.

But Nancy's sense of sense in fact wreaks utter and ongoing havoc with that key metaphysical distinction, as we have seen in the case of his deft deconstruction of the body/mind divide in Descartes via the *unum quid*, or his deployment of the Kantian monogram as the schematic intersection of image and concept. Far from distinguishing assiduously between different senses of sense, Nancy as often as not deploys the multiple meanings of the word "sense" in ways that obligate us to rethink what we mean by sense, in any sense at all: not just the apparent trinity of meaning, sensation, direction, but also their various possible intersecting conjugations, intersections, and displacements. The point is certainly not, as we have also seen, to conflate or collapse the distinction between the sensible and the intelligible into some indistinct continuum but rather to elaborate the irreducible set of *differences* that can occur under the term of "sense" and that perhaps do not universally allow themselves to fall on one side or the other of the sensible/intelligible divide, which Nancy reminds us in *A Finite Thinking* is "the most powerful distinction that philosophy has to offer."[4] Moreover, he continues, "we could easily show that there is no philosophy, no poetry, which hasn't claimed, in one way or another, to have overcome, dissolved, or rendered dialectical this double aporia," situated at "the most extreme point of metaphysics," whereby "what senses in sense is the fact that it includes what it senses, and what produces sense in sense is the fact that it senses itself producing sense," and yet "nothing tells us what it might mean 'to sense sense' or 'to understand sensing'" (*Finite Thinking*, 6). Sense, for Nancy, is indubitably caught within this auto-reflexive regression of sense sensing itself ad infinitum, whether as sensation or as understanding. Indeed, he concludes, "the 'other' sense of the word sense is only 'other' in terms of this sameness" (*Finite Thinking*, 5). That infinite regression is also at the same time an indefinite progression, whereby the "each and every time" finite, punctual singularity of sense in turn produces more sense, be it the very "end" of sense in its infinite deferral and difference, the endlessness if you like of sense sensing itself. Moreover, sense never stops sensing itself, in whatever sense of the word "sense" one chooses: "Sensing senses nothing if it doesn't sense itself sensing, just as understanding understands nothing if it doesn't understand itself understanding" (*Finite Thinking*, 5). But before we conclude a kind of ipseity such as modeled by Paul Valéry's Monsieur Teste, "I am being and seeing myself; seeing me see myself, and so forth,"[5] we need to heed Nancy's claim that the vertigo of sense sensing itself ad infinitum is "first and foremost the fissure, the gap, the spacing of an opening," a "being-other of the self as neither 'self' nor 'other,'" to the extent that "sense depends on relating to itself as to another or to some other" (*Finite Thinking*, 6–7). Sense, in whatever sense we might take it, partakes in a structure of difference, of endlessly proliferating differences, that far from becoming reabsorbed in an overarching identity as per the ideals of classical philosophy (Subject, History, God, Idea) only succeeds in underscoring its inappropriable singularity each and every time, the limitless singularity of being that is the insuperable finitude of existence, the sense of singularity that demands the rigor of a finite thinking that "is only ever able to think to the extent that it also touches on its own limit and its own singularity" (*Finite Thinking*, 5). Sensing singularity is sense sensing what escapes sense, what has no sense or cannot be sensed, or more properly what is at the very limit of sense, where the meaning of sensation, the experience of sense (meaning), and the sensing of meaning all converge into the linguistic singularity of a hapax. "Sense" thus undoes the Fregian distinction between meaning and reference to the extent that sense is its own concept and reference.[6]

In addition to this critique of the verticality of sense sensing itself, Nancy is quick to dispel any horizontal concept of a "common sense": "Senses *don't touch each other*, there's no 'common sense,' no sensing 'in itself.'"[7] Nancy supports this position by referring, ironically perhaps, to Aristotle, the very philosopher credited with conceptualizing the sense of a common sense as that by which we integrate our individually distinct sensory perceptions into a coherent view of the world, informed by a general underlying sense of a self. Proceeding somewhat differently, Nancy states that "Aristotle knows this, saying that each sense senses *and* senses itself sensing, each on its own with no overarching control, each one withdrawn, as sight, as hearing, as taste, smell, touch, each delighting and knowing that it delights in the absolute apartness of its delight" (*Corpus*, 119). The Nancean logic of retreat/withdrawal reappears here as the very sense of sense, "each one withdrawn" from the "overarching control" of what might have been a so-called common sense. The self-sensing of each sense is perhaps then the retreat of common sense, or at least of any sense in common. Indeed, Nancy goes so far as to claim that it is the very "apartness" of the senses, their apparent singularity, that is the "starting point" from which "all theory of art issues" (*Corpus*, 119), such as music's appeal to our sense of hearing or painting's play on our sense of vision.

For Aristotle, on the other hand, it is precisely this ability to sense ourselves sensing as well as to sense the *difference* between the senses that justifies the hypothesis of "something that is one and single," not an additional sense per se, but a "common sensibility" or faculty "with which we perceive that [the senses] are different." Moreover, "what asserts this difference must be self-identical, and as what asserts, so also what thinks or perceives."[8] The coordinating function of this sense that is not a sense is also the basis of what Aristotle calls the soul—and elsewhere the underlying *hypokeimenon* or sub-ject—whose "distinctive properties" include "local movement" as well as the interrelated but distinct activities of "thinking, understanding, and perceiving."[9] And under the hands of a host of commentators from Aquinas through Locke and Kant, the vicissitudes of the term have moved from that of sense coordination to a kind of normative knowledge or fundamental human rationality, the very seat of human subjectivity, of the subject. In the opening line to the *Discourse on Method*, Descartes famously quips about the supposed equanimity of the common sense when he refers to "good sense" as being "the best distributed thing in the world: for everyone thinks himself so well endowed with it that even those who are the hardest to please in everything else do not usually desire more of it than they possess."[10] From a *sensus communis* that functions as sensory coordinator to a common sense that is the equitable quota of reason in each one of us (our supposed common-sense reasoning, or the common sense we are incessantly admonished to use on a day-to-day basis), one also sees the philosophical extrication of mind from body, or (which is the same thing) that of the intelligible from the sensible, as well as a general suspicion for any thinking that might challenge our common sense understanding of the way things are, hence, a concomitant and generalized antipathy to speculative thought. To the contrary, and in an ironic rebuke to Descartes's witticism, Nancy states in the very first sentence of *A Finite Thinking* that sense is "the least shared thing in the world" (3).

The Body of Sense

Confronting this drift from sense to sense, or the wavering direction between sensation and meaning, Nancy imagines the body as "the intervallic space [*entre-deux*] between two *senses*—amongst which the intervals between right and left, high and low, before and behind, phallus and cephale, male and female, inside and outside, sensory sense and intelligible sense, merely interexpress each other" (*Corpus*, 65). There is no common sense (either in Aristotle's or Descartes's sense), nor even sense in common, but an ever-shifting set of gaps *between* different senses, whose singular points of articulation, convergence, and divergence *instantiate* a space, an areality, perhaps even a world, that we can call the "body" (or perhaps just a body, any body, some body, my body), the literal incarnation of sense as "inter-expression," or the mutual translation of senses, the ones into the others. As such, the senses are inseparably different, while partaking in the singular plural of their being. Sense thus remains transcendent, even transgressive, always on the outside posing as inside, but also inside posing as outside, wreaking havoc with the very senses of inside and outside. If the body is indeed the intervallic space between senses, then one can no longer speak confidently of an inner (body) and outer (world). All the more so if we read Nancy's French, which states *entre-deux*, creatively but not incorrectly rendered by translator Richard Rand as "intervallic space." While the "space" in between the intervals of what is here called "sense" suggests something like the physical volume we tend to associate with the deep space and resonance of the "body," that space as *entre-deux* also gears down to a mere space or spacing of difference, a betweenness that at its limit is no more than the trace of that difference between (at least?) "two senses" or two senses of the word "sense," whose "inter-expression" would chart the transcendence or translation of one sense into the other. What we could call the body is but the ongoing transcription and relay of these differences. The so-called body serves as the inter-expressed difference or differance of sense, be it but the in-betweenness of the *entre deux*, an interval, the gap between two valleys, the ridge of some high ground, point or line, if not the very space or place of articulated sense.

If we still want to call the body a space, it would have to be in the place of this "inter-expression," a curious formulation worth unpacking. It certainly complicates the usual conundrum, frequently elaborated by Nancy, of expression as im-pression, or more precisely ex-position as the basis for an interiority that only exists as an effect of our being exposed, the very basis of our *ex*-istence, or *ek-sistence*, to follow the Heideggerian formula. But what exactly is an "inter" expression? There is indeed not only the sense of a mutual co-positing but also of an exchange, where the one is expressed in and through the other. That "inter" is also the *entre deux* of expression, a kind of interdiction, as what is both said and not said, or as Nancy defines it, as "the diction or saying that is said *between*" [le dire qui se pronounce "entre"].[11] Elsewhere, Nancy describes the inter-dict as "what falls between words": "To say or show stupor, a form of commotion made of fright, trouble, and torment—desire tormenting itself, exceeding itself in accord with its most intimate movement—comes back to saying or showing the *inter-dict*: what falls between words, there where showing is no longer possible, if all showing consists of a 'here it is!'"[12]

What falls between is the relaying back (or *"renvoi"* between the senses that makes sense possible and impossible, the *entre-deux* that is at once inter-diction and inter-expression, the expression of inexpressibility itself or the inexpressibility that nonetheless lurks at the heart of every ex-pression, the exorbitant that is the only center we can know: "For there is no sense without relay—to the same or the other, which amounts to the same (that is, the other), provided that there is relay. What is needed is a call, recall, restitution, reper-cussion, resonance, return, reprise, reflection, reproduction, so that there can be a coming—and coming is needed for there to be a stay [*séjour*]."[13] There is necessarily relay from sense to sense, in every sense of the word. The senses are necessarily iterative or allusive or referential (*renvoi*). It is always a question of what "sounds like" or "looks like" or "feels like," whence the presumed "du-plicity or unreliability" of the senses, as per the traditional skepticist critique that the senses "lie."

Does this then posit singularity as truth? But how? And what do we make of the context, space, time, uttering, iterating, commonality of the senses in dissonance? Con-text is not what surrounds or englobes or contours the "text," but is nothing other than the very situation of the event, or eventness, of the situation, the very event of utterance, of in- or ex-scription. The sense of exis-tence is always there and then (*Da-sein*), singularity occluded by the very sense that senses it, that makes sense of it. Singularity as lost horizon is always re-ceding as the (un)common ground of what we sense as the sense of our exis-tence, or *ek-sistence*. Singularity cannot be said to exist in space and time but at or as its very edge, as event horizon, as (vanishing) point, of what comes to be, of the partaking of the world. It is the taking place of place and of taking place (*l'avoir lieu du lieu*). Like but not a *Ding-an-sich*, not a phenomenon (that can be sensed, or as a "construct" of sense/perception/meaning) nor a noumenon (as some kind of selfsame object beyond or anterior to sense), but the very iteration, the ceaseless coming and going of what patently is.

And what then is the sense of the relation between the relation of senses in the *entre-deux* of their inter-diction? There is a "point," writes Nancy in *Cor-pus II*, "where we might have to grant that a relation [*rapport*], whatever it is, makes something like some sense [*fait quelque chose comme du sens*], even if that is initially simply directional sense (the relation of setting in motion), then sense-able [*sens sensible*] (the relation of skin to the skin it touches, or of an eye to the color that delights it). Or that it caresses and then relates significa-tion, which both a direction (even if it must go in both directions [*dans les deux sens*]) and a sensibility (because the saying touches [*car le dire touche*]. . . ." (7). Nancy's clarification here is precious: there is a "point" where the senses intersect in every possible sense—a point of convergence, however fleeting or asymptotic, that is also the lower limit of their inter-expression—building up from their most rudimentary sense as directionality through the sensing of the senses up to the "relation of signification," which itself also appears to encompass both direction and sensibility. If, as he concludes, "saying touches," then meaning is also directional sensing and vice versa. The apparently vertical move up through these meanings of sense is less a true hierarchy (from direction to sensation to meaning) than a complex and mutual invagination whereby each sense of the word "sense" is found in each and every other possible sense. Thus is realized at least one mode of inter-expression between sense and senses, intersection and/as inter-diction.

Can physical sensation, in other words, be perceived—sensed—as anything other than meaning, be it the senselessness of what remains meaningfully without meaning? In turn, meaning is only meaningful if sensed, say through the *materiality* of language, written or oral, or sensorially by visual or auditory representation, or even by the many registers of corporal gesticulation. Such a conundrum of sense recalls the Saussurian theory of the sign, split between a "sound-image" or signifier and a "concept" or signified. While countless buckets of ink have been spilt on Saussure's claim that the relation between signifier and signified is "arbitrary," less attention has been paid to the *necessity* of the relation between the two parts of the sign, what Saussure describes as the two sides of a coin, or of a sheet of paper, recto and verso.[14] And this necessary interdependence of signifier and signified can help us think through the equally necessary interdependence between sensation and meaning, perception and understanding, less as two parallel and competing systems of cognition than as two inextricably linked ways of making "sense" out of the world in which we are thrown, or as "two aspects or modes of a single disposition to sense" (*Sexistence*, 30).

And if it appears as the "point" where sensation and meaning initially occur, directional sense can also arise out of this inter-expression of sensation and meaning, as a further inter-expression of what it feels or means to be somewhere, be that somewhere a nowhere, the very sense of being lost and unsure of one's bearings. One thinks again of the floundering Descartes, swept up in a bottomless abyss of doubt, whose desperately sought Archimedean point of leverage comes with the iterative interruption of the cogito, the repeated stating or thinking of *ego sum, ego existo* as the very high ground of sense (sensation, meaning, location) between the valleys whose inter-expression provides the bearings of our existence, literally incarnated in and as our body, not as the ship wherein the mind is ensconced as mere pilot, but as the differance of self-(dis)articulation, *unum quid*. Inter-expression is thus also the reversal of terms whereby senselessness, meaninglessness, and placelessness flip into the foundation of sense as subjectivity, the reputedly unshakeable and indubitable point from which sense can be deduced in an endless chain of ever greater knowledge, the great directional narrative of science as progress. A further elaboration can be found in Hegel, for whom so-called sense-certainty is the starting point for his own developmental narrative powered by the dialectic whose "magical power of the negative" leads in a self-canceling but progressive direction from sensory cognition to perception to understanding and eventually up to the comprehensive meaningfulness of "absolute knowledge." But while Hegel does not so much as raise the question of coordination between the different senses—that is, he seems to eschew the entire question of a common sense—he does insist on the relation between sense perception, any sensing, and the necessary co-positing of a mind or consciousness that determines the object sensed as "mine" [*meinem*] while giving meaning [*Meinen*] to that sensed object.[15] As with Aristotle, the disparities of sense, in every sense of the word, are contained and controlled by the existence of a "sensible" subject of knowledge.

But whether we are speaking of the relation between mind and object or that between different senses, a co-positioning or co-exposition is the operative effect of the body's *entre-deux* as the liminal space of inter-expression. What Aristotle imagines as common sense dissolves into the mere trace of difference, inscribing a network of reversals, inversions, reconcatenations, translations, and transcodings of and between all senses of sense, the intervallic place of *articulation*, a word that incidentally applies to corporal flexibility as well as linguistic facility, to the free play of limbs as well as the dexterity of tongue or hand holding pen (indeed, "articulation" gives the sense of the Latin word *ars*, from which we derive the word "art"). A networking system not unlike how we currently imagine the brain itself and its neuronal matrix as the putative organ of whatever we might still want to call common or perhaps even uncommon sense. "Speech," writes Hegel, "has the divine nature of directly turning the 'mere' meaning right round about, making it into something else."[16] How is the intervallic space of articulation, a.k.a. the body, different then from "art" and from language itself—that is, from the meaningful play of differences (or the play of meaningful differences)?

At the limit, the body as articulation of differences comes down to the skin itself as the line that demarcates the inter-val, the *entre-deux*, or betweenness that constitutes Nancy's sense of the body as *corpus interruptus*. We are an ever-shifting network of membranes, a vibrantly interstitial space of manifest volatility, where every shift marks what we call a sense, whether perception, conception, or orientation (and beyond that, we can understand the reticulated skein of the world as itself a skin and a very "fragile" one at that).[17] But "sense" then marks an irredeemable externality, the infinity of an internal finitude, whose "inter-expression" is incarnated in or as the organ we call skin, arguably the largest organ in the body. And no matter how deeply we penetrate into the body, we can only ever uncover more layers of skin, be they the mere membranes of difference, between our body and what supposedly lies outside, between the different organs within our body, between the cells that make up those organs, between the molecules that make up the cells, and so forth until we reach that sub-atomic level where, so quantum mechanics tells us, particulate matter both is and is not. In an all too real sense, our sense is only ever external; you can't feel the "inside" of your body, only the difference that is skin,[18] the internal is only ever felt as external. And if the body reveals itself through endless layers of skin, as the infinity of the finitude of flesh, that does not exclude at all those supplementary layers of pseudo-skin we call clothing, a dynamic semiosis of perceptible meaning or sensible sense that can serve to manifest gender, social status, cultural or religious belonging, professional identity, or institutional affiliation (not only but especially when such identity is signaled by the kind of clothing called "uniform"), all this over and beyond the reputed truth of nudity, of bared skin, as the very metaphor of *aletheia* traced by Nancy and Ferrari in *Being Nude: The Skin of Images*.[19] The unveiling of a striptease aims to reveal the meaning of the sensed body in the absence of the supplement of dress but only ever shows more skin and its hint of ever-deferred meaning: "Nudity, considered as pure denudation, is an abstraction. All denudation is the index of an even more intimate stripping, perhaps bottomless or unattainable" (*Sexistence*, 10). The revealed existence of skin as nakedness always nevertheless retains endless opportunities for (re)inscription, ornamentation, tattooing, scarification, painting, dyeing, "cosmetics" of all kinds,[20] as well as those other, less intended markings of age and stress: wrinkles, crow's feet, hair loss, stretch marks, all manner of scabs, scars, discolorations, and distensions. The body as skin is always already ex-scribed as it is inscribed, the "inter-expressive" play of sense and senses, where intimacy is always already "extimacy."

Pain and pleasure only occur as ex-scribed, even when conceived as auto-affection, as the singularity of senses sensing themselves, as skin touching skin. And all the more so for that experience physicians call "referred pain," where the sensation one feels refers not to where it might actually arise but elsewhere, to some other part of the body, such as when heart troubles are felt as a pain in the left arm. More generally, however, bodily pain (and pleasure) might always be said to be "referred," signaled as it is via the neural network that links the violated surface of our limbs and organs to the apperception of the brain. Numbness, too, works as the referred pain of no pain, as the debilitating absence of sensation that is nonetheless an overwhelming (of) sensation in its own right, in a kind of obverse to the amputee's phantom sensation of feeling in a lost limb.

Pain and pleasure are thus caught in a web of communication, a "com-union" (or a union that is only "like" a union, that is not a union at all, *unum quid*), that no matter how prolonged or repeated, is always experienced as singular, as this particular pain or that particular pleasure, the finitude of a touch, lingering in its anticipation or in its memory, the space-time of its *reference* necessarily delayed by its neuronal trajectory, the each time singular inter-expression of sense and sense.

The Sense of Bodies

But doesn't the body as the space of "inter-diction/inter-expression" between not only multiple senses but the very multiplicity of senses (in every sense of the word), also paradoxically express its converse—namely, that sense occurs in/as the "intervallic space" between (at least) two bodies, the vibrant *entre-deux* of their corporal contact, their intercommunication or inter-penetration, the chiasmus of reciprocal invagination, be it coitus, or mere conversation, or even the most casual of street encounters, as in Baudelaire's famous poem "A une passante" [To a Passerby], which Nancy cites in its entirety at one point (*Sexistence*, 87–88). There is in fact no one body, no body at all, in the sense of some self-subsisting physiognomic identity, but rather *some bodies*, bodies in perpetual motion, bodies thrown together by the incessant clinamen of their *entre-deux*, of their own metamorphoses, bodies generating other bodies, bodies subsisting as other than themselves, "sexisting," as Nancy, true to neologistic form, proposes in *Sexistence*. The *entre-deux* is the space of sex, but also, says Nancy, that of language, as well as that of *tekhnè* in all its senses: technique, technology, art. Alternatively, sex could be said to occur at the "point" (like the point we saw earlier with the difference between senses) when the difference between bodies and the difference within bodies becomes indecidable and so potentially ecstatic, the orgasm of inter-expression across bodies and senses as the essence of fucking: "Proximity heightens the incommensurable: a slight, infinitely diminutive but infinitely maintained distance, contact, touch, the *point* where representation blurs and the vertigo of presence begins. There where the simulacrum—the thin film of the other—ceases to simulate or rather never ceases to tumble into a simultaneous real. At once, fucking and its fiction" (*Sexistence*, 114; emphasis added).

Between bodies, between senses, such is the world Nancy gives us to think: the "fragile skin" of existence as iterated singularity or as singular iteration, as the "singular plural" of (inoperable) community and (inter-dictal) communication. Sex is what happens between and within bodies and between senses, both sensually and senselessly. So too does language occur between bodies and between senses, between ears and mouths and eyes, as meaning and as signification, be it at the limit of what can be uttered as sense, be it the inchoate ecstasy of polymorphous perversities ("silence, sigh, spasm," *Sexistence*, 44). So too with *tekhnè* as what happens between bodies and between senses, as transformation, transcendence, or transgression of our relation to ourselves, to the world. But what happens in all three is nothing other than existence, whether as sexistence, as logexistence, or as technexistence, to cite more Nancean neologisms (*Sexistence*, 72).

Tekhnè, logos, eros: these are in fact the classic markers of human exceptionality, the anthropocentrism that defines "man" as the only creature that makes or uses tools (*homo faber*), or the only creature that speaks or writes, or the only creature that is endlessly available sexually (unlike the limited mating "seasons" or estrus and highly specific conditions that limit copulation in most animals) and thus capable of unrestrained sexual pleasure and love beyond the mere business of reproduction. Of course, none of these exceptions are true, in and of themselves, and biological research teems with examples to the contrary from the tool-making capacities of birds to the language of dolphins to the unbridled reproducibility and observed non-reproductive sexual behavior of many animals, including masturbation and homosexuality, among others. But the point here is not a concern with the long tradition of trying to define human beings as somehow different from and implicitly superior to other animals and thus to deny the very animality of our being human. Nor would the subsequent humanist claim of defining our species as the sole possessor of *all three* distinctive behaviors be the issue at hand. It is not a question of whether humans' distinctive sexuality, communication, and technology do or do not define our species' essence as human. Rather, in one of the more challenging chapters of *Sexistence*, titled "Technics and Transcendence," what Nancy seems to propose is an analysis of sexuality, technology, and language as well as their possible points of convergence and intersection, the various *entre-deux* of their inter-expression. Not a defense of some putative "human nature" per se, but rather an inquiry into what lies *between* what we call "nature" and what we call "human": "Between the two, or rather, beyond their distinction, unfolds a regime that we call 'technics' and that seems to take the place of all possible appropriations—mastery, the setting of goals, the production of goods" (42). Within this regime, Nancy continues, "our own relation to ourselves is transformed into technique," including both sexual and linguistic technique. But this twin technical transformation that traditionally defines the specificity of "human" existence nonetheless both assumes and arises out of "this supposed nature and its presumed order" (43), nevertheless as a kind of excess and exception: "Language excepts itself from all orders of communication between living beings and human sex excepts itself from all orders of the reproduction of species." This exceptionality, according to Nancy, "consists in the fact that the function, of language or of sex, takes itself for an end in itself at the same time as it operates as a means of communication or reproduction." But a function turning itself into its own end also means that it "no longer functions in the same manner." Thus "exception is excessive," while "it emerges from nature and from life."

This paradox of an exception that also follows the "natural course" of things, of an excess that still remains within a presumed natural order, refers us back to Aristotle again, for whom technology was grasped as a kind of "fundamentally natural means of supplementing certain of the human animal's insufficiencies," as nature's compensation for human weakness and vulnerability, lack of protective fur or claws, lack of speed, agility, and so forth. For Aristotle, according to Nancy, such compensatory technology would not exceed certain limits, "which, it must be understood, was more or less achieved in Aristotle's time." Such an equilibrium, Nancy cautions, is nonetheless contradicted by the fact that, ever since then, "technology has not ceased to exceed limits and to exceed itself." Does this mean that technology "has become less 'natural?'" asks Nancy, before concluding that "the question makes no sense."

How so? And what do we mean by "nature" and, for that matter, by "human"? Nancy elaborates:

> Nowhere does "Nature" occur in a "natural" state. Human beings have not always been there; but when they arrive the nature within them humanizes itself—that is, displaces itself in a new way. What was originally a movement without principle and or goal—energy, turbulence, clinamen, life and death, metabolisms, evolutions, circumvolutions, revolutions, mutations—is now expressed as such: as sense always being born (*nasco, natura*) and always disappearing (silence, sigh, spasm). (43–44)

Whatever we can call "human nature" is but the self-expression of the chaos that nature is and that never appears as such, in its "natural state," except as expressed or displaced through the human (barring, Nancy adds, "the possibility that other games are being played at the same time and unbeknownst to us" [45]). Human nature is nature humanizing itself as the retreat of sense, always at once arriving and receding, being born (as per the etymology of the word "nature" itself) and dying—i.e., the very demise of sense itself in "silence, sigh, spasm." Sense appears (and disappears) as and at the *point* of human existence, as the *entre-deux* between those indeterminate entities of nature and human, and thus also between and within human bodies, as sex, as language, as technology, each of which exceeds itself in/as its exceptionality of/as an end in itself. This auto-telic detour that gives birth to sense is how the regime of technology "deploys" or literally unfolds nature, albeit in "a singular mode, certainly, because it implies the renewed opening of an *ex nihilo*" (44). This formulation reasserts the paradox of a human species that follows "the natural course of things" that is also ipso facto followed by "the mutations and revolutions of technology" itself, while acknowledging, on the other hand, that "the 'natural' course of things comes with a denaturation or a transnaturation." But that is also to acknowledge that while a transhumanism "might understand itself as a transformation, or even a transgression, it actually belongs to the course of things" (44). What we presume to call nature is "by essence transhuman or transcendent." Its course is not one that "is oriented in a certain direction or proceeds at a constant or accelerated speed" (i.e., no apparent directional sense), but one that "signals, rather, the emergent forms of excess, leaps, or ruptures," without any "determinate progression" (44). And all this despite the apparent "advances in power, speed, and discriminating capacities" that stem from technological developments such as the harnessing of "steam, electricity, the atom, and informatic circuits." "Technology is transcendence," concludes Nancy, a proposition he terms "scandalous," but that in fact merely restates the earlier recognition regarding the necessary externality of our relation to ourselves, "what relates us to ourselves as beings in excess of ourselves" (42), whether that relationality be dubbed sexual, linguistic, or technological, the latter as we saw being singled out as the very "regime" of transcendence.

At the same time, though, and in an implicit nod to the lessons of psychoanalysis, sex seems to emerge as the primary element of this triad, as the very driver of human culture, the "something more" that Aristotle pinpoints as the basis of political life, of human social organization as being together, not just as meeting the bare necessities of bare life, not even just as the virtue of societal reproducibility enabled by sexual procreation: "It is through sex that human technology activates nature by practicing selective reproduction or hybridization, which is the condition for what is known as *culture*. The sexual relation is also the principle of an indefinite proliferation of these differences" (*Corpus II*, 10).

As such, sex names the relationality of the *entre-deux*, which is nothing in and of itself but the very essence of existence, not presence but the coming to presence, and toward the event of sense, not as absence but as receding, as retreat, the disappearing from presence, toward an infinite yet ever-deferred vanishing point. It is the event of sense perceived, understood, and directed toward the endless horizon of a singularity, which is itself not a horizon but a *point*, the very heart of being, so to speak, where the one crosses into the other, the other in oneself and the self in the other.

The Heart of Being

"At the heart of being" is where Nancy situates love in his early essay, "Shattered Love" [L'amour en éclats],[21] where he extrapolates upon the proposition that "love is the extreme movement, beyond the self, of a being reaching completion" (86), an insight from which he concludes that "one cannot separate sex from love even in their most incompatible forms," and that accordingly, "love is aroused by sex just as sex is excited by love" (*Sexistence*, 106). In "Shattered Love," he expounds at length:

> Love arrives, it comes, or else it is not love. But it is thus that it endlessly goes elsewhere than to "me" who would receive it: its coming is only a departure for the other, its departure only the coming of the other.
> What is offered by transcendence, or as transcendence, is this arrival and this departure, this incessant coming-and-going. What is offered is the offered being itself: exposed to arrival and to departure, the singular being is traversed by the alterity of the other, which does not stop or fix itself anywhere, neither in "him" nor in "me," because it is nothing other than the coming-and-going. . . .
> Transcendence will thus be better named the crossing of love. What love cuts across, and what it reveals by its crossing, is what is exposed to the crossing, to its coming-and-going—and this is nothing other than finitude. Because the singular being is finite, the other cuts across it (and never does the other "penetrate" the singular being or "unite itself" with it or "commune"). Love unveils finitude. Finitude is the being of that which is infinitely inappropriable (98).

Such is the very definition of love according to Nancy: "Love takes place, it happens, and it happens endlessly in the withdrawal of its own presentation" (97), as an incessant coming and going, an ever-recurring retreat that unveils the fundamental finitude of our being together. Love is orgasmic, not necessarily the "big O" but an O like no other, a singular experience, if not the very experience of the singular in the person of the loved one, as Nancy eloquently writes elsewhere.[22] Love is singularly transcendent or transcendence itself, a "crossing" that can never be realized or occur as a penetration, nor even as inter-penetration, but perhaps as the inappropriable incompossibility of a mutual invagination: "No penetration without being penetrated yourself. Swallowing the other and being swallowed by them" (*Sexistence*, 70).

What does this have to do, then, with the so-called "heart of being," where love is said to be situated? Nancy writes, "It is necessary that being have a heart, or still more rigorously that being *be* a heart" (88, Nancy's emphasis), yet at the same time he qualifies that necessity in the following way: "'The heart of being' means nothing but the being of being, that by virtue of which it is being." But, he continues, for such an expression to be "endowed with meaning, it would be necessary that the essence of being is like a heart," and yet "this heart of being is not a heart." Is the heart then the metaphor of being? But then, what exactly is meant by this "heart"? We seem to have returned to our earlier conundrum whereby a metaphor tells us less about what it supposedly figures than about the figure or vehicle of the metaphor itself. In these pages, Nancy describes the heart as "that which alone is capable of love" (88) while also insisting that it is "not an organ, and neither is it a faculty" (99), so what is it? Rather than simply acknowledging a negative presentation of what it is not, it might be more useful to grasp it for the colloquial symbol that it is in the strong sense of the term as the bringing together of different attributes, *sym-bolein*, or indeed as another form of syllepsis where the literal beating heart that preserves life at the bodily core of our singular being is also the figural embodiment of what we call "love," as in those slogans that read "I ♥ x," and love is of course the ostensible topic of this article on "Shattered Love" and, as we saw earlier, in a kind of inextricable, inseparable, and mutually excitable dance with what we have been calling sex—that is, what occurs both between and within bodies.

As such, the heart points to an inflexion in the way of being, an alternative to the dialectic (though not a contradiction, which would indeed be sublatable and thus well captured within dialectics), which Nancy calls "exposition," a key concept in his thinking, one of the earliest elaborations of which is found in this same essay. The difference is crucial: "If the dialectic is the process of that which must appropriate its own becoming in order to be, exposition, on the other hand, is the condition of that whose essence or destination consists in being presented: given over, offered to the outside, to others, and even to the self" (89). The dialectic, most especially in its classic Hegelian form, remains an economy of the same and presupposes a subject who can appropriate whatever lies outside into itself by way of a kind of return. The heart, on the other hand, lives or "beats" under what Nancy terms the "regime of exposition"—that is to say, a crossing with the other to which one is irretrievably vulnerable or liable: "It is not a matter of posing or opposing and then of resorbing the same and the other . . . the affirmation 'I love you' is given over to that which is neither contradictory nor noncontradictory with it: the risk that the other does not love me, or the risk that I do not keep the promise of my love" (90). The transcendence of the heart is of another order than the immanence of dialectic, for the "coming-and-going" of love, "this crossing" is what "breaks the heart": "The break is nothing more than a touch, but the touch is not less deep than a wound" (98). As such, the heart is always already "broken," a fracture that makes its beat possible. Nancy makes this most important point as a paragraph-length parenthesis:

> (Actually, the heart is not broken, in the sense that it does not exist before the break. But it is the break itself that makes the heart. The heart is not an organ, and neither is it a faculty. It is: that *I* is broken and traversed by the other where its presence is most intimate and its life most open. The beating of the heart—rhythm of the partition of being, syncope of the sharing of singularity—cuts across presence, life, consciousness. That is why thinking—which is nothing other than the *weighing* or testing of the limits, the ends, of presence, of life, of consciousness—thinking itself is love.) (99)

I find these sentences among the most consequential in all of Nancy's work, buried as they are in a parenthesis in a relatively obscure early article, better known perhaps since an English translation was published as an addition to *The Inoperative Community* in 1991 and a revised French version appeared in *La pensée finie* in 1990 (English translation published in 1994). To say there is no heart that is not broken, that everyone's heart is broken from the get-go, might sound like a bad reprise of a Bruce Springsteen song. But much more is at stake, especially if we take care to read this passage from Nancy understanding the term "heart" less symbolically than sylleptically—that is, reading the relation between literal and figural hearts as equivalent but irresolvable, like two parallel lines meeting at infinity or another example of *unum quid*. If "it is the break itself that makes the heart," then the organ only beats because of the pause, or, to use a classic Nancy word, because of the *interruption* that not only happens between beats but defines the actual beating such as it is, as an intervallic time, the gap between two pulsations that defines us as living, perhaps even as present or conscious, as per Descartes's iterative cogito. At the same time, being heartbroken is the very condition of our being "traversed by the other," of being in love and hence by definition vulnerable to loss or disappointment at the hands of that other. In both cases, we are talking about an externality felt "where one's presence is most intimate and one's life most open" (translation modified), hence a profound "extimacy" (to use another Nancean neologism, this time borrowed from Lacan: *Corpus II*, 18) or exteriority located in one's innermost core or corpus. Much later, Nancy will revisit this conundrum under the sign of the "intruder" to reflect upon the meaning of the heart in the wake of his own transplant. It is remarkable, though, that his basic insight into the intrusive heart is already fully articulated a good decade before his operation described in *Intrus*. As such, the heart in both senses is *at* the very heart of being: "The beating of the heart—rhythm of the partition of being, syncope of the sharing of singularity—cuts across presence, life, consciousness." The rhythm of that beat in turn reminds us that time phrases singularity (in the musical sense), not as some kind of even or even uneven flow but as singular interruption, the incessant iterative gap between now and then, the intervallic point always "between two senses."[23]

Finally, thought itself is said by Nancy in the same passage to be "love" to the extent that thinking (with reference to the etymology of the French word *penser* and as reflected in English, "to ponder" or even "ponderousness") is "nothing other than the *weighing* or testing of the limits, the ends, of presence, of life, of consciousness."[24] Love is thus the meaning of *philosophy* itself, as the love of making sense but only insofar as this "love of knowledge" or *philo-sophia* is open and available to the heartbreak of the traversal of the other, the transcendence of the crossing of love, to the risk and passion of the aleatory and the unsaid. As such, "the heart of the singular being *is* that which is not totally one's own, but it is thus that it is *one's* own" (99; translation modified). The horizon of thought, of sensation and meaning, the finitude of existence is not the border of a plane but the singularity of a point, an instant, or the gap between a point and the sense of its iteration, the interruption of a "comme-union" (16), the as-if of the *unum quid*, or of something like the communism of a being in common that can never be anything but uncommon. As such, the horizon is always already lost, vanishing into an instantaneous point, the very definition mathematically of singularity. Singularity is not a thing, nor an object, nor a concept but the necessarily unstable state of an occurrence, of what is happening, the pulse of time itself as the singularity of existence. . . . It is what is, but what it is is always already in retreat, withdrawn as it is redrawn, sensed only as the "then" of an ever receding "now."

In astrophysics, the singularity that is a black hole, the collapsed core of what once was a star, is a point of infinite density, whose gravitational mass is such as to prevent anything, including light, from escaping, hence, the term "black hole" (despite the fact that such an object is in itself neither black nor a hole). That singularity is nonetheless surrounded by the halo of an event horizon, the horizon, if you will, of the very event that is space-time, a horizon beyond which nothing can be sensed. For Nancy, the singularity of existence is in the here and the now, the very spacing that is space-time, its inevitably lost horizon, its origin or *ursprung* from which it emerges but also its vanishing point. Singularity can be defined mathematically as the point where dimensionality collapses, or where dimensions vanish into or as a point. The word "point" also implies the previously discussed convergence of sensation, meaning, and direction, of *eros*, *logos*, and *tekhnè* as we point in the direction of a place and time, a virtual point, that escapes all space and time. Singularity thus marks a retreat of sense in every sense, the infinite curvature of meaning, its differance, meaning as always already deferred, in retreat, yet forever (re)iterable.

The Point and Pulse of (S)existence

It is the "point," to recall Nancy's exact formulation "where it is perhaps necessary to posit that a relation, whatever it may be, makes something like some sense." The point where we *may* need to posit the point of a "rapport," a relation, or perhaps even a point of inter-expression, that somehow, somewhere "makes sense," or makes some sense (*du sens*), makes some kind of sense, be it the direction of being set in motion, or the sensation or sensed sense (*sens sensible*) of skin touching skin, or the very "relation of signification" that combines direction and sensation. It is the "there is" of sexual relation, the being of (s)existence, or more precisely, to follow Nancy's formulation, sex is the "there is" of relation (21), and the "body as the place of the sense of relation" (18), which we can interpret as the place of the space between senses.

How does this work, and what exactly does Nancy mean by "sexistence," another neologism, one that conjugates sex and existence? The book *Sexistence* was published in 2017, a decade and a half after *The "There Is" of Sexual Relation* (2001; English translation published in 2013 in *Corpus II*), and offers a significant amplification upon the arguments proposed in the earlier study, which represents in itself a deepening of the analyses first pursued in *Corpus*, whose earliest iterations date back to 1990 with revised and expanded editions up through 2006. To sum up what we have seen, the intervallic space of the body, its existence as *entre deux*, realizes itself in the inter-expression of sense and senses, the ever-reiterated interruption of a singularly beating and broken heart. The issue of sexual relations, in turn, raises the question of the *entre-deux*, of betweenness, as what happens both between and within bodies.[25] "Sex" is the name for this inter-expression, this inter-penetration, the intimacy of exscription or the extimacy of inscription, the "there is" of relation that is at once the drawing of boundaries and their transgression. Sex is the conjoining and disjoining of bodies, not only within as well as without, but as the very coming into and out of existence of bodies, the finitude of their birthing but also their dying (both the "little death" of the loss of selfhood in orgasmic ecstasy and the inevitability of physiological demise itself), the inescapable but ever receding horizons of life itself.

Sexistence takes these insights to the level of existence itself, the first and most direct iteration of which is found, curiously, buried in a footnote: "Eros remains foreign to 'being' understood in terms of 'beings,' substance or *subjectum*. It is also in this sense that, in my own way, I would like to understand *existence*—that is, being-outside-self, as signaled in a primordial manner by the drive (*poussée*) called "sex": a "sexistence" (125n). The sexual impulse or drive thus "signals in a primordial manner" the experience of ecstasy, the being-outside-of-oneself that is also the fundamental condition of what we call existence, or ec-stasis as ek-sistence. Not being an entity or a substance, not a being, sex is driven by either anticipation or recollection of that coming that escapes us, our being lost in the moment of orgasm and ecstasy where we stand outside ourselves, in the bliss of a presence that is lived as absence to ourselves, the "little death" signaled or sung by the poetry of love.

Nancy translates German *Trieb*, the concept so dear to Freud and typically rendered into English as "drive" and into French as *"pulsion,"* and then adds an entire constellation of words derived from the French word *pousser*, or push, including "pulsation, impulsion, expulsion, compulsion, pulsar, pulse, push [*poussée*]" (*Sexistence*, 17), all of which are identical in French and English, except for the last two—namely, the pulse of a beating heart and "push" itself. But if sex is a kind of push, so too is the act of pushing itself a sexual designator (both index and icon), as in Herbie Mann's scandalous album cover for his 1971 recording of "Push Push," displaying two naked torsos fully exerted in overt missionary-style coitus, whose immodesty is both veiled and revealed, bathed as they are in the orange glow of a diffused lighting.

But pulsation also offers an alternative astronomical reference in the form of a pulsar and thus a metaphorical avenue for the coinciding of sex with existence itself, not just human or animate but the workings of the cosmos itself. Nancy extrapolates:

> A pulsar (pulsating star) is a celestial body that periodically shines very brightly. It is plausible to say that every existence is such a celestial body, plausible also to wonder up to what *point* all the realities in the world participate in such a pulsation. This is to say, in fact, up to what *point* every reality (living or not) is fundamentally constituted of an ex-pulsion of nothing toward nothing [*de rien vers rien*]—of *res* toward *res* that is nothing other than being in general, that is to say, in particular. . . .

In other words, the drive [*pulsion*] is nothing other than existence itself—eksisting, exsisting." (20, trans. modified)[26]

It seems we are back to the heart of being again, but then what or where is this "point" of existence? What is this point at which literally *every* thing is pulsating or has a pulse, the point at which every *thing* [*res*] partakes in the ex-nihilo of ex-pulsion, from *res* to *res* (*res* being the Latin word for "thing" while also serving as the etymological source of the French word *rien*, meaning "nothing")? With respect to the word *pulsion*, which triggers this line of argument, Nancy notes, "This is a redoutable word, much like its equivalents in other languages [as seen in the almost identical set of English equivalents]. It designates at once a force and its effect; its notion is situated between a source of energy and the energy itself, added to which is a value of *élan*, dispatch, excitation" (17). "Pulsion," he concludes, "pushes and is itself pushed. Or rather, it is itself the pushing, the impulsing" (18, trans. modified). But how are we to understand this impulsive pushing if not by the very imagery of the sexual act, that physicality of the push-push, skin slapping skin, heart beating against heart: "Added as well, as the semantic family demonstrates, is a rhythmic value linked to an emphasis upon the impetus of the pulse [*coup d'envoi de la pousée*], the rap or beat of a given *élan*" (17). We are back to the coital image of "push push," but now as the very designation of the conundrum of existence itself, as the singular beat of a coming-and-going, as the very retreat of being in the existent.

Sex would appear synonymous with being itself, and so Nancy first introduces the word *sexistence* in the actual body of the text, as referring to "a sort of ontology of sex," to which we are "led by the adventures of modern thought since Plato" (21). But then doesn't this sexual ontology, whether an ontology of sex or a sexualization of ontology, suggest in turn nothing less than a certain retreat of sex itself, or of sex as the very structure of retreat and withdrawal? Such a retreat of sex itself would justify Nancy's skepticism about "sexual liberation" in the opening pages of *Sexistence*. Moreover, Nancy describes the conundrum of sex as an impulse that "in all rigor, it is out of reach. One doesn't arrive. One arrives by not arriving. . . . Sex tends towards its own exasperation. . . . It knows that if it comes [*s'il jouit*] it can undo its coming just as well as come again [*il peut se déjouir autant que se réjouir*]" (21–22; translation modified). Unpleasure can excite just as much as pleasure, not just as some alternative form of pleasure that plays with pain such as sadomasochism, but as the very pulsating rhythm that makes (its) pleasure possible in the first place. Or, to translate this back into a more traditional discourse, the intensity of desire depends upon the rhythm and circumstances of its (un)satisfaction. A later section of *Sexistence* overtly confirms the point of this translation: "Desire desires itself and desires to be devoured by itself. Devouring itself it renews itself and annihilates itself in the same movement. It consumes itself and is reborn from its ashes. From nothing [*rien*], that is" (58). Sex, or rather, "sexistence," appears at first to be but another version of *mitsein* as per *The Inoperative Community*, but in many passages such as these, it seems to emerge as another name for the retreat of being itself. Or, to rephrase a prior problematic, in terms of the fundamental relation of existence, are we dealing with community or with world? The answer to this apparent dilemma is a rigorous understanding that "community is made of the interruption of singularities, or of the suspension that singular beings *are*" (*Inoperative Community*, 31) as well as a capaciously finite understanding of the world as "the essential co-belonging of existence with the existence of all things."[27] World creation means the world as place of existence as such, as the "there is" of its taking place, the very *relation* of sense and singularity that is also the partaking of other in self, of self in other, sexistence. This sharing and this transmission of sense make for space-time as the field/fold of its difference, as world. We are thus always already sensing a singular world, such is what remains of (un)common sense, as iterative embodiment of our singular being, *singuli*, which as Nancy reminds us, is necessarily "always in the plural," never as one in or of itself (*Corpus II*, 11).

From Sense to Sex and Back Again

Perhaps we need to find our way back to the question of sense via the trio of sex, language, and technics and specifically by examining their inter-relations, or more likely, how they "inter-express" what happens in the *entre deux* of existence as interrupted or crossed and crisscrossed by the other. Chapter 2 of *Sexistence* directly addresses the relations between *eros* and *logos*: "On the one side, there is the friction of sexual coming-and-going, the caress, the approach, the parade: the other is occupied by the friction of words, the departure-return of speech acts, the translation of languages [*langues*], and their untranslatability. Not to mention the two significations that Latin idioms offer of the word *tongue* [*langue*]" (*Sexistence*, 30). But there is more here than two sides of the same coin, so to speak. And it is sense itself that turns out to be what is at stake in the relation between sex and language, which looks more and more like a structured non-relation:

> The sense of the word, the sense of coming (*jouissance*), or the sense of having a child are a matter of lifting ever further off. Sense, properly speaking—that is, always improperly—inheres in its arising, its uprising,

its rebellion against any requirement to abide or to signify. This is how sense is double—sensible and intelligible, not as the double regime of an incompatible opposition but, on the contrary, as the necessary division whereby each interrupts the other. Language and sex mutually intercut one another. The first defies the other to say itself, the second defies the first to do itself. (29).

Linguistic sense and sexual sense challenge each other as saying is to doing, and vice-versa, which is not at all to say they are unrelated, and certainly not that they are aligned one with the intelligible and the other with the sensible. Rather, it is the way they intersect with or cut across each other, their mutual interruption and calling out to each other, their nonetheless impossible convergence that clues us into the sense of sense itself, whether sensible or intelligible, sex or language, perception or meaning, touching or conceiving, feeling or thinking.

Sense, in every possible sense, is about referral from one sense to the other. Sense is fundamentally a sending. Sense "does not only inhere in the sending [*envoi*] of existents to one another: this sending—this liftoff, this raising up—always expedites itself outside of itself" (29). Sense sends its sense beyond itself, which means that there is no sense alone in and of itself but only in its expediting structure, as *envoi* or *renvoi*, whether sensible or intelligible, or between perception and meaning, as what takes place "between" or combined with what is sending and what is receiving. With regard to the sense of singularity, sense can sense it but only to the extent that it can re-iterate it—that is, to deny its singularity as such. Nancy elaborates:

> Just as there is no "being," there is no "with." Herein arises the formidable ambivalence and ambiguity of everything that pertains to the *com*: communication, commerce, copula (which consists of *co* plus *apio*, to link). The "with" is never a thing, a substance, nor a subject. It is the element of sense alone, in all of its senses, that is, in all the ways of sensing, of receiving, or repulsing an outside, of not being "inside" without this outside that comes and distances itself [*s'écarte*]. (29)

Sense is nothing in itself, it is the in-between, the *entre-deux*, that links the two as "with," as what comes between, as the pre-fixing co- or com-, nothing in itself except sense in all its senses, including the sense of an inside that only exists insofar as it implies an outside of itself, an in-trusion that is the ex-pediting of sense itself. It is the nothing of a *mitsein* ("there is no 'being,' there is no 'with'"), without which there would be nothing at all, the ex-intrusion that we call language or that we experience as sex, the never resolvable friction of an endless if endlessly interrupted coming-and-going. "Language and sex make truth of one another: that is, an interruption of sense. Suspension of continuity, discontinuity as point of apparition" (30). The "interruption of sense" here is to be understood as subjective as well as objective genitive, not just sense as interrupted but sense as interruption itself, to the extent that sense sends itself. All sex is *coitus interruptus* to the extent that it is always "coming-and-going," always stopping and starting again. Language, too, depends upon the interruption that is the articulation of elements, made discreet by the work of differance. But not only are they each structured as discontinuity and interruption, but each is discontinuous and interruptive of the other, the one saying in order to do and the other doing in order to say, invaginating the very unsteady relation between the supposedly intelligible and the sensible as the "necessary division whereby each interrupts the other." As such, the intelligible and the sensible again do not constitute for Nancy a conceptual opposition but rather two different aspects of "a single disposition to sense": "This is where the grand affair of the 'mind' and the 'body' plays itself out. It does not play out between envelope and contents, but between two aspects or modes of a single disposition to sense, that is at once that of the communication of life and of the transmission of truth—or of truth as transmission" (30). The sense of sense, its "truth," is in its transmission, its sending, its relay, whether feeling, perception, meaning, or even direction. Whatever the difference between these versions of sense may be, it is the transmission between or the communication "with" that matters. That in turn makes possible their inter-relation or inter-expression while marking the differentiations that indeed make sense what it is, no matter how we understand it. We tend to speak of our means of perception in the plural, as "the senses," while confining the ways of meaning to the singular, as in "making sense" or making "some sense," but never as making senses, even if we can all readily grant the existence of plural meanings. "That is what we call 'the senses' when we give to the (sensible, sensuous) senses the sense of being external to signification."[28] Nancy invites us to transgress this residue of the metaphysical opposition between the intelligible and the sensible and to ponder their difference as "two aspects" of a "single disposition," that disposition being by definition an undoing of position itself, a literal dis-position or dispossession, in the course of the transmission or transmissiveness that defines sense itself as the singular plural of perception and meaning, but a singular plural whose essence is that of transmission itself, or iteration as difference in repetition, as "push push."

If, on the one hand, sex and language would seem to operate as flip sides of each other, differing slopes that challenge each other to the extent that they cannot converge as saying is to doing, and, on the other hand, we've also encountered that singular "point" where they do converge, in that passage from *There Is*, where meaning encompasses both feeling and directional sense, where we recall that "saying is a touching [*le dire touche*]." And one would be equally justified then in arguing that touching can also be a saying, whether the reassurance of a hug or the erotic intent of a lover's caress.[29]

Technique and Invagination: A Punctual Crossing

We should also recall our earlier discussion of technology as the regime under which both sex and language take on their particular, human dimension. While technology in one version seems to subsume the other two components of this trinity, in actuality, as we have seen, Nancy elsewhere writes as if sex is the encompassing term, but of course by dint of that writing we can also argue that language, too—not the heart of being, perhaps, but the reputed "house" of being—is the foundational category from which sex and technology emerge as modes of existence. Each of the three is inside the others and foundational to them in a convoluted if seamless mutual invagination: "That existence has three dimensions implies that it does not have one unique sense . . . at stake is the triple self-relation of what does not subsist in itself" (*Sexistence*, 133n). *Tekhnè, logos, eros*: all three reinscribe the fundamental transcendence of existence or ek-sistence, literally standing outside oneself as what defines oneself as such. What this means is that "an other of the other appears: outside immanence, outside being-in-itself, an outside that authorizes, opens the possibility of an inside that is only a place of emission, sending, raising. Interruption and relaunch" (*Sexistence*, 30).

Transmission thus presupposes transcendence and transgression, and vice versa. The untranslatability of sex, language, and technology into each other is also the very condition of their "inter-expression," a paradox we can probe by considering the role of art and aesthetics in general, of synesthesia in particular, and of "simulation" (*Finite Thinking*, 21–24) in the transmission of sense, or rather sense as transmission. Skeptics have long argued their case on the basis of the so-called unreliability of the senses, that the representation of the world they offer is at best false, deceptive, and incorrect. Radical skepticism argues that sense itself in terms of meaning is impossible, given the deception of the senses as organs of perception. That said, mainstream Western philosophy has also gone along with this distrust of the senses, but precisely by instituting the metaphysical opposition between the intelligible and the sensible, from Plato's cave through Kant's distinction between the phenomenal and the noumenal, and Hegel's dialectic overcoming sense certainty. All these interpretations propose some form of subjectivity or reason that enables thought to sift through the untrustworthy "evidence" of the senses to arrive at some higher truth that would be the real Sense of the world. Indeed, the history of philosophy could be told as the sequence of attempts to interpret the unreliability of sense data correctly and sensibly. Such an agenda typically relies again upon various versions of Aristotle's notion of the "common sense," situated in a subject able to adjudicate differing sense input and correct "misrepresentations" through the coordinating functions of an underlying sense-making entity, *hypokeimenon*, or subject.

But not all philosophers agree with this view of the senses as bad representation of the world we perceive. Ernst Mach notably argued that "the senses represent things neither wrongly nor correctly," and Gilbert Ryle famously quipped, "It is as absurd to call a sensation 'veridical' as to call it 'mistaken.' The senses are neither honest nor deceitful."[30] While Mach's work has often been taken as the basis for the Viennese and later British traditions of logical empiricism, his insights into the analysis of sensation have been retained by those traditions at the cost of maintaining an insuperable distinction between the sensible and the intelligible. Freud and Heidegger, in their different ways, also took account of Mach's insights, in the one case seeing human consciousness as overcoming sensory overload by selectively filtering out sense data, the process better known as "repression," and in the other, by decisively shifting the paradigm of what constitutes truth from a representational model to the workings of disclosure or *aletheia*, literally an "unforgetting" of what has been forgotten or covered over by the retreat of being. In both cases, sensing is not mere passive input to be rationalized by the subject of common sense but part of sense-making itself, a way of being in the world, the very stuff of existence itself. As such, Freud and Heidegger would seem to meet at the point of infinity, where the ontic/ontological difference intersects the very mechanisms of (sexual) repression as the divide between conscious and unconscious, as the discontented civilization of being there, of *da-sein*, thrown in the world. Or, sex in its ontology as the "there is" of relation that justifies Lacan in his Freudo-Heideggerian pronouncement that "there is no sexual relation," on which Nancy comments at length in his work by that title in *Corpus II*.

In Nancy's case, we seem to have a critical articulation or inter-expression of the two if we consider the following from among many passages in *Sexistence*:

> Language and sex desire one another without thereby forming subjects. Each relates to itself without consisting in anything other than this relation. A subject perhaps occurs there where the two intersect: a point where sex is named (presented) and where language is engendered as proper (I speak "in my name"). This punctual intersection,

always put back into play, does not prevent the double élan of sense from preceding every subject and succeeding all of them. (32)

Language and sex would seem here to take the place of the intelligible and the sensible as the difference between sensation and meaning, between the senses and sense, as their double impetus [*élan*], but more precisely, language and sex can meet each other by way of a "punctual crossing" only because they *each* cross the so-called divide between the intelligible and the sensible, and not only in those particular cases already noted where sex "talks" and language "touches." It is in the last section of the last chapter of *Sexistence* that Nancy raises the question explicitly: "How to bring about the crossing or the melee of sex and language—aside from silence or the cry into which they each plunge together or separately?" (115). As if to signal the inescapable singularity of such a "punctual crossing," Nancy offers not a general answer but instead six different *examples* of such possible "melees" that range from speaking/hushing silence to silencing the word to "a chiasmus of words that can amount to sensate flesh" to the suggestive ellipsis of a dash to say what cannot be said, among others, perhaps many others. Notably, each of these examples is taken from a literary source: Henry Miller, William Carlos Williams, Walter Benjamin, Paul Celan, Emily Dickinson, Heinrich von Kleist. But not to overemphasize this final crescendo of meaningfully evocative citations, it should be noted that such citations appear all throughout *Sexistence* and define its innovative form in the use of literary passages, not just to illustrate but to advance the philosophical work of the text.

Thus we arrive back at the question of art, which Nancy indicates as a form of technics, that third mode of existence that enables the singular encounter of sex with language:

> That's why the only possibility for saying, here, arises there where sex and language happen to cross one another and for once to mix—to (dis)continue one another. There where, one might say, *logos*, *tekhnè*, and *eros* together become, for a time, the trinitarian condition of the self-relation of what is selfless (of what pulses). Speech that in saying acts—for no text is erotic through its "object" without being so through action as well. An art (technique) of doing that thereby converts itself into a supposed object (pornography). Desire of the desire to say its own act. An art that is supposedly practiced by those who listen (or read) as much as those who speak (or write), Sex ex-pressing itself. (115)

Art is a practice of making as well as of communing or communicating, the "comme-union" of an artifice or artfulness that is a kind of "coming" together for maker and beholder, writer and reader, performer and spectator. And while Nancy's attention here is directed specifically toward erotic art, we might also ask, with an appropriate gesture to Freud, to what extent all art is erotic, whether sublimated or overt.

Art as a kind of technique can be situated at the point where eros, logos, and *tekhnè* intersect in that "punctual crossing" where "for a moment" they share the "trinitarian condition" of a self-relation to what is not itself, the singular experience of existence. But the singularity of that point is what art in its transcendence transmits, or reiterates, in and as sense. Art senses that singularity but by sensing it—that is, by sending it, by necessarily redoubling it—the singular vanishes except as the absence negatively signaled (primordially?) by its artful presencing (which it should be noted is not a re-presenting or representation, a *Darstellung* rather than *Vorstellung*). The repetitive work of sensing is that of a drive, a pulsating, and as such the origin of art: "If all art proceeds from the drive [*pulsion*], from the pulsation of desire, the arts are works turned toward others whereas the flesh is a work turned toward the inside of the beast with two backs—an empty inside, an interval, the space between skin and skin, the rubbing and whacking of each other at a harrowing rhythm amidst clutching, raging, and interlocked bodies" (*Sexistence*, 130). Art is the push push directed outward, to others, a pushing and a sensing, a crossing and a sending, the impulsion of an expulsion.

What is the relation between this "pushing" and sensing? Between cum, coming, *comme*, and *con*? How can we understand this *poussée*, or *poussay*, if not as the push of a certain "pussy"? This cross-language homophony may be unjustified, even outrageous, but it does nonetheless suggest a further refiguring of pulsating/pushing, the double push-push of iterative embodied motion, the "figuration of the unfigurable" (*Sexistence*, 113). Linking "pushing" to "pussy" in fact reinforces the skepticism about penetration as never "other than being penetrated" (*Sexistence*, 70), even as the vagina is no less a pulsating pushing organ, not just during the act of giving birth when midwives typically advise the mother-to-be to "push" and help expel the baby from the womb, but also even during "hetero-normal" coitus when the female genitals can grip, and squeeze and push back on the male organ, not to reject it but to encourage and welcome its potential, thus hastening climax for both partners. This is why the second "push" matters, as the "coming-and-going" between and within bodies, staging and sensing "a slight, infinitely diminutive but infinitely maintained distance, contact, touch, the *point* where representation blurs and the vertigo of presence begins" (*Sexistence*, 114). For Nancy, it matters not whether the aim here is reproduction or orgasmic pleasure, representation or presentation. On the other hand, we see here a reciprocal and perhaps unexpectedly gynocentric understanding of sex and sense. Not penetration but abandon, openness, receptivity, Kant's "art of receiving," and thus also of birthing, the retreat of the mother or the mother as retreat (as we saw earlier). What Nancy calls the paradoxical "trans-immanence" of sexistence, at once immanent and transcendent, is thus trans-invagination where any orifice can "come" in the place of any other: vagina, mouth, anus, eyes, nostrils, ears, even the penis as itself but an elongated orifice:

> Sex is at the crossroads, where the turbulence of desire becomes love, where renunciation might renounce itself and open toward a higher art. Kant sees in sex a relationship between natural power and the art of receiving this power—masculine and feminine aligned with nature and culture. Freud does not think that love can appease destructive rage—but the parallel that he traces between sex and art upholds the drive's [*pulsion*] ability to find a form. That is, a way to make sense. (*Sexistence*, 119)

Beyond the gender inversion attributed here to Kant whereby the traditional Western misogynist association of nature with the feminine and culture with the masculine is reversed, the pushing that underpins both sex and art, their impulse in common, allows for—or at least does not inhibit—the invention of form, or the "making" of sense. I use the word "invention" here in its ancient sense, not as some kind of creation ex nihilo (as enshrined in Christian theology or the romanticist ideology of creative genius, or in our own contemporary tech culture of "innovation") but literally as a coming upon or across, *in-venio*, something you find or stumble upon as if by accident. Form, or sense, is what you receive, or conceive, or give birth to, by an abandonment to what is, by an "art of receiving" that is, in turn, a kind of donation, a giving (in) to the other that is also the ex-position of self in what is without self, the risky inter-vention or selflessness of love, despite not being able to "appease" the destructiveness of rage.

But the invention of form and the making of sense take place in and as the proliferation of differences, just as the "art of receiving" tells us that there is no limit to what can or cannot be an erogenous zone, or a sexual identity, or a genre of art. Rather than simply adding further letters to the sexual minority alphabet of LGBTQ, which he sees as "only an approximative sense for the real multiplicity of practices and dispositions" (*Sexistence*, 75), Nancy proposes the singular concept "that there are only idiosexes, just as there are only idiolects: speech only exists—and through it, language—in manners, accents, intonations, lexical and syntactic choices, and mimicry, in each person's pragmatics. And just as the idiolect itself is never simply one, nor unified, nor unitary, but rather is diffracted according to circumstances, registers of expression, and interlocutors, so sex is neither unique nor unified in any person" (*Sexistence*, 76). Is idiosex anything other, then, than the singular plural of existence itself?

The Arts Singular Plural

This proliferation of differences driven by the invention of form and the making of sense is not just an affair of sexistence. Much earlier, in the first chapter of *The Muses* (1994), "Why are there several arts and not just one?," Nancy offers his most sweeping depiction of the necessary and the singularly interrelated multiplicity of the arts, senses, and worlds. All "singular plural" yet not, despite the attempts of Western philosophy, coincident with each other. Nancy deftly demonstrates how the arts do not match onto the senses, neither of which map onto the world as the representation of some artful common sense. Each one's heterogeneity is not "homothetic" to the others: "The classical distribution of the five senses either does not refer to five arts or raises infinite problems of the 'minor' ones (e.g., cooking, perfumery)" (*Muses*, 11). And with regard to the "heterogeneity of the senses," that too "is impossible to decide":

> One may, for example, consider the role of what Aristotle calls "common-objects" (movement, figure, size), or one may look at pain as a specific sense, or yet again one may take account of contemporary physiology and considerably exceed the five senses so as to envision, beyond the common-objects of Aristotle, the senses of acceleration or the tension of organs: what is more, one can attempt to take in the whole of the animal kingdom and envision distributions via "mechanoreceptors" (pressure, contact, vibration, stretching, etc.), "thermoreceptors," "photoreceptors," "chemoreceptors," "electroreceptors," or yet again, according to different criteria, via "exteroreceptors," "proprioreceptors" (actions of the body upon itself), "interoreceptors" (digestion, arterial pressure, urogenital sensations, etc.). (*Muses*, 11–12)

No news here that what senses we do attribute to ourselves can only provide a very partial sensing or reception of the world we inhabit. Even the classic five senses remain extremely limited in what they can sense within their respective domains. We can only see within a very limited spectrum of light and hear within a very narrow range of tones and decibels. We are by definition partially blind and partially deaf, and so on. The sensing of our senses sensing themselves is the very sign of our finitude and the necessary finiteness of our thought. And such finitude is less lifted than reinforced by technological advances in sensing techniques and devices, which no matter how expansive, can only underscore even more what we cannot know or sense. Every expansion of sensing technology can only point to a further beyond of what that technology can *not* sense. It must sense that there is always what lies outside of what it senses, thus self-sensing its own sensory finitude. Even so-called artificial intelligence, despite its misleading name, is nothing more than the feedback loop of a self-sensing technology that can adjust itself only in very limited and indeed deliberately "programmable" ways to changes in what is sensed.[31]

So, what then of the relation between art(s) and sense(s)? The answer lies not in trying to match them up with or against each other but rather in coming to terms with their insuperable heteronomies, heteronomies it should be underscored that themselves remain resolutely without equivalent and incommensurable, or "non homothetic," to each other (*Muses*, 11). And yet, at the same time, this is not at all to say there are no relations between the arts and the senses. On the contrary, "what does art do if not finally touch upon and touch by means of the principal heterogeneity of 'sensing'?" (*Muses*, 18). Touch, that sense that Aristotle termed the one essential sense and that Derrida makes the focus of his reading of Nancy, *On Touching*, becomes the very metaphor of the relation between whatever we call "art" and whatever we call "sense," in at least two senses of the word: literally, on the sense of touch itself, "at once on the 'self-touching' inherent in touch and on the 'interruption' that is no less inherent in it"; and figuratively perhaps: "'to touch on' in the sense of shaking up, disturbing, destabilizing, or deconstructing" (*Muses*, 18), touching on as interruption. Touch is the syllepsis of a metaphor, or a metaphor of syllepsis, undecidably literal and figural. Touch senses itself, like all senses, hence the irreducible immanence of a self-touching, but only insofar as it feels its own finitude, its own transcendence, not only in terms of feeling some hardness or softness, smoothness or roughness, penetrability or impenetrability, outside itself, but also in terms of its limited duration. An uninterrupted touch becomes senseless, and thus, its sensuousness depends upon a certain touching-and-going, a rhythm or beat of the touch, like the beat of the heart, or the pulsar, or like the invaginated push push of bodies in the interval between touching and not touching each other. At the same time, this sensuous literality of touch spaces a certain heterogeneity that also meaningfully figures and disfigures, disposes and dislocates, our very sense of being in the world, beginning with the very being of sense itself, as indecidably fractured between the so-called sensible and the intelligible. In this way, what we call art "touches on the living integration of the sensuous," and thus touches on "the synthetic unity and the continuity of a world of life and activity," but, continues Nancy, "in the final analysis, that world is less a sensuous world than an intelligible world of markers, functions or uses, and transitivities—in the final analysis less a world, perhaps, than a milieu, an *Umwelt* (that of the '1 percent of information')" (18). Art "touches on" this world to the extent that it "isolates or forces there the moment of the *world* as such, the being-world of the world, not as does a milieu in which a subject moves, but as exteriority and exposition of a being-in-the-world, exteriority and exposition that are formally grasped, isolated, and presented as such" (18). Art thus exposes the worldliness of the world, its "being-world" as such, but that is at the same time to "dis-locate" the world into "plural worlds, or more precisely, into the irreducible plurality of the unity 'world'" (18).[32] Nancy describes this dis-location as "the *a priori* and the transcendental of art"—that is, both its condition of possibility and that by which it exceeds whatever it touches on: "It makes appear that the appearance of a world is always first of all that of phenomena, each of which is 'phenomenon-of-world.' It brings out that a sense-of-world, and consequently the sense of the world, is only given by dis-locating at the origin its unique and unitary sense of 'sense'" (18–19). Art phenomenologizes the world, it ex-poses the evidence of the world as phenomenon, as dis-located or deconstructed sensuous sense.

Nancy clarifies this dis-location of the sense of sense a few pages later when he returns to address that primary distinction between not just the intelligible and the sensible, but "intelligible sense" and "sensuous sense," whose inevitably chiasmatic relation "is nothing other than the necessary double encroachment of one sense on another, which is far more radical and constitutive than one might be led to think by what seems to stem from a linguistic contingency" (*Muses*, 28).[33] In what may be Nancy's most incisive analysis of the question of sense, he pursues:

> (Sensuous) sense senses only if it is oriented to an object and if it valorizes it in a meaningful, informative, or operational context; reciprocally, (intelligible) sense makes sense only if it is, as one says, "perceived" and the "intuitive or perceptive relation to *intelligible sense* has always included, in finite being in general, an irreducible receptivity." (Sensuous) sense makes (intelligible) sense; it is indeed nothing but that, the intellection of its receptivity as such. (Intelligible) sense is sensed/senses itself; it is indeed nothing but that, the receptivity of its intelligibility. But receptivity consists *ea ipsa* in its singular plural. (28)

The dis-location of sense is not a simple translation from one sense into the other, but a "double encroachment" of one sense upon the other, again in every sense of the word. "Sense makes sense" is not a proposition to be construed as tautological, for sense always makes more sense. Phenomenologizing the world is also, inevitably, to assign meaning and direction to it, to give it sense in the course of sensing it, so sense making sense. Sense making is also, as Nancy makes clear, "nothing but" the chiasmatic relation between the "intellection of its receptivity" and the "receptivity of its intellection." Sensuous sense and intelligible sense make sense through their "double encroachment," as they touch on each other, the push push or the heartbeat of a pulsating interval that is the very embodiment of (s)existence, and of course, the "art" of our openness and vaginal receptivity, which Nancy after Kant affirmatively codes as cultural and feminine.

Sense and Synesthesia

The "inter-expression" of senses with other senses, the *entre deux* of sensuous with sensuous, sensuous with intelligible, intelligible with intelligible—a generalized synesthesia, in short—defines our very sense of embodiment, our being in/as a body, which is also to say, our being-in-the-world, our existence as such. Synesthesia here means the senses refer to each other, respond to each other, or *correspond* with each other (as per Baudelaire),[34] sense sensing itself, but that self-sensing is necessarily at every point sensing itself as other. But then, what do we mean by "the signification of the sensuous—by which path does it lead to its intelligibility?" (28–29). Nancy considers this a "technical question," one "in which sense demands from itself its own condition of production, but in which it thus *demands itself*, tensed toward its own activity as toward the reception of its own receptivity, toward a *logos* that would be the *pathos* of *pathos*" (29). Synesthetic perception, which is "the rule" according to Merleau-Ponty,[35] is not just differing senses corresponding or communicating with each other but also sense communicating (with) itself as "meta-sense," the sensory reception of sensory reception, what Nancy terms the "*pathos* of *pathos*," which is to say its own logos or intelligibility. Intelligibility is thus at least one kind of meta-sense (most probably not the only one, if one thinks of classic synesthesia such as the visualizing of sounds). The intelligible is not the opposite or complement of sensation but its meta-sense, its self-transcendence, or trans-immanence as sense of sense—that is, as the sense of sense sensing itself, but as necessarily and irredeemably un-common in the unending iterations of its difference.

The Sense of Sense I: Touch

There is a bifurcation in Nancy's work as regards this sense of sense. Touch appears, on the one hand, metaphorically perhaps, as the sensuous sense of sense; and on the other hand, metonymically speaking, art and especially poetry as the intelligible sense of sense in its inherent dis-location as what art "touches on." Both touch and art are seen to ex-pose the patency of the world and the discontinuous singularity of existence, an otherness that is "only 'other' in terms of this sameness" (*Finite Thinking*, 5), but let us track out the workings of this apparent discrepancy.

Following upon a long philosophical tradition that views touch as the "one essential sense" (Aristotle) and as "the sense of the body in its entirety" (Lucretius), and as both following up *and* anticipating Derrida's capacious discussions of touch with specific reference to Nancy's own work, Nancy provides his most pointed and eloquent analysis of the primacy of touch in the same opening chapter of *The Muses*: "Touch is nothing other than the touch or stroke of sense altogether and of all the senses" (17). Touch appears as the ur-sense or archi-sense, always already meta-sense to the extent that it is not only the sense of sense but the sense of all the senses, their very sensing as such: "It is their sensuality as such, felt and feeling." But what do we mean by sensuality "as such" if not again the insuperable, vertiginous, and perhaps even infinitely regressive sense of sense sensing itself at once as itself and as other? "But touch itself—inasmuch as it is a sense and consequently inasmuch as it feels itself feeling, or more than that, inasmuch as it *feels itself feeling itself*, since it only touches by touching also itself, touched by what it touches *and* because it touches—touch presents the proper moment of sensuous exteriority; it presents it *as such and as sensuous*"(17). Touch is both just one sense among others, "*a* sense," and what presents every sense in itself, what presents sensuous sense itself, or sense in all its sensuality, and in all its manifold senses as the very essence or *es-sense* of sense, "the proper moment of sensuous exteriority," sense "as such and as sensuous."

And yet, what makes this sense make sense is that it is interrupted in its very sense-making, that it is always already split from itself, as in reference to itself in the interval from itself that makes it itself, as Nancy cites Derrida on interruption, which is of course one of Nancy's core concepts: "the interruption, which constitutes the touch of the *self-touching*, touch *as self-touching*" (17). Nancy extrapolates, "Touch *is* the interval and the heterogeneity of touch," before continuing, "Touch is proximate distance. It makes one sense what makes one sense (what it *is* to sense): the proximity of the distant, the approximation of the intimate" (17). Given his thinking in *Sexistence* and other texts, one might also see (or *feel*) touch, touch touching as the distance of the proximate, and the exposing of the "extimate," even in that always "infinitesimal gap" between bodies that comes and goes in the push push of sex. But while touch seems to emerge as the very metaphor of sense and sensuality, Nancy nonetheless concludes that touch "has no 'primacy' or 'privilege' except insofar as it subordinates nothing to it: it is or it gives but the general extension and particular extraposition of sensing." The *sense* of touch is also the zero degree of sense, nothing more than the very tension or extension of what we feel as feeling, the mere sense of sense. Touch models the very interval between two senses, between the interruption of sensation, that defines our very sense of embodiment. Touch is no more than this, but that is also to say that it "touches upon" everything, including most notably what it is *not*: "Sensing and the sensing-oneself-sense that *makes* for sensing itself consists always in sensing at the same time that there is some other (which one senses) and that there are other zones of sensing, overlooked by the zone that is sensing at this moment, or else on which this zone touches on all sides but only at the limit where it ceases being the zone that it is. Each sensing touches on the rest of sensing as that which it cannot sense." By a kind of punctual crossing, the finitude of sense touches on the other senses as what it cannot sense. A sense of (un)common sense returns here but only negatively as "the singular 'unity' of a 'between' the sensuous domains, that 'existential communication' turns out to take place in the element of the outside-itself, of an exposition of existence" (23). Nonetheless, this "auto-heterology of touch" (17) "forms" the body not only as the interruption, the interval of the senses, which is to say as sense itself always already split and doubled, as the very *entre-deux* or betweenness of "two senses" that is inscribed in sense itself, but also as the very sense of finitude, as the limit, one wants to say, the skin, of what can sense, of what senses in/as the interval of at least two senses—namely, the body as *corpus interruptus*. Touch is the sense of sense to the extent that it models or "touches on" what Nancy calls the "trans-immanence of being-in-the-world," or on the "heterogenesis of existence as interruption and discontinuity, at once transcendent and immanent." Sense is inherently dis-located as the immanence of the body to itself outside itself, as transcendent. Hence, the dislocation of sense would then be "the transcendence of immanence as such, the transcendence of an immanence that does not go outside itself in transcending, which is not ex-static but ek-sistent. A 'trans-immanence'" (34–35). To conclude: "The touch or stroke of the sense may thus be distributed and classified in as many ways as one likes: what makes it into the touch that it is is a dis-location, a heterogeneity in principle" (17–18).

The Sense of Sense II: Poetry

If touch as the figure of sense in general can thus be described as a dis-location that is fundamental, heterogeneous "in principle," this brings us back again to Nancy's conceptions of art and the other pathway of his thinking through sense and singularity: "What does art do if not finally touch upon and touch by means of the principal heterogeneity of 'sensing'?" (18). Art, in other words, "dis-locates 'common sense' or ordinary synesthesia, or causes it to touch itself in an infinity of points" (22). No longer just that "point" where the differing senses of the word sense may come together, art triggers an "infinity" of (singular) points (of interruption) where sense touches itself, beyond what Nancy here calls "common sense" in scare quotes or its equivalent "ordinary synesthesia," by which we can only understand the inter-expression of two or more senses, a "common" sense only by dint of its uncommon connection between different senses. In "a way opposite to the abstract breakdown [of perception] into sensations," art "isolates what we call a 'sense,' or a part or a feature of this sense, it isolates it so as to force it to be only what it is outside of signifying and useful perception" (21)—that is to say, by stripping sense of what we could call its informational value. In this way, "art forces a sense to touch itself, to be this sense that it is" (21). But this is to say that in forcing a sense to touch itself, art by the same stroke touches *on* it, dislocates it and thereby "exposes another world, not a 'visual' or 'sonorous' world but a 'pictorial' or 'musical' one" (21): "It makes of the 'sonorous' or 'auditory' regime, for example, a world composed of equivalents, pitches, scales, harmonic relations, melodic sequences, tonalities, rhythms, timbres, and so forth—a world one of whose faces, the written and calculated one, has nothing to do with sound and another of whose faces is taken up in the always unpredictable quality of a singular 'interpretation' or 'execution.'" (21). This dis-integration or singularization of phenomenal perception into an infinity of points that are "not geometric and without dimension"—that is, singularities as rigorously defined, does not exclude and, on the contrary, "combines heterogeneous sensuous values without homogenizing them: *this* red is also a thickness, a fluidity, a figure, a movement, a flash of sound, a taste, or an odor" (21). Art thus deconstructs sense, or occurs as deconstructed sense, as the dislocation of its dislocatedness, as a further heterogeneous twist of its irreducible "auto-heterogeneity." If sense is always already meta-sense, then art acts as a further degree of meta, a meta-meta-sensing that opens onto a nominalist infinity, an endless proliferation of singularities: "an infinity of points, in an infinitely divisible *locality*, even though its 'points' are not geometric and without dimension" (21).[36]

Art, in sum, "disengages the senses from signification" (22), and thus do we give "the (sensible, sensuous) senses the sense of being external to signification" (22). This distinction, however, between "the senses" in the plural and "sense" (meaning, signification) in the singular is the gap opened by art and exploited by metaphysics as the difference between the sensible and the intelligible. This spacing, which is "not spatial but ontological," also opens onto the invention of metaphor, or the difference between figure and ground. This is again because "the heterogeneity that spaces out sensitive or sensuous plurality . . . is itself at least double: it divides very distinct, incommunicable qualities (visual, sonorous), *and* it shares out among these qualities other qualities (or the same ones), which one might name with 'metaphors' (such as the *dark*, the *brilliant*, the *thick*, the *soft*, the *strident*, etc., but also, through a generalized metaphorical circulation, *taste* or *flavor, odor, tone, color, flesh*, etc.), but which are in the final analysis meta-phors in the proper sense, effective transports or communication across the incommunicable itself, a general play of *mimesis* and *methexis* mixed together across all the senses and all the arts" (24). If art, by one stroke, breaks down any zone of the senses into endless, incommunicable singularities, then by another it reinstitutes intelligible sense as figurable meaning, figures that communicate the incommunicability of the singular, the transport of metaphors that raises forms or figures "less in relation to a 'ground' (perhaps there is no ground for all these figures, no other 'ground' than their differences) than it raises some in relation to others, all of them being thus grounds or figures for one another" (24). As such, "the arts or the senses of the arts endlessly meta-phorize each other."

It is in terms of this production of sense that Nancy sees the arts as *"technical"* (24) to the extent that "technique means knowing how to go about producing what does not produce itself by itself" (25). *Sexistence*, we recall, advanced the "scandalous proposition," whereby "technique is transcendence" (45), in its transformative potential, as the exteriority of pro-duction, its very exceeding ex nihilo of existence, as technexistence: "Technique is a—perhaps infinite—space and delay between the producer and the produced, and thus between the producer and him- or herself. It is production in an exteriority to self and in the discreteness of its operations and its objects" (25).

But this transcendence of production that defines technics and the arts is not to be confused, despite a long tradition of such confusion, with the myth of creation that would posit a pre-existing creator, whose genius stands outside the world of that creation ex nihilo and thus "closes art into the aporia of a divine autism" (26), as the "bursting of a blossom into bloom" (25), or a "disenclosure [*déclosion*]," such as Nancy addresses at length in his two-volume *Deconstruction of Christianity*. On the contrary, "art-technique exposes an exteriority of the work to its production or to its subject, just as it exposes an exteriority of its end" (26). It is a matter of transcendence rather than immanence, or at the very least, the transcendence of an immanence whereby "art lacks origin and end": "Technique is the obsolescence of the origin and the end: the exposition to a lack of ground and foundation. . . . Technique extends a withdrawal (*retrait*) of the 'ground'" (26). Nancy offers a radical rejection of classical and romanticist notions of creation (artistic, technological, divine) as the making of forms ex nihilo and argues instead for a theory of art as the retreat of ground, its withdrawal and reinscription: "Not the cutting out that lifts up a figure against a ground, but the cut of a form inasmuch as a form *is a ground that withdraws*, that removes or ex-poses itself of itself, different from itself as ground. . . . A form is the force of a ground that sets apart and dislocates itself, its syncopated rhythm" (31–32). Or again, citing the work of Gérard Lépinlois, "A figure is never entirely detached from the ground. It is always, more or less, the ground that comes forward as figure and that will soon move back away to become again simple space."[37] Never a beginning but an ever-recommenced recommencement: never an end, but "linking endlessly to other techniques and asking again endlessly for, as its most proper end, yet another technique, and consequently its end that appears to itself in the mode of a perpetual 'means,' for an endless end" (26).

We can readily recognize in this formulation that of our contemporary technological reality as the forever or structurally unsatisfied need for ever greater "innovation," or what Silicon Valley calls "disruption," but what about the arts? More than even meta-sensible, art appears to be meta-technological for Nancy, as "nothing other than the second-degree exposition of technique itself, or perhaps the technique *of the ground* itself" (26). If technique is production, then the question becomes, as Nancy states it, "How to produce the ground that does not produce itself: that would be the question of art, and that would be its plurality of origin" (26). Before addressing the question of how to produce that which does not produce itself, we might reflect for a moment on what a "technique of the ground" might mean here, if not a kind of production—that is, a drawing out that is also a withdrawing, a drawing that is inescapably a re-drawing, a *re-trait* or retreat of whatever we mean by "ground" itself, assuming of course that ground has an "itself" to draw out. So, then, what is this ground that is not produced? And what is it that is produced by the meta-sensible, meta-technological exposition that is art?

Nancy answers the first question by in turn asking the question of how to produce the ground, playing on its double meaning in French of fund or foundation (*fonds*), "if the *ground* is not *one* and is not a *grounds* or a *fund* from which to draw one's resources" (26)? Such a ground that "does not produce itself and is not produced in any manner" is nothing but the very "obviousness or manifestness of Being: existence, with which one cannot have done, . . . existence as the 'infinite multiplicity of the world'" (27), citing a phrase from Alan Badiou, which the author of *Being Singular Plural* not surprisingly revises with a nod to Wittgenstein: "But the multiplicity of the world does not remain even the multiplicity of *a* world: it qualifies the world as heterogeneity of worlds *in which consists the unity of the world*" (27).

If the ground (not) produced by the arts is thus the very ground(lessness) of existence in its infinite multiplicity and heterogeneity, what is "produced" by the arts if not sense itself, including notably intelligible sense? "In other words, the sensuous and technical plurality of the arts is bound up with intelligible sense. And it is thus that there is an art, or rather, once again, arts of intelligible sense, that is, arts of language, on which all the other arts touch according to modalities that irresistibly lead to attempts to inter-express them through the category of 'poetry'" (27). If the body was the locus of inter-expression between senses, then the specific art of poetry as meta-sense and meta-technique becomes the locale for any attempted inter-expression of the arts. As such, with poetry we see "simultaneously the renewal of the arts beneath the unity of a pure production of sense *and* the sensuous dis-location of sense" (27). It is not just a question, though, of poetry's distinct imbrication of sensible sense with intelligible sense, but of the poetic production of sense as in itself sensuous, at once the intellection of the sensible and the sensuousness of the intelligible. It is the epitome of sense sensing itself, yet it also reveals the paradox of the production of sense, what Nancy labels "a literally untenable tension" between the sense that is produced and what would precede it. Specifically, what "produces" this sense "is the fact of its being first of all received, felt, in short, *sensed* as sense" (28). This "tension" between reception and production, or in technical terms, between aesthetics and poetics, between sense and sense sensing itself, is "literally untenable" to the extent that what comes between reception and production, between their touching, is *interruption*, "and that is why there is no poetry that does not bear upon the extremity of its own interruption and that does not have this movement for its law and technique" (28).

Sense produced as what is first of all received is sense sensing itself, sense as auto-reflexive meta-sense, which in terms of its self-sensing assumes the very interruption of its sensing itself, according to "the law of touch." This conundrum of poetic sense not only speaks well beyond what we classically call poetry, but more dynamically, as per Nancy's fleeting reference here to the German sense of *Dichtung*, toward the category of the "poetic" as embracing the many other arts that engage some version of the difference between the sensible and intelligible, such as "prose poetry," so-called "creative non-fiction," the theatre in its many forms, film and video, the multiple ways of orchestrating lyric with music, not to mention other "arts of language" and any number of "cultural practices."[38]

More generally, "poetry" for Nancy becomes the very figure and ground of technique itself, to the extent that it "presents itself simultaneously as *pars pro toto* of art and *totum pro parte* of technique" (28). It is one among the arts and that among which technique is one. If touch is multiply the metaphor of the senses, poetry is the multivalent metonymy of the arts-techniques, of meta-sense in general, of the sense of sense. And to the extent that it responds or corresponds to the "demand to sense sense sensing (itself)" (29), poetry, according to Nancy, both "permanently" subsumes the arts under itself and assumes a "no less permanent and irreducible face-to-face" with philosophy.

Rather than engage in a major detour here through the long history of the standoff between poetry and philosophy, Nancy leans on Hegel to cut to the chase: "Thinking is only a reconciliation between reality and truth within thinking itself. But poetic creation and formation is a reconciliation in the form of a *real* phenomenon itself" (29).[39] To which Nancy adds that the "poetic" reconciliation takes place "in an irreconcilable mode"—that is, according to a double exteriority, "at once the exteriority of the phenomenon as such or of the sensuous as being-outside-itself, *and* the exteriority of the poetic reconciliation in relation to the thought reconciliation inasmuch as the latter is 'only . . . within thinking'" (29). Poetry offers an irreconcilable reconciliation that highlights the double exteriority of thought to what it can only think or sense outside itself, both the "thing" itself that is the "exteriority of the phenomenon as such" and "the sensuous as being-outside-itself," on the one hand, and on the other, poetry "as sensuous assumption of sense itself that thinking only thinks" (29–30). What the consequential dilemma of thinking (or "philosophy," as Nancy indicates before deploying the word "thinking") reveals in turn is the very finitude of thought itself, and this passage gives rise to an early iteration of "finite thinking," here defined as what "separates [thought] from the thing, from its most proper thing, *and* precisely renders thereby sensuous the stakes of thinking" (29). In other words, thinking as finite feels or senses itself outside itself, "feels its weight, its gravity," adds Nancy in another bow to the etymological sense of the French word for thought, *pensée*, as weight. In its ponderousness, finite thinking senses itself twice "outside itself," once with regard to the thing and once with regard to poetry, "which together form the ex-position of thought" (30). Thinking remains caught within "thinking itself," sensing itself outside itself, ex-posed, in what it cannot grasp except within itself as "within thinking itself." This apparent circularity of thought, though, does not mean it is insensible, so to speak, to its ex-position, and to what Nancy terms the "extension and tension" between thing and poetry, the *poiesis* of the *thing* itself, which in a mystical or romantic model would be that "sui generis" or self-canceling concept that is called "creation," but that Nancy identifies more rigorously as "a *technique* of the world," which in turn "can only be understood in the plural of techniques that have neither the point of origin of a *fiat* nor the endpoint of a *sense*"(30). Technique opens up the singular plural of art as what is "destined to repeat itself," not yet begun and always already ended. As Nancy says, "The end of art was always yesterday" (30), meaning an irreducible untimeliness of what can only take place, like the Cartesian cogito, each and every time as a singleton or singularity:

> Each one of the arts exposes in its way the unity of "art," which has neither place nor consistency outside this "each one"—still more, the unity of a single art is ex-posed in this sense only in its works one by one. Each work is in its fashion a synesthesia and the opening of a world. But it is this insofar as "the world" as such, in its being-world (the being of that *to* which opens a being-*to-the*-world), is plurality of worlds.
>
> Thus, the "in its fashion" of each art, of each style, and of each work, its *manner* or incommunicable technique, is not an expressive variation on the ground of an *identical* theme. (31)

The unity of art as meta-sense lies in the utter singularity of its singular style or fashion, its each time this one, into the singularity of the world it opens in the synesthetic *entre-deux* of the senses, as a singular world or world of singularities. This is the radical heterogeneity of the arts in general, and poetry above all. It speaks to the very innumerability of their styles and genres, and to the irreducible transcendence of their ex-position, which is, in turn, the very sense of sense: "Poetry names its proper outside, or the outside as the proper: the sense of sense" (30). Whether reception or intellection, sense is always ex-posed, always sensed as what lies outside, as the proper name of the between ourselves, our bodies, our sense of sensation. Poetry is the name of this ex-position, forever outside itself, endlessly recommenced and endlessly over, "without synthesis or without system" (37). Art is its own end as the infinite vertigo of each-time finite meta-sense. "Art is always *coming to its end*," which is "always the beginning of its plurality," but "it could also be the beginning of another sense of and for 'technics' in general" (37). Or else, adds Nancy, the "technicity of art" means its *désoeuvrement*, its coming undone in its very coming, its inoperability at loose ends with itself, "the 'out-of-workness' of the work," or "what puts it outside itself," what "dislodges [the arts] endlessly from aestheticizing repose," thus "always *coming to its end*" (37). Poetry names the (uncommon) sense of sense, "the infinite sense that touches itself finite (that interrupts itself sensibly" (33–34), as ex-position, as "the proper outside." As such:

> ... art is the transcendence of immanence as such, the transcendence of an immanence that does not go outside itself in transcending, which is not ex-static but ek-sistent. A "trans-immanence." Art exposes this. Once again, it does not "represent" this. Art is its ex-position. The trans-immanence or patency of the world takes place as art, as works of art. (35)

The Sense of Sense III: The Patency of the World

Nancy returns to the "sense of sense" a few pages after its poetic "naming," but oddly enough this time as the very definition of "truth," or at least as its substitute, and as the equivalent of the world in its "patency": "Truth, in fact, or sense of sense, is the patency of the world" (33). What we could call Nancy's critical ontology of sense and singularity comes down to this cryptic sentence that articulates truth, the sense of sense, and the "patency" of the world, which we can also understand indeed as the very "sense of the world," the title, of course, of one of his subsequent books. A critical explication, then, of this sentence can bring our own reading of the relation between sense and singularity to a point of conclusion, if not necessarily to an "end."

Unpacking the sentence in reverse order of its equivalent terms seems the most propitious path to follow here. What does Nancy mean by "the patency [*patence*] of the world"? The word, and the entire expression for that matter, underscores Nancy's most striking rejection of classic phenomenology. It is clearly not about revealing or unveiling some latent or hidden (noumenal) truth about the (phenomenal) world, a sense that would represent the sense of the world as appearance to some consciousness, something given to or intended for someone, be that the absolute consciousness of divinity. Rather, for Nancy, the ever heterological sense of sense, the very singular plural of the arts-technique, points to the very limits of phenomenology, since "the single theme of an 'appearing' cannot respond to the clear-cut—and cutting—discreteness of a ground that withdraws and that retraces itself in forms" (32). It is not a question of an appearance, or an appearing, a coming to presence, but rather, in a familiar move, of a retreat, a withdrawal and retracing. It is not about a coming of the world, much less any supposed coming into the world, "a matter neither of a donation nor an intention, nor even a signifying": "The coming of the world is not even a coming. The world is simply *patent*, if one may understand by that an appearance that does not 'appear,' no immanence of a subject having preceded its transcendence, and no obscure ground its luminosity" (33). The patency of the world is the utter, infinite exorbitance of what is, such as it is, the singular plural of ex-sistence in its occurrences, in its passages, in the touch or pulse, in the interruptedness of its coming and going, in the fact that "there is only the world" (33), in its nonapparent appearing, in its manifestness or "evidence." This infinite patency recalls, as Nancy notes, Spinoza's concept of truth as that which "discloses itself (*qui se ipsum patefacit*)" (33), as that which is in itself patent. The patent is what we invent in the sense of what we come upon, what we stumble across, what we find in/as the world in which we are thrown, the very singularity of existence at any given moment or location. Disclosing this disclosure, evidencing what is patent about patency, ex-posing this presentation *as* presentation, is what falls to art as "the presentation of presentation" (34). Art as "sense of sense" or meta-sense is thus also meta-presentation (but not representation, which would "relate presentation to a subject for which or in which it would take place," whereas the presentation of presentation "relates it to itself" [34]), nor is it the unveiling of some latency in the world: "By touching on presentation itself, or on patency, one touches on nothing, one does not penetrate a secret; one touches on obviousness, and the obviousness is such that one cannot be done with it, that it multiples itself in its very immanence: color, nuance, grain, line, timbre, echo, cadence . . ." (36). Touching on the obvious is to particularize it to infinity, to gesture toward endless singularity, and at the same time, to underscore the singular plural of the arts. For that reason, art disappears or comes to an endless end each time it happens: "As soon as it takes place, 'art' vanishes, it is *an* art, the latter is *a* work, which is *a* style, a manner, a mode of resonance with other sensuous registers, a rhythmic reference back through indefinite networks" (36). Each work is singular even as it presents the singular plural of the sensed world, its trans-immanence or patency. At the same time, by dint of its singularity, its meta-sense as art disappears into the endless networking of sense, into the infinite chain of reference upon reference, the pulsating rhythm of interruption between sense and sense, the beat of their intervallic space, the critical *entre-deux* between reception and intellection or between intellection and reception. The "privilege" of art is that of "an index, which shows and touches, which shows by touching," or, to prolong Nancy's thought, which touches by showing. "It is not the privilege of a superior revelation" (36), but "the ground-figure of presentation of patency" (38). Presenting patency in its trans-immanence through the incessant retreat of ground/figure, "art" comes to its end each and every time, as a "one off," as what disappears in/as art in its very appearance, its singularity nonetheless denied or sublated in its relay as sense, as whatever meaning of "art" contemporary circumstances strive to attribute to it. "In this manner, a certain determination of 'art,' which is ours—in other words, that of the period that will have named 'art' as such and absolutely—is perhaps coming to its end, and with it the categorization of the 'fine arts' that accompany it, and with these a whole aesthetic feeling and judgment, a whole sublime delectation" (37–38).

There is nothing new about this sense of the end of art, it is indeed part and parcel of our "modernity," and of modernism itself as the aesthetic/technological project of our times that urges the incessant overcoming of one art form by another yet to be invented. Nancy cautions, however, in a characteristic move we have seen from the beginning of this study, that this coming to an end of a certain "determination" of "art" today "is not an end, but a renewed demand to grant rights to the naked presentation of the singular plural of obviousness—or of existence: it's the same thing" (38). This demand is in fact a "duty," "a duty for art to put an end to 'art'" (38), which is not to say to pit "puritanically" "an 'ethics' against an 'aesthetics,'" nor even to pursue an "ethics of the aesthetic," but a duty that "utters *sense as ethos*" (38).

The ethical or categorical imperative is a sense-making duty, one that puts an end to art as the sense of yet another art to come. This response to the "renewed demand" to present the patency of existence (or "the singular plural of obviousness") is sense *as* ethics, a duty that "imposes art, or it imposes 'some art'—but not Art": "But it is not Art that comes, it is the *tekhnè* of existence" (38). It is truth as the sense of sense that presents the patency of the world, or the obviousness of existence as ever renewed, as iterative trans-immanence. Existence is not mere *phusis*: "Its—obvious—patency is not the blooming of a rose," (38), not the disenclosure that models the Christian concept of creation. What art does is to give sense to ethics, or as what Nancy calls, "the *ars* of existing—not an 'art of living,' but technique as relation to endless ends" (38). But that art or *ars*, to highlight again the etymological sense of art as "articulation," such as the articulation between senses that defines the finitude of our embodiment as singular plural, puts an end to itself as it directs itself (as directional sense, or sense of direction) teleologically toward an ever-renewed series of ends. That relation is the technique of existence, not an "art of living" per se, but the imperative of transcendence, of trans-immanence, of exposition as ek-sisting for what is to come, and *as* what is to come.

Freedom, Singularity, and the Return of the Mother

This technique of existence summons us back then to the trio of *tekhnè, logos,* and *eros*, or more generally, to lived existence as the heterogeneous areality of the never-ending *entre-deux* within and between bodies and words and things—that is, the world (by definition, the plurality of worlds) as discontinuous, disruptive, interrupted in every way. Existence is as heterological as the world is patent in its trans-immanence. The arts-techniques form the meta-sense or the meta-presentation of the world in its patency as the ethos of our being-in-the-world, in our singular existence, in our existence as singular.[40] At stake is what Nancy calls a "materialism of the present understood as singularity of existence and not as appropriated presence" (*Experience of Freedom*, 191n). This existential materialism ex-posed in and as art/technique is also the "experience of freedom," which is "the recognition of the freedom of being in its singularity" (*Experience of Freedom*, 13), a recognition that takes the form of thought itself, of philo-sophy lived as the singularly shattered love of making sense but only insofar as it is, as per Kant's "feminine" art of receptivity, or Nancy's own retreat of the mother, open to and affected by the pulse or heartbreak that is the traversal of the other, the transcendence of the crossing of love, the singular risks and passions of the aleatory, the unsaid, and the unsensed.

That figure of the mother, not to mention the question of her "retreat," is curiously absent from *Corpus, Corpus II*, and even from *Sexistence*, despite some referencing of gender difference and the final Kantian allusion to "feminine receptivity." *Coming* is a bit more engaged, especially when Nancy admits the variable outcomes of sexual behavior, not just pleasure but also procreation (whether the latter be viewed as aim or risk). That leads him to the statement that "starting from nothing," sex is "the site of creation: making children or forming forms, assemblages and configurations, rhythms and resonances" (97). He even embarks on a long analysis of birth as the becoming distinct of two bodies, as "the child emerges from the womb and in turn becomes a belly that can swallow and spit out" (103). The problem, though, with this child-centric narrative is the disappearance or effacement of the mother's body except as the "vessel" from which the child essentially births itself. Despite the issue here of a transformative *mitsein* between mother and child leading to the interruption of this singular condominium in the actuality of birth, the mother really does seem to be all but absent, withdrawn, in retreat, albeit only in the objective genitive rendering of the expression, retreat of the mother.

Nancy does, however, significantly revise this scenario in his *Cruor: Corpus III*, which is also his last book (2021), and where the mother does reappear quite dramatically, in a context where the "retreat of the mother," without that expression being deployed as such, receives an ultimate reformulation that addresses both the subjective and objective senses: "Now the belly is also the womb [*la matrice*], another push [*poussée*] of the other, toward the other as self. Another self detaches. Another other. Otherwise other. The amplitude of the body is never as ample than with the belly of a pregnant woman" (39). The swelling of the mother's womb is the sign not only of the trans-immanence of sex, but a fortiori the trans-immanence of existence, whereby the self can only be itself in its own othering, be that the singular othering of a wholly other self. Hence, the retreat of the mother does not end with the birth or expulsion of the child, who is "newborn but always to be born anew, always to become self until it comes to an end one day" (39). Birth as coming into the world is incessant and iterative, not a simple beginning but an endlessly repeated interruption, the recurring retreat of the mother that is both affection and rejection: "For this reason, the mother is never completely distinct from the world (or from the id) and for the same reason she can be rejected as much as loved, since being in the world also means no longer being the world itself with its indistinct identity" (116). And while Nancy, in a section of the book oddly called "longing for the father," and in a nod to classical psychoanalysis, subsequently tries to reintroduce the father as the principle of "detachment itself" and as the "possibility of an outside-the world, of autonomy," he quickly finds himself in a situation that "forces us to step back from Freud," to the extent that the retreat of the mother implies at once maternal embrace and paternal rejection: "If we were to pursue this reasoning, we would see how the mother and the father are intertwined, or how thrownness (*être-jeté*) and being-in-the-world are correlated, as well as how this correlation involves the collective or plurality of egos since on the father's side there can only be exclusion of unicity and on the mother's side there is the world, which supposes the alterity and the circulation of distinct elements of sense" (117). What Nancy presents here as the virtual sketch of a larger project implies an utter scrambling of traditional psychoanalysis. No longer the Oedipus complex of old with desire for the mother blocked by the castration threat of the father, but the retreat of the mother as bi-parental ambivalence, as the affective sense of our singular but common *Geworfenheit*: "affective ambivalence: love and hate for what threw me forth and what opened the world to me" (117). The retreat of the mother, in all its ambiguity, may not only be the essence of the political that is not political, but the essence of existence that is not existential, of sense that is not sense, of life that is not (yet) life.

Within this maternal retreat, the womb names "the possibility of transformation by which a form begins to emerge and then comes away, distinguishes itself" (41). As such "it is the origin insofar as it is neither a principle nor a cause, but an expansion that has begun well before, that has always already begun and of which a singular womb [*matrice*], penetrated by another singularity, is but a particular scansion, the beating proper of a self/other" (41). What we call "conception" or "birth" or "life" is each time but the singular interruption of a body that is nothing other than interruption, and sense but the iteration of those multiple singularities, revealing the patency of the world in the singular crossings of *eros*, *logos*, and *tekhnè* that we call birth, poetry, and art, or "the site of creation: making children or forming forms, assemblages and configurations, rhythms and resonances" (*Coming*, 97).

In *The Experience of Freedom*, Nancy writes, "Existence is above all what is singular. It happens singularly and only singularly" (*Experience of Freedom*, 190–91n). Existence as at every point singular and multiply singular, but its *sense* as iteration—that is, the self-sensing that senses sense as such—re-marks the retreat of the singular as such, while by the same stroke retracing the very interruption of identity that is sense, the pulsing or pushing that makes sense what it is by the rhythm of its endless sending and transmission, by its referral and referencing. The singularity of existence, for that matter, is not the field or place or space or milieu of singularity, but its fundamental *areality*—that is, an "incalculable spacing" (*Experience of Freedom*, 146) that is the ontological if not spatial punctuality of an "unreal area" that is the ever-receding horizon of ex-perience, the all-too real retreat—or the double gesture of withdrawal and retracing—of reality that by dint of interruption re-marks at any point the "singularity" of existence. So too, a certain representation of the origin of philosophy as the "retreat of sense by which sense arrives" (*Oubli de la philosophie*, 108), philosophy as interruption, the iterative monogram of finite thinking itself, where "freedom expends itself in the withdrawal from every determination" (*Experience of Freedom*, 57), or "in and as the being-singular of being" (*Experience of Freedom*, 205n). Existence is singular, but sense is iterative, hence singular plural, meaning that in its iteration the *event* of any given sense is also in and of itself singular, an experience of freedom.

This literal ex-position or exscription (as experienced through the singularity of touching and in particular the *sense* of skin) thus defines an ethics and aesthetics of exteriority in line with a finite thinking that is open to both the singular and plural, repetition and difference, open and available to the creation of world, and especially open to the singularly unheard, the unseen, the unsensed, the unknown or unknowable—in other words, says Nancy channeling Kant, the "feminine" potential to receive the pulse and potential of the other, an artful passivity or passibility (*Sexistence*, 119). The *sense* of singularity and the *singularity* of sense together draw and redraw the lines of our *exposure* to what is finite, each and every time, yet endlessly, infinitely, reinscribed, hence our exposure to the ecstasy of being drawn out, of a finite thinking that is surprised each and every time by its own freedom and the unsuspected inventiveness of its philosophical *poein* or world creation, by the pain or pleasure of existence itself.

Acknowledgments

It has been my repeated honor and pleasure to encounter Jean-Luc Nancy in different situations and contexts over a long period of time, notable as much for its many interruptions as well as reiterations. My first encounter dates back to my undergraduate days, when as an overly arrogant French major at Reed College who had read just enough theory to make problems for me, my fellow students, and especially my teachers, I was invited by one of my professors, Jane McLelland, to a seminar by a visiting speaker, an occasion, so she said, for me "to crack my teeth on a real French philosopher." That visitor was Jean-Luc Nancy, and far from this being an occasion for me to show off how smart I was, I was utterly stunned by what seemed to me to be his encyclopedic knowledge and uncanny ability to move with dexterous ease between what I had been taught as the very separate worlds of philosophy, literature, and intellectual history. That startling seminar on the Witz, a modest version of which later appeared as the chapter "Menstruum universale," in *The Birth to Presence*, not only urged me to completely rethink my senior thesis on Marivaux's novels but also, and transformationally, to seek a doctoral degree where I could work at the nexus of literature and philosophy. I assiduously followed Nancy's career through his first publications in English (*MLN*, *Glyph*), which were the grounds for much discussion while I was a graduate student at Cornell. While on a fellowship in Paris in 1981, I regularly attended the meetings of the Centre de Recherches Philosophiques sur le Politique, directed by Nancy and Philippe Lacoue-Labarthe (I later translated Lyotard's lecture to this group as *Enthusiasm: The Kantian Critique of History* [Stanford: Stanford University Press, 2009]). Later, I was invited to present a paper at the Lyotard colloquium at Cerisy-la-Salle in 1982, where I encountered Nancy again as a keynote speaker. At Miami University, beginning in 1986, I organized with Peggy Kamuf the first discussion group in the U.S. in response to Nancy's *Inoperative Community*, which resulted in a major conference and eventually a volume, where I served as primary editor, published by the University of Minnesota Press as *Community at Loose Ends* (1991). And when Helen Tartar launched the generous project of bringing Nancy's work to an Anglo-American readership, she requested my service repeatedly as an external reviewer for such key works as *The Muses* and *Being Singular Plural*.

In addition to his work's serving as a major influence on my work, I went on to write articles specifically on Nancy, "Singular Remarks," in the first special issue dedicated to his work for the journal *Paragraph* 16, no. 2 (1993); "Lost Horizons and Uncommon Grounds," in the widely read volume on his work edited by Darren Sheppard, Simon Sparks, and Colin Thomas and published by Routledge as *On Jean-Luc Nancy: The Sense of Philosophy* (1997), 12–18; and much later on "Monograms: Then and 'Now,'" in the *Nancy Now* volume, edited by Verena Andermatt Conley and Irving Goh, for Polity Press (2014), 59–89. Some portions of the first two pieces ended up in the Introduction to this volume, and the last essay served as the basis for Chapter 2. Revised versions or extracts of these texts are here reproduced with the permission of Edinburgh University Press through PLSclear, Informa UK Limited through PLSclear, and Polity Press, respectively. Finally, a version of Chapter 1, "Descartes's Iterative Cogito," has also just appeared in Irving Goh, ed., *Jean-Luc Nancy Among the Philosophers*, out from Fordham University Press earlier this year.

Only recently did I realize that the impossibly vast opus I've been trying to write for years on "The Retreat of French Thought" essentially included an entire book on Nancy, which is what has come together here under the title of *Sense and Singularity*. Decades later, and after innumerable creative "interruptions," I am still trying to crack my teeth on the incalculably profound work of this most real of real French philosophers. This book represents, of course, only the most minimal repayment for the debt I owe him for the exemplarity of a thinking he has pursued with uncommon care and dedication over many, many years. And while I shared parts of this volume with him before his untimely death, I was sadly not able to present him with the finished whole before we lost him. Given this turn of events, this book also stands as a (necessarily pagan) requiem in his honor. In addition to the reviewers for the press, I would like to thank a number of people who have inspired or supported this project, especially Jane McLelland, William Ray, Philip Lewis, Peggy Kamuf, Verena Andermatt Conley, Irving Goh, Juliet Flower MacCannell, Darryl Chagi, and Andrew Benjamin (who early on encouraged me to pursue my work on Nancy, and I wish I had followed his advice earlier). Special thanks and appreciation to Tom Lay for valiantly chauffeuring this work to editorial completion. And all my love and gratitude to Beryl Schlossman for endlessly and lovingly supporting me on this project despite my own foibles and disagreeableness. Finally, I dedicate this book, in addition to Jean-Luc Nancy, to the memory of Helen Tartar, whose editorial foresight and courage remain peerless.

Notes

Introduction: From the Interruption of Sense to the Poetics of Finitude

1. Frank Kermode, *The Sense of an Ending: Studies in the Theory of Fiction* (Oxford: Oxford University Press, 1966).

2. Jean-Luc Nancy, *Adoration: The Deconstruction of Christianity II*, trans. John McKeane (New York: Fordham University Press, 2013), 18. The "salute" or *salut* of a "salutation without salvation" refers to the final page of Jacques Derrida, *On Touching—Jean-Luc Nancy*, trans. Christine Irizarry (Stanford, Calif.: Stanford University Press, 2005), 310: "a benediction without any hope of salvation, an ex-hoped-for *salve*, an incalculable, unpresentable salutation in advance renouncing Salvation (as should any salute worthy of the name). Just *salut*, greeting without salvation; just a *salut* on the way." Nancy's moving response, "*Salut* to you, *salut* to the blind we become," appears as an appendix to this same volume, 311–14.

3. Jacques Derrida, "Sur un ton apocalyptique naguère adopté en philosophie," in *Les fins de l'homme: À partir du travail de Jacques Derrida*, ed. Philippe Lacoue-Labarthe and Jean-Luc Nancy (Paris: Galilée, 1981), 471–78; my translation, emphasis added. Derrida raises the question, however, whether the exemplary revelation that is "the apocalyptic wouldn't be a transcendental condition of all discourse, of all experience even, of every mark or of every trace" (471), that it emerges in its most radical form as an "apocalypse without apocalypse," where the "*without* marks an internal and external catastrophe of the apocalypse, a *reversal of sense* not to be confused with the catastrophe announced or described in apocalyptic writings yet without being foreign to them either. Here, the catastrophe would perhaps be that *of* the apocalypse itself, its fold and its end, an enclosure without bounds, an end without end" (478; emphasis added).

4. Nancy, *Adoration*, 11.

5. Nancy, *Doing*, trans. Charlotte Mandell (2016; repr. London: Seagull, 2020), 68, trans modified. Hegel's remark comes from the Preface to Georg Wilhelm Friedrich Hegel, *The Philosophy of Right*, trans. T. M. Knox (London: Oxford University Press, 1952), 13: "Die Eule der Minerva beginnt erst mit der einbrechenden Dämmerung ihren Flug." See also Nancy, "Monogrammes II," *Digraphe 21* (1979): 133–38, analyzed in Chapter 2, and more recently, Nancy, *The Fragile Skin of the World*, trans. Cory Stockwell (2020; repr. New York: Fordham University Press, 2021), 28, 77.

6. In *La fin des fins*, coauthored with Federico Ferrari (Paris: Kimé, 2017), Nancy reflects on the degree to which the discourse of things coming to an end, so prevalent in his own work but also indelibly linked with the heyday of "poststructuralism," is either merely "generational" or else fundamentally "ontological." This dialogue with Ferrari, presented as a play in three acts, offers one of Nancy's most acute reflections on the sense of both beginnings and endings, and where he displays his characteristic suspicion of the idealism of those two concepts as well as the necessity of their use. Ultimately, there is neither beginning nor ending, only what is in-between: "Perhaps there is no beginning and no end, and always an in-between [*entre-deux*] always a passage, a middleplace that is not a place [*un milieu qui n'est pas un lieu*] but an element where that floats between a start and a finish which have never taken place" (24). On the one hand, he concludes that "beginning and end are perhaps nothing other than the *rupture* of continuity and homogeneity" (26, emphasis added), or "interruption," to use the related term, also omnipresent in Nancy's writing, that guides my thinking through these conundrums.

7. Nancy, "'You Ask Me What It Means Today . . .': An Epigraph for *Paragraph*," *Paragraph* 16, no. 2 (1993), Special Issue on the Work of Jean-Luc Nancy, ed. Peggy Kamuf, 108.

8. Nancy, "Exscription," in *The Birth to Presence*, trans. Brian Holmes et al (Stanford, Calif.: Stanford University Press, 1993), 319; translation modified.

9. Nancy, *Adoration*, 95.

10. Nancy, *L'oubli de la philosophie* (Paris: Galilée, 1986).

11. See Nancy, *The Dis-Enclosure: The Deconstruction of Christianity*, trans. Bettina Bergo, Gabriel Malenfant, and Michael B. Smith (2005; repr. New York: Fordham University Press, 2008), x.

12. Nancy, *After Fukushima: The Equivalence of Catastrophes*, trans. Charlotte Mandell (2012; repr. New York: Fordham University Press, 2015); *An All-Too-Human Virus*, trans. Cory Stockwell, David Fernbach, and Sarah Clift (2020; repr. New York: Fordham University Press, 2021).

13. Nancy, *The Inoperative Community*, trans. Peter Connor, Lisa Garbus, Michael Holland, and Simona Sawhney (1983; repr. Minneapolis: University of Minnesota Press, 1991), 1; translation modified. On Nancy's "misquoting" of Sartre, see Richard Terdiman, "On the Dialectics of Postdialectical Thinking," in *Community at Loose Ends*, ed. Miami Theory Collective (Minneapolis: University of Minnesota Press, 1991), 118.

14. Nancy, *Corpus*, trans. Richard A. Rand (1992; repr. New York: Fordham University Press, 2008), 43.

15. See, in this regard, especially *Le mythe nazi*, with Philippe Lacoue-Labarthe (La tour d'Aigues: L'Aube, 1991).

16. Nancy, "We Need . . . ," in *The Birth to Presence*, 308.

17. Arthur Rimbaud, "Lettre: à Paul Demeny," Charleville, May 15, 1871, in *Poésies complètes*, ed. Pascal Pia (Paris: Livre de Poche, 1963), 220.

18. Nancy, *Dis-Enclosure*, 129. Interestingly, for Nancy, the philosopher who most dramatically exemplifies this dissatisfaction with philosophy and hunger for poetic expression is none other than Kant: "He is one of the very few philosophers to complain about not having the language he needs to expound his thinking. He wishes a poet could come along and do what he is unable to do"; Jean-Luc Nancy and Alain Badiou, *German Philosophy: A Dialogue*, ed. Jan Völker, trans. Richard Lambert (Cambridge, Mass.: MIT Press, 2018), 13. Much earlier, Nancy addressed this question at length in his *The Discourse of the Syncope: Logodaedelus I*, trans. Saul Anton (1975; repr. Stanford, Calif.: Stanford University Press, 2008): "[There] is the moment in which philosophy explicitly designates its own exposition as *literature*. . . . This is the moment of Kant" (18–19). And it is under the Kantian term *monogram* that Nancy will undertake some of his most overt experiments in the *style* of writing philosophy. I analyze these writings at length in Chapter 2 of this study.

19. "Ideas are to objects as constellations are to stars"; Walter Benjamin, *The Origin of German Tragic Drama*, trans. John Osborne (London: Verso, 1998), 34.

20. Stephen W. Hawking, *A Brief History of Time* (New York: Bantam, 1988), 186.

21. On monstrous singularity in the sixteenth century, see Jean Céard, *La nature et ses prodiges: L'insolite au XVIe siècle* (Geneva: Droz, 1977); and Marc E. Blanchard, *Trois portraits de Montaigne: Essai sur la représentation à la Renaissance* (Paris: Nizet, 1990), 281–82. Also see Georges Van Den Abbeele, "Duplicity and Singularity in André Thevet's *Cosmographie de Levant*," *L'Esprit Créateur* 32, no. 3 (Fall 1992): 25–35.

22. The expression "community at loose ends" was first coined by Peggy Kamuf to translate the title of Nancy's *La communauté désoeuvrée*. "Community at loose ends" subsequently became the title of a colloquium on Nancy at Miami University in October 1988 and then of the volume containing the proceedings of that conference, which were edited by the Miami Theory Collective and published in 1991 by the University of Minnesota Press.

23. William J. Kaufmann III, *Black Holes and Warped Spacetime* (New York: W. H. Freeman, 1979), 84.

24. Hawking, *Brief History of Time*, 46.

25. Ibid., 50.

26. Ibid., 173.

27. Ibid., 47. Perhaps its theological conformity makes sense given its direct affiliation with the big bang theory first conceived by a Belgian priest, Georges

Lemaître. On the anxiety of singularity, see Samuel Weber, *Inquiétantes singularités* (Paris: Hermann, 2014).

28. Ernesto Laclau and Chantal Mouffe, *Hegemony and Socialist Strategy: Toward a Radical Democratic Politics* (London: Verso, 1985).

29. As Nancy makes utterly explicit in *Being Singular Plural*, trans. Robert D. Richardson and Anne E. O'Byrne (1996; repr. Stanford, Calif.: Stanford University Press, 2000).

30. Nancy, *Le partage des voix* (Paris: Galilée, 1982).

31. I note the curious absence of any entry on Nancy's key use of the term "singularity" in *The Nancy Dictionary*, ed. Peter Gratton and Mare-Eve Morin (Edinburgh: Edinburgh University Press, 2015), even while "sense" is given a precise and nuanced treatment by Jeffrey Librett (213–15).

32. For such a comprehensive overview of Nancy's philosophical contributions, see Ian James, *The Fragmentary Demand: An Introduction to the Philosophy of Jean-Luc Nancy* (Stanford, Calif.: Stanford University Press, 2006); Marie-Eve Morin, *Jean-Luc Nancy* (Cambridge: Polity, 2012); and B. C. Hutchens, *Jean-Luc Nancy and the Future of Philosophy* (Montreal: McGill-Queen's University Press, 2005). On Nancy's relations with other thinkers, see *Nancy among the Philosophers*, ed. Irving Goh (New York: Fordham University Press, 2022).

33. The decisive importance of Nancy's reading of Descartes in *Ego Sum* for his further philosophical development is also reflected by Derrida's insistence on this text early on in his *On Touching—Jean-Luc Nancy*, 20–35.

34. Among such continuations of Nancy's "monograms," see his *Philosophical Chronicles*, trans. Franson Manjali (2004; repr. New York: Fordham University Press, 2008); *After Fukushima*, trans. Charlotte Mandell (New York: Fordham University Press, 2015; *An All-Too-Human Virus*, trans. Cory Stockwell, David Fernbach, and Sarah Clift (New York: Fordham University Press, 2021); *Mascarons de Macron* (2020; Paris: Galilée, 2021).

35. Jacques Derrida, "The *Retrait* of Metaphor," trans. Peggy Kamuf, in *Psyche: Inventions of the Other*, ed. Peggy Kamuf and Elizabeth Rottenberg (Stanford, Calif.: Stanford University Press, 2007), 1:48–80.

36. Nancy, *Corpus; Corpus II: Writings on Sexuality*, trans. Anne O'Byrne (New York: Fordham University Press, 2013); *Sexistence*, trans. Steven Miller (2017; New York: Fordham University Press, 2021); *Corpus III: Cruor and Other Writings*, trans. Jeff Fort (New York: Fordham University Press, 2022).

1. Descartes's Iterative Cogito, or the *Sum* of Each and Every Time

1. Jean-Luc Nancy, *Hegel: The Restlessness of the Negative*, trans. Jason Smith and Steven Miller (1997; repr. Minneapolis: University of Minnesota Press, 2002); *The Banality of Heidegger*, trans. Jeff Fort (2015; repr. New York: Fordham University Press, 2017); *Derrida, suppléments* (Paris: Galilée, 2019).

2. Jean-Luc Nancy, *Ego Sum: Corpus, Anima, Fabula*, trans. Marie-Eve Morin (1979; repr. New York: Fordham University Press, 2016). Reduced versions of three chapters appeared in translation as follows: "*Dum scribo*," trans. Ian McLeod, *Oxford Literary Review* 3, no. 2 (1978): 6–21; "Larvatus pro deo," trans. Daniel Brewer, *Glyph* 2 (1977): 14–36; "Mundus est fabula," trans. Daniel Brewer, *MLN* 93, no. 4 (1978): 635–53, all ironically published before the actual French publication of *Ego Sum*, an irony that makes the long delay in the book's subsequent translation into English even more remarkable.

3. Jacques Derrida, *On Touching—Jean-Luc Nancy*, trans. Christine Irizarry (2000; repr. Stanford, Calif.: Stanford University Press, 2005), 20–35.

4. The actual expression, "I think, therefore I am," only appears in the French text of the *Discourse on Method* and in the never published *Recherche de la vérité*; René Descartes, *The Philosophical Writings of Descartes*, trans. John Cottingham, Robert Stoothoff, and Dugald Murdoch (Cambridge: Cambridge University Press, 1984), II:417. Further references to this English translation will be indicated in the text only as CSM, followed by volume and page number. References to either Descartes's Latin or French will be to the standard eleven-volume *Oeuvres de Descartes*, ed. Charles Adam and Paul Tannery, rev. ed. (Paris: Vrin, 1964–76), indicated as AT, followed by volume and page number (in the current case: AT VI:32); or to the three-volume *Oeuvres philosophiques*, ed. Ferdinand Alquié (Paris: Garnier, 1963–73), which Nancy prefers to cite. References to this edition will be indicated as Alquié, followed by volume and page number (in the current case: Alquié II:1,136).

5. Nancy's signature affection for giving Latin titles to his works, and well beyond those focused on Descartes, is worth reflection, especially given the following remarks from "Lapsus Judicii," in *L'impératif catégorique* (Paris: Flammarion, 1983), where he questions the becoming juridical of philosophy when it moves from Athens to Greece: "If philosophy is Greek, then it is the *Latin* question of philosophy; if Rome is the dissolution of philosophy, then it is the *philosophical* question of Rome. . . . If Roman law substitutes itself for philosophy, or imposes its mask upon it, this is also perhaps because metaphysics, in Rome and since Rome, begins to speak through the law. There would thus be, intimately woven within the *Greek* discourse of metaphysics, a *Latin* discourse: juridical discourse" (36–37). Does Nancy's repeated use of Latin titles signal and thus *expose* an awareness of the implied juridical aspect of critical philosophy per se (and Kant figures well in this discussion as well), its embeddedness in or as a discourse of judgment and legitimation? ("Lapsus Judicii" also closes with or opens up a strong line of discussion with the Jean-François Lyotard of *The Differend*.)

6. The basic lineaments of Martin Heidegger's evolving critique of Descartes can be found in *Being and Time*, trans. Jane Stambaugh (Albany N.Y.: SUNY Press, 1996), 83–93; *Nietzsche*, ed. David Krell, trans. F. A. Capuzzi, vol. 4 (New York, Harper and Row, 1982), 85–138; *What Is a Thing?*, trans. W. B. Barton Jr. and V. Deutsch (South Bend, Ind.: Gateway, 1967), 98–108.

7. But even as traditional a Descartes scholar as Ferdinand Alquié recognizes the problem in his critical edition of the *Meditations*: "There is certainly, in this sense, at the point of departure, an ontological experience of the self as existent (*ego sum, ego existo*, says the Latin text) . . . experience [that] positions us far away from idealist interpretations, which would like to see Descartes begin with thinking in general, or with a properly cognizant subject" (Alquié II:416n).

8. In the preface to the translation of *Ego Sum*, Nancy himself concedes that the expression *ego sum* "tautologizes its 'I' since the Latin word *sum* already contains the first-person pronoun and has no need of *ego*" (xii). I tend to see the line less as a clean tautology that would close and totalize the utterance than as the striking excess of pleonasm, and as such, a harbinger of the iterative, non-identitarian work of what we too readily call "the" cogito.

9. As I've already indicated, Nancy's philosophical work is marked by an insistent foregrounding of contemporary actuality, which is not at all seen as diverging from a rigorous philosophical praxis, on the contrary. As such, Nancy deftly evades the pitfalls, on the one hand, of a fashionable taking of positions at the expense of an openly critical thinking, and on the other hand, of an abstract detachment that fails to rise to the level of comprehending the sense of the world in which we live. More on this tendency in Chapter 2 and following.

10. Irving Goh is a major exception. See his *The Reject: Community, Politics, and Religion after the Subject* (New York: Fordham University Press, 2014). Nancy's query about "who comes after the subject" dates back to at least 1991 with the publication of the volume by that same title edited by Eduardo Cadava, Peter Connor, and Jean-Luc Nancy *Who Comes after the Subject?* (New York: Routledge, 1991).

11. See especially Nancy, "The Surprise of the Event," in *Being Singular Plural*, trans. Robert D. Richardson and Anne E. O'Byrne (Stanford, Calif.: Stanford University Press, 2000), 159–76; and Verena Andermatt Conley and Irving Goh's perceptive remarks in their introduction to *Nancy Now* (Cambridge: Polity Press, 2014), 10–11.

12. Nancy, it should be said, is neither the first nor only one to note this performative aspect of the cogito. See especially Jaako Hintikka, "Cogito, Ergo Sum as an Inference and a Performance," *Philosophical Review* 72, no. 4 (1963): 487–96. Moreover, Nancy's resulting depiction of Cartesian subjectivity as interrupted or intermittent also foreshadows the later stage in Nancy's development analyzed by Jeffrey Librett, "On an Intermittent Subject in Jean-Luc Nancy," *Diacritics* 42, no. 2 (2014): 36–58.

13. Jacques Derrida, *Limited Inc*, trans. Samuel Weber and Jeffrey Mehlman (Evanston, Ill.: Northwestern University Press, 1988), 7. What does it mean to read Nancy under the sign of a key concept developed by his mentor, Jacques Derrida, but that as far as I can tell he never has used himself? On the other hand, *iter* and iterability and their derivatives do seem to intersect in all kinds of unanticipated ways with much of Nancy's critical vocabulary: interruption, areality, ex-perience, ex-position, and even the sense of his deployment of the word, sense.

14. Now, this term, *cogito* (or *cogitus*) *interruptus*, seems easy enough to accept in our post-Freudian, post-Lacanian, post-Althusserian, post-Deleuzian world where

unconscious processes are freely acknowledged to determine and inform what consciousness we think we have, but the expression also has a separate history dating to Umberto Eco's devastating review in 1967 of books by Sedlmayr and McLuhan (reprinted in *Travels in Hyperreality*). For Eco, the illogicality and misguided belief of these two authors in a "world inhabited by symbols or symptoms" represents a deliberate failure of thought or *"cogito interruptus"*; Umberto Eco, *Travels in Hyperreality* (San Diego: Harcourt, 1986), 222. More recently, Eco's idea has been explicitly deployed by Kyoo Lee in her astute and challenging reading of the correspondence between Descartes and the Palatine Princess Elizabeth, yet her concept of *cogito interruptus* is more focused on the literal interruptions of thought in the course of embodied life and the "intersubjectivity" of dialogue; Kyoo Lee, *"Cogito Interruptus*: The Epistolary Body in the Elisabeth-Descartes Correspondence, June 22, 1645–November 3, 1645," philoSOPHIA 1, no. 2 (2011): 173–94. More colloquially, as evidenced by even a quick googling of the term, *cogitus interruptus* seems to have cropped up as an explanatory concept in all kinds of business and corporate thinking regarding ways to overcome the constant interruptions and distractions workers experience in the contemporary digital or wired environment and that would result in countless amounts of lost time, productivity, and profits. See, for example, Dan Markovitz, "Cogitus Interruptus: The Case for Focus," which begins, "Cogitus Interruptus is the disease of the modern workplace. Its symptoms are familiar to any executive: the inability to complete a thought or a task without losing focus under the onslaught of relentless interruptions. It results in a lack of efficiency, a loss of time to solve problems, to think strategically, to plan, to dream—to get your company from here to there. But there's hope: there are techniques to help you regain the opportunity to think without interruption"; https://www.socialmediatoday.com/content/cogitus-interruptus-case-focus. The author is indicated as the president of something called TimeBackManagement.

15. Nancy, *The Inoperative Community*, trans. Peter Connor (1983; repr. Minneapolis: University of Minnesota Press, 1991), 43–70.

16. One can only reflect on the irony of strikingly conflicted or even duplicitous "anonymity" of Descartes's *Discourse on Method*,(CSM I:109–51; AT VI:1–78) whose princeps edition amounted to a mere 200 copies printed without the author's name but each one then individually signed by Descartes and mailed to his interlocutors. See Adrien Baillet, *La Vie de Monsieur Des-Cartes* (Paris, 1691), 275–79; Étienne Gilson, *René Descartes: Discours de la méthode; Texte et commentaire* (Paris: Vrin, 1947).

17. See especially Nancy's critical rejection of Heidegger's statement that "the stone is without world," arguing instead that the stone is "nonetheless toward or in the world," and concluding that "all bodies, each outside the others, make up the inorganic body of sense. The stone does not 'have' any sense. But sense touches the stone"; Nancy, *The Sense of the World*, trans. Jeffrey S. Librett (1993; repr. Minneapolis: University of Minnesota Press, 1997), 59–63.

18. Perhaps nothing speaks of Descartes's reputed solipsism louder than his questioning of whether the people he sees outside his window are "any more than hats and coats which could conceal automatons" CSM II:21), yet this line from the Second *Meditation* (CSM II:21) following right upon the discussion of the piece of wax emphasizes rather the perils of relying *solely* on the evidence of the senses in favor of critical intellection. The lines here make it clear that while what I *see* is nothing more than ambulatory "hats and coats," I do *judge* them to be people rather than automatons underneath the outerwear.

19. See Georges Van Den Abbeele, "Fabel," in *Historisch-Kritisches Wörterbuch der Marxismus*, ed. Wolfgang Fritz Haug (Berlin: Argument-Verlag, 1999); English translation in *Historical Materialism* 16, no. 4 (2008): 233–38; *A World of Fables*, ed. Brenda Schildgen and Georges Van Den Abbeele (Berkeley, Calif.: Pacific View Press, 2003), ix–xvi.

20. As Nancy notes elsewhere, this more famous reiteration of the *ego sum* supplies both a *content*, "thought," and a *logical sequencing*, "therefore," that are not otherwise justified: "Between *The World* and the *Meditations*, the *Discourse* represents . . . the weakest model in that the extremity of the withdrawal [*retranchement*] is immediately covered over, saturated, and guaranteed by the name of thought and by the formal mark of reasoning (*therefore*, I am). But the 'concept' of this name and its demonstrative 'reason' reside in fact . . . in their impossible articulation"; Nancy, "*Ego Sum*, 83; Nancy's emphasis.

21. It is tempting, of course, to read in this early use of the word *dis-enclosure* an anticipation of Nancy's much later work on Christian theology: *Dis-Enclosure: The Deconstruction of Christianity*, trans. Bettina Bergo, Gabriel Malenfant, and Michael B. Smith (2005; repr. New York: Fordham University Press, 2008); and *Adoration: The Deconstruction of Christianity II*, trans. John McKean (2010; repr. New York: Fordham University Press, 2013), a temptation at least somewhat justified by the "pro deo" revealed here to underlie Cartesian discourse. Emmanuel Martineau's translation of Rudolph Boehm's *Entdeckung* (*La métaphysique d'Aristote, le fundamental et l'essentiel* [Paris: Gallimard, 1976]) as disenclosure is well noted, but nowhere do I claim Nancy's invention of this term, only that it appears much earlier on (ES, 1979) than in its full-blown deployment in *Dis-Enclosure: The Deconstruction of Christianity*.

22. The intrusion of purity here reflects again the meaning of *mundus*, as Nancy explains it: "This is no word play. It is the same word, *mundus*, pure, clean, proper, well-disposed, well-ordered world. This is what, according to Plutarch, Pythagoras meant by the word *kosmos*. The world is nice arrangement, clear, clean, pure, and proper. The world is that which is not impure [*immonde*]" (ES, 66–67).

23. Cf. Nancy, *Sense of the World*, 156: "Without this coming toward the world that the world in turn spatializes, an 'ego' purely present there would not properly speaking be (this is what Descartes cannot see) or it would be immediately all of given sense (and this is what philosophy desires from Descartes to Husserl)."

24. See Antonia Birnbaum, "To Exist Is to Exit a Point," in Nancy, *Corpus*, trans. Richard A. Rand (1992; repr. New York: Fordham University Press, 2008), 145–49.

25. And much more recently, in *An All-Too-Human Virus*, trans. Cory Stockwell, David Fernbach, and Sarah Clift (2020; repr. New York: Fordham University Press, 2021), Nancy with reference to Descartes returns to the uncertainty of experience itself:

> Every experience is the experience of an uncertainty. Certitude, knowledge assured in itself and by itself, forms the distinctive mark of Cartesian truth. Far from being exclusively French, this certitude orders all our representations of knowledge: scientific, technological, societal, political and nearly cultural. It is thus the entire order of our assurances and confidence that is put to the test. For this reason, we truly undergo an experience: we are pushed outside of our programming. . . . To undergo an experience is always to be lost. One loses one mastery. In a sense, one is never truly the subject of one's experience. Rather, experience is what foments a new subject (78–79).

26. See *Corpus*, 131, where Nancy completes this rethinking of Descartes: "For Descartes, thought is sensing, and as sensing, it touches upon the extended thing, it's touching extension. . . . for Descartes, the *res cogitans* is a body."

27. The critique of any historical concept of "man" pursued by Nancy in the closing pages of *Ego Sum* also reveals his intervention within the famous polemics between Derrida and Foucault regarding the latter's argument that Descartes's rejection of the possibility of his being mad also inaugurates a certain idea of "man" whose legacy lies in the subsequent development of the human sciences. See Michel Foucault, *History of Madness*, ed. Jean Khalfa, trans. Jonathan Murphy (1961; repr. New York: Routledge; 2006); the only complete English translation of Foucault's *Folie et déraison: Histoire de le folie à l'âge classique* (Paris: Plon, 1961); and Jacques Derrida, "Cogito and the History of Madness," in *Writing and Difference*, trans. Alan Bass (London and New York: Routledge, 1978), 36–76.

28. On this mouth without a face, see Sara Guyer, "Buccality, in *Derrida, Deleuze, Psychoanalysis*, ed. Gabriele M. Schwab (New York: Columbia University Press, 2007), 77–104; and Derrida, *On Touching—Jean-Luc Nancy*, 20–25.

29. Or are we giving too much credit to the mouth as the privileged opening of the body and the areality of the space between, or as body and soul, but why not the vagina, for instance, the very locus of birth as the spacing of bodies, of the human being as "that which spaces itself out, and which perhaps only ever dwells in this spacing" (ES 112), as the very locus of our birth to presence in the particular "being with" of mother and child? Or we could go even further, imaging a kind of vaginal mouth, as in Magritte's famous painting of a face with the features of a naked woman, where breasts stand in the place of eyes and a vagina for a mouth. Might we pursue *unum quid*'s "convulsion of thought" as orgasm or ecstasy, as the non-*sum* of passionate being with one another? Or, alternatively as the violence of violation and intrusion?

30. The rapprochement between thinking and sensing might occasion a rereading of Pierre Gassendi's defense of sense-based knowledge and concomitant critique of the mind-body split as well as Descartes's response in the "Fifth Set of Objections" to the *Meditations* (CSM II:179–277; AT VII:256–412).

31. The French word *dérober* means to steal or rob, but Nancy in this passage and in others also plays upon the buried sense of disrobement, hence my translating it variously as to strip or take away.

32. Nancy, "Finite Thinking," trans. Edward Bullard, Jonathan Derbyshire, and Simon Sparks, in *A Finite Thinking*, ed. Simon Sparks (1990; repr. Stanford, Calif.: Stanford University Press, 2003), 31.

33. Nancy, *Le poids d'une pensée, l'approche* (Strasbourg: Le Phocide, 2008), 13.

34. One can see Nancy's conceptualization of what thinking is as a radicalization of Heidegger's notion of *gelassenheit*; Heidegger, *What Is Called Thinking?*, trans. J. Glenn Gray (New York: Harper and Row, 1968). For Nancy, it is not just a question of being "open" but of thought "always surprised by its own freedom"; *A Finite Thinking*, 15.

35. Birnbaum, "To Exist Is to Exit a Point," 149.

2. Monograms: Writing Singular Plural

1. Nancy, *Monogrammes I*, *Digraphe* 20 (1979): 131–37; *Monogrammes II*, *Digraphe* 21 (1979): 133–38; *Monogrammes III*, *Digraphe* 22–23 (1980): 221–29; *Monogrammes IV*, *Digraphe* 24 (1980): 131–40; *Monogrammes V*, *Digraphe* 25 (1980): 199–208. Based on the short length of these texts, citations from these and all subsequent *Monogrammes* will include the series number but not specific page numbers. All translations are by Georges Van Den Abbeele.

2. Nancy, *Monogrammes VI*, *Futur Antérieur* 10, no. 2 (1992); *Monogrammes VII*, *Futur Antérieur* 11, no. 3 (1992); *Monogrammes VIII*, *Futur Antérieur* 12–13, no. 4–5 (1992); *Monogrammes IX*, *Futur Antérieur* 14, no. 6 (1992); *Monogrammes X*, *Futur Antérieur* 15, no. 1 (1993); *Monogrammes XI*, *Futur Antérieur* 16, no. 2 (1993): 141–44; *Monogrammes XII*, *Futur Antérieur* 17, no. 3 (1993); *Monogrammes XIII*, *Futur Antérieur* 18, no. 4 (1993); *Monogrammes XIV*, *Futur Antérieur* 19–20, no. 5–6 (1993). All translations are by Georges Van Den Abbeele.

3. Nancy, *L'Impossible: Monogrammes* XV, XVI, and XVII, published respectively in *L'Impossible* 10 (February 2013), 12 (April 2013), and 13 (Summer 2013).

4. Nancy, *Philosophical Chronicles*, trans. Franson Manjali (2004; repr. New York: Fordham University Press, 2008); *After Fukushima: The Equivalence of Catastrophes*, trans. Charlotte Mandell (2012; repr. New York: Fordham University Press, 2015); *The Fragile Skin of the World*, trans. Cory Stockwell (2020; repr. New York: Fordham University Press, 2021); *An All-Too-Human Virus*, trans. Cory Stockwell, David Fernbach, and Sarah Clift (2020; New York: Fordham University Press, 2021); *Mascarons de Macron* (Paris: Galilée, 2021).

5. The website address is https://www.multitudes.net/author/Nancy-Jean-Luc/. When accessed December 26, 2021, the link for *Monogrammes* X, *Futur Antérieur* 15,

no. 1 (1993), was no longer functioning; and the link for *Monogrammes* XI, *Futur Antérieur* 16, no. 2 (1993): 141–44 was missing entirely. All other links were still viable as of this date.

6. The French word *actualité*, as used by Nancy, presents a number of challenges in translation. *Actualité* in common French designates what is current, recent, or happening now, as in the plural form, *actualités*, which is the French term for news or current events. It thus has an overridingly temporal significance. At the same time, *actualité* is the technical French translation for German *Wirklichkeit* [English, actuality], in the Hegelian philosophical sense, to describe the unity of essence and appearance. The *actual* is thus to be distinguished from the real or mere existence (*Dasein*) insofar its essence is objectively revealed, or "actualized," by self-conscious thought, leading to his famous dictum that "the actual is the rational and the rational is the actual." Nancy in his *Monogrammes* moves between the differing though not entirely contradictory meanings of the term, which I am thus sometimes obliged to translate as "current" situation, current events, currentness, timeliness, etc., and sometimes as "actual." In many cases, I am stuck using the neologistic expression "actuality" to refer to what is in fact both "current" and *wirklich*. Clearly, a sustained analysis of the "actual" in Nancy remains to be done, but that is beyond the scope of the present work.

7. "The real question is philosophical: all duplicity set aside, to *take on the figure* of the philosopher [*faire figure de philosophe*], *to pass oneself* off as a philosopher [*se donner pour philosophe*], that is to give (produce, present, take) philosophy as that which can take on a *figure*, and as a figure which henceforth can *speak*, and which in speaking, can *announce* a given truth whose announcement is, precisely, sanctioned by the voice and the figure of a philosopher—this comes down to a misunderstanding of philosophy. It is to misunderstand, in effect, with a dizzying ignorance and carelessness, that which makes for the very question of philosophy, at least since Kant and Hegel (since the *double bind* of metaphysics in Kant and Hegel): the possibility, or rather the (im)possibility that it *presents itself*, that it takes on a *figure*"; Nancy, *Monogrammes I*.

8. The question of the monogram as "out-line," contour, or de-lineation demands a critical comparison with what Jacques Derrida calls the "parergon," in Derrida, *The Truth in Painting*, trans. Geoff Bennington and Ian McLeod (1978; repr. Chicago: University of Chicago Press, 1987).

9. The text appears in Nancy's collective volume *Sur l'ex-Yougoslavie, Actes de la journée du 6 mars 1993* (Paris: Collège International de Philosophie, 1993).

10. Here again, the reference to Jean-François Lyotard's *The Postmodern Condition*, trans. Geoff Bennington and Brian Massumi (Minneapolis: University of Minnesota Press, 1979), imposes itself, most notably in Lyotard's discussion of the role of performance as the pervasive criterion of legitimation under postmodern conditions.

11. Nancy, *All-Too-Human Virus*, 110.

12. "As soon as one attempts to find, to produce and, in the first place, to posit and to thematize the non-given conjunction of power and sense (what we shall call

'democracy'), politics at once gets defined as that which has still not taken place but rather demands its place at the point where the disjunction between power and sense reigns. It is, therefore, not so much utopia that is first of all political, but, rather, it is politics that is always utopian"; Nancy, "In Place of Utopia," trans. Patricia Viera and Michael Marder, in *Existential Utopia: New Perspectives on Utopian Thought*, ed. Patricia Viera and Michael Marder (New York: Continuum, 2012), 8; translation modified. The text was first published in French as "Au lieu de l'utopie," in *Les utopies et leurs représentations: Colloque franco-japonais, Tokyo, 2000* (Paris: Le Quartier, 2002). On the proposed notion of "exonomy," Nancy writes, "We will not oppose autonomy with heteronomy, with which it forms a pair. Being heteronomous toward another subject that is itself autonomous changes nothing, regardless of whether this other autonomous thing is named God, the market, technics, or life. But, in order to open a new path, we could try out the word *exonomy*. The word would evoke a law that would not be the law of the same or of the other, but one that would be unappropriable by either the same or the other. Just as *exogamy* goes outside of kinship, *exonomy* moves out of the binary familiarity of the self and the other"; Nancy, *Philosophical Chronicles*, 9–10.

13. Immanuel Kant, *Critique of Pure Reason*, trans., ed. Paul Guyer and Alan Wood (Cambridge: Cambridge University Press, 1999), 272.

14. Karl Wilhelm Friedrich von Schlegel, *Athenaeum Fragmenten*, in *L'absolu littéraire*, ed. Jean-Luc Nancy and Philippe Lacoue-Labarthe (Paris: Seuil, 1978).

15. The exact citation reads as follows: "Die Eule der Minerva beginnt erst mit der einbrechenden Dämmerung ihren Flug" [The owl of Minerva begins its flight only when twilight falls]; Georg Wilhelm Friedrich Hegel, "Vorrede," in *Grundlinien der Philosophie des Rechts* (Leipzig: Felix Meiner, 1911), 17 (my translation).

16. One might compare Montaigne's lonely castle and redoubt, on the one hand, and Descartes's sense of beneficent isolation in the very heart of urban Amsterdam, on the other ("amidst a great and populous nation, extremely industrious and more concerned with their own business than curious about other people's, while I do not lack any conveniences of the most frequented cities, I have been able to live a life as solitary and retired as though I were in the most remote deserts"); René Descartes, *Discourse on Method*, CSM I:126. These and other examples are the subject for a forthcoming work.

17. Heidegger glosses this line to read, "The schemata of the pure concepts of the understanding 'determine' time," which follows from his inference that "time is the schema-image and not just the form of intuition which stands over and against the pure concepts of the understanding"; Martin Heidegger, *Kant and the Problem of Metaphysics*, trans. Richard Taft (Bloomington: Indiana University Press, 1997), 73–74; also see Nancy's invaluable commentary on Heidegger's reading of Kant in *The Ground of the Image*, admirably translated by Jeff Fort (New York: Fordham University Press, 2005), 80–99).

18. "Each single one of the memories and expectations in which the libido is bound to the [lost] object is brought up and hyper-cathected, and detachment of the

libido is accomplished in respect of it"; Sigmund Freud, "Mourning and Melancholia," trans. Richard Strachey, in *The Standard Edition of the Complete Psychological Works of Sigmund Freud* (London: Norton, 1976), XIV:244.

19. Mary McCarthy, *Birds of America* (New York: Harcourt Brace Jovanovich, 1965). Among other instances: "From his present vantage point, he could confirm that he had been living not just in a fairy tale but in a paradise, in which his love for his mother coincided with his love of Nature" (30); "With her light-brown hair and gray eyes and rosy skin, his mother was like an American bird—the rose-breasted grosbeak, for instance."

20. William Shakespeare, *Hamlet* (I.ii.65).

21. On the question of the "future of philosophy," Nancy writes, "Philosophizing always turns itself towards the 'to-come' (*avenir*) of philosophy. But this coming is not exactly a future. A future is predictable, calculable, appreciable or imaginable. A 'coming' is incalculable and inappreciable. In a sense, philosophy is always, in essence, 'to-come.' It is not ever given, never already done or befallen. It always begins, as the essential beginning of an inchoate thinking that knows itself as such"; In B. C. Hutchens, *Jean-Luc Nancy and the Future of Philosophy* (Montreal: McGill-Queens University Press, 2005), 162.

22. On this "foresight" of the schema, see Nancy's remarks in *The Ground of the Image* on Heidegger's deployment of the word *Vorbild* in connection with his reading of Kant: "the *Vorbild* (fore-image) or the model of a 'being that is yet to be created or produced.' . . . a model of the fore-vision of the unity that anticipates itself in the precession of its own succession: time as a series of time, which forms the first of the schemata." (95).

23. Jean-Luc Nancy, *Dis-Enclosure: The Deconstruction of Christianity*, trans. Bettina Bergo, Gabriel Malenfant, and Michael B. Smith (2005; repr. New York: Fordham University Press, 2008), 6.

24. Ibid., 11.

25. Ibid., 12.

26. *Philosophical Chronicles*. All citations to follow are from the first lecture, pp. 1–3.

27. Nancy, *After Fukushima; The Fragile Skin of the World; An All-Too-Human Virus; Mascarons de Macron*.

3. The "Singular Logic of the Retreat": Interruptions of the Political

1. Martin Heidegger, *Being and Time*, trans. Joan Stambaugh (Albany: SUNY Press, 1996), 110–22. "Being-with is also a version of what Irving Goh has variously termed prepositional sense or prepositional existence"; Goh, ed., "The Prepositional Senses of Jean-Luc Nancy (1)," *Diacritics* 42, no. 2 (2014); and Goh, *L'existence prépositionnelle* (Paris: Galilée, 2019).

2. Jean-Luc Nancy, *Ego Sum: Corpus, Anima, Fabula*, trans. Marie-Eve Morin (1979; repr. New York: Fordham University Press, 2016).

3. Nancy, *The Inoperative Community*, trans. Peter Connor (1983; repr. Minneapolis: University of Minnesota Press, 1991); and *Being Singular Plural*, trans. Robert D. Richardson and Anne E. O'Byrne. (1996; repr. Stanford, Calif.: Stanford University Press, 2000).

4. Jacques Derrida, "The *Retrait* of Metaphor," trans. Peggy Kamuf, in *Psyche: Inventions of the Other*, ed. Peggy Kamuf and Elizabeth Rottenberg (Stanford, Calif.: Stanford University Press, 2007), 1:48–80.

5. See especially Philip Armstrong, *Reticulations: Jean-Luc Nancy and the Networks of the Political* (Minneapolis: University of Minnesota Press, 2009); Pierre-Philippe Jandin, *Jean-Luc Nancy: Retracer le politique* (Paris: Michalon, 2012); Oliver Marchart, *Post-Foundational Political Thought: Political Difference in Nancy, Lefort, Badiou and Laclau* (Edinburgh: Edinburgh University Press, 2007); Marie-Eve Morin, *Jean-Luc Nancy* (Cambridge: Polity, 2012); Frédérique Neyrat, "No/us: The Nietzschean Democracy of Jean-Luc Nancy," *Diacritics* 43, no. 4 (2015): 67–72.

6. Among many other instances and by no means suggestive of an exhaustive inventory, one can track the vicissitudes of retreat/withdrawal all across Nancy's work: in *The Inoperative Community*, "community necessarily takes place in what Blanchot has called "unworking"[*désoeuvrement*], referring to that which, before or beyond the work, withdraws from the work, and which, no longer having to do either with production or with completion, encounters interruption, fragmentation, suspension. Community is made of the interruption of singularities, or of the suspension that singular beings *are*" (IC 31); "Unworking takes place in the communication of this withdrawal of singularity on the very limit where singularity communicates itself as exemplary, on the limit where it makes *and* unmakes its own figure and its own example" (IC 79; also 58, 70, 78). *L'oubli de la philosophie* (Paris: Galilée, 1986): "that withdrawal of sense by which sense arrives" (108; also 84, 99).

The Experience of Freedom, trans. Bridget McDonald (1988; repr. Stanford, Calif.: Stanford University Press, 1993), 92: "Freedom is the withdrawal of being, whose existence founds itself"; 128: "In evil the existent withdraws existence into the abyss of being—pure immanence or pure transcendence—instead of letting being withdraw into the existentiality of existence"; 140: "Now decision, as singularly existing and as engaging relation and sharing, engages the withdrawal of being. If decision keeps itself as decision, it also keeps being in its withdrawal, as withdrawn. . . . What is thus saved is the finitude of being. . . . Finitude is what, in singularity and as singularity, withdraws from the infinite grasp, from the molar expansion and furious devastation, of an ego-ity of being. Being withdraws into finitude." Also, 33, 41–42, 57, 59, 84–85, 103, 105, 139, 167, 184–85n, 193n.

Being Singular Plural, 47: "The retreat of the political and the religious, or of the theologico-political, means the retreat of every space, form, or screen into which or onto which a figure of community could be projected. . . . The retreat presents itself in two ways at once: on the one hand, the theologico-political withdraws into the realm of law; on the other, it withdraws into a self-representation that no longer refers to an origin, but only to the void of its own specularity"; 80: "'Love' is the abyss of the self in itself; it is the 'delectation' or 'taking care' of what originally escapes or is lacking; it consists in taking care of this retreat and in this retreat. As a result, this love is 'charity': it is the consideration of the *caritas*, of the cost or the extreme, absolute, and, therefore, inestimable value of the other as other, that is, the other as the self-withdrawn-in-itself. This love speaks of the infinite cost of what is infinitely withdrawn: the incommensurability of the other." Also, 6, 37.

Corpus, 119: "Each sense senses *and* senses itself sensing, each on its own with no overarching control, each one withdrawn, as sight, as hearing, as taste, smell, touch, each delighting and knowing that it delights in the absolute apartness of its delight."

The Sense of the World, trans. Jeffrey S. Librett (1993; repr. Minneapolis: University of Minnesota Press, 1997), 73: "the world as a world of examples, as a world of the withdrawal of singularities in their very exposition." "*Un jour, les dieux se retirent . . .*" (Paris: William Blake 2001), 8: "Truth and narration thus separate. Their separation is traced by the very trait that is upon the retreat of the gods." *The Inoperative Community*, trans. Peter Connor (1983; repr. Minneapolis: University of Minneapolis Press, 1991), 143: "It is with the withdrawal of the gods that community came into being"; also 10, 110, 114, 115, 118, 120, 122–43.

La pensée dérobée (Paris: Galilée, 2001), 15: "How to be born and die here and now? Or else: how to be naked? What then is the presence of nakedness? Is it not a presence essentially exceeding and withdrawing from [*en excès et en retrait de*] its present and its presentation?" *The Birth to Presence*, trans. Brian Holmes et al. (Stanford, Calif.: Stanford University Press, 1993), 6 and 141: "What I have called 'political jurisdiction' requires, from the very center of and by the avowal of the philosophical thought of the political, an essential *withdrawal* of the Political as subject and as organicity. A withdrawal which responds to relation, which brings relation back everywhere in 'union'—which 'desocializes,' one might try to say, organic sociality, and which 'depoliticizes' the political subject."

The Creation of the World, or Globalization, trans. François Raffoul and David Pettigrew (2002; repr. Albany: SUNY Press, 2007), 40: "It is not an accident if, since Marx, the 'world' and the 'worldly" have remained uncertain determinations, overly suspended between the finite and the infinite, between a new and former world, between this world and an other: in short, one may assume that the 'world' has fallen short [*resté en retrait*] of what it should be, of what it can be, perhaps of what it already is, in some way that we have not yet determined."

The Truth of Democracy, trans. Pascale-Anne Brault and Michael Nass (2008; repr. New York: Fordham Univeristy Press), 32: "Democratic politics is thus a politics that withdraws from making assumptions" [*en retrait d'assomption*].

7. Walter Benjamin, "The Task of the Translator," in *Illuminations*, trans. Harry Zohn (New York: Schocken, 1968), 69–82; Philip E. Lewis, "Vers la traduction abusive," in *Les fins de l'homme: À partir du travail de Jacques Derrida*, ed. Philippe Lacoue-Labarthe and Jean-Luc Nancy (Paris: Galilée, 1981), 253–61. A modified translation of this text appears as "The Measure of Translation Effects," in *Difference*

in Translation, ed. Joseph F. Graham (Ithaca: Cornell University Press, 1985), 31–62. Also see V. N. Volosinov's persuasive remarks on the inherent foreignness of language in *Marxism and the Philosophy of Language*, trans. Ladislav Matejka and I. R. Titunik (Cambridge, Mass.: Harvard University Press, 1973), especially 73–79.

8. Nancy, "Hyperion's Joy," trans. Christine Laennec and Michael Syrotinski, in *Birth to Presence*, 68.

9. Sigmund Freud, *Beyond the Pleasure Principle*, in *The Standard Edition of the Complete Psychological Works*, trans. James Strachey (London: Hogarth, 1953–74), 18:1–64. All further references to Freud will be to this edition and will be indicated by the initials "SE" followed by volume and page numbers. References to the German text of Freud will be to *Gesammelte Werke* (London: Imago, 1940–52), and will be similarly indicated by the initials GS followed by volume and page number. On the child's game of fort/da, see Jacques Derrida, *The Postcard*, trans. Alan Bass (Chicago: University of Chicago Press, 1980).

10. Philippe Lacoue-Labarthe and Jean-Luc Nancy, "Le peuple juif ne rêve pas," in *La panique politique* (Paris: Christian Bourgois, 2013), 72. The volume reprints this essay (read at the 1980 colloquium at Montpellier, "La psychanalyse est-elle une histoire juive?"), along with its companion piece, "La panique politique," originally published in *Cahiers confrontations* 2 (1979): 33–57. Both essays also appeared together in German in the March 1989 issue of the journal *Frag-Mente*: 29–30. An English translation of "La panique politique," but without its companion piece appears in Philippe Lacoue-Labarthe and Jean-Luc Nancy, *Retreating the Political*, ed. Simon Sparks, trans. Céline Surprenant, Simon Sparks, Richard Stamp, and Leslie Hill (Oxon: Routledge, 1997), 1–31. Sparks has carried out an inestimable service by putting together this edited volume, which collects and translates much of the relevant work by Nancy and Lacoue-Labarthe, including their joint as well as individual contributions to Nancy and Lacoue-Labarthe, eds., *Les fins de l'homme: À partir du travail de Jacques Derrida* (Paris: Galilée, 1981), *and* their jointly edited volumes, *Rejouer le politique* (Paris: Galilée, 1981), and *Le retrait du politique* (Paris: Galilée, 1983), as well as a number of other texts and documents relative to the establishment of the Centre de recherches philosophiques sur le politique.

11. Jacques Derrida, "Pas," *Gramma*, no. 3/4 (1976): 111–215.

12. Derrida, *"Retrait* of Metaphor," 1:80.

13. The un-forgetting of being (*Unverborgenheit, aletheia*) that Heidegger figures as truth also defines the closure of Western metaphysics, whose history "would be a vast structural process where the *epochè* of Being withholding itself, holding itself in withdrawal [*en retrait*], would take or rather *would present* an (interlaced) series of guises, turns, modes, that is to say, of figures or tropical movements that we might be *tempted* to describe with the aid of rhetorical conceptuality"; Derrida, "The *Retrait* of Metaphor," trans. Peggy Kamuf, in *Psyche: Inventions of the Other*, ed. Peggy Kamuf and Elizabeth Rottenberg (Stanford, Calif.: Stanford University Press, 2007),1:65 (Derrida's emphasis). Metaphysics "would correspond to an essential *withdrawing*

[*retrait*] of Being: unable to reveal itself, to present itself except by dissimulating itself. . . . Being does not let itself be named except through a metaphorico-metonymical divergence" (1: 65; Derrida's emphasis). Derrida carefully describes this "temptation" in the conditional mode, since despite the evident figuration that attends the withdrawal of Being, its apparent metaphoricity, none of this can be described as *stricto senso* metaphorical or even figural: "Being being nothing, not being a being, it cannot be expressed or named *more metaphorico*. And therefore it does not have, in the context of the dominant metaphysical usage of the word 'metaphor,' a proper or literal meaning that could be intended metaphorically by metaphysics" (1:65–66). It can be spoken of "only *quasi*-metaphorically, according to a metaphor of metaphor, with the overload of a supplementary trait, a re-trait" (1:66).

14. Derrida, *"Retrait* of Metaphor," 1:70; Martin Heidegger, "Letter on Humanism," in *Basic Writings*, trans. David Farrel Krell (New York: Harper and Row, 1977), 213.

15. Martin Heidegger, "The Nature of Language," in *On the Way to Language*, trans. Peter D. Hertz (San Francisco: Harper and Row, 1971), 81–82.

16. Derrida, "Le retrait de l'apocalypse," radio interview, Montreal 1983. A tape recording exists in the Critical Theory Archives at UC Irvine, box 40, folder 2.

17. "Annexe," in Lacoue-Labarthe and Nancy, *Retreating the Political*, 138–40.

18. Jacques Rancière, "La représentation de l'ouvrier ou la classe introuvable," in Nancy and Lacouse-Labarthe, *Le Retrait du politique*, 89–111.

19. Cf. Nancy, "The Jurisdiction of the Hegelian Monarch," trans. Mary Ann and Peter Caws, in Nancy, *The Birth to Presence* (Stanford, Calif.: Stanford University Press), 110–42.

20. Michel Henry, *Marx: A Philosophy of Human Reality*, trans. Kathleen McLaughlin (Bloomington: Indiana University Press, 1983).

21. Sigmund Freud, "The Theme of The Three Caskets," in SE 12:289–302.

22. Hannah Arendt, *The Origins of Totalitarianism*, rev. ed. (New York: Houghton Mifflin, 1968), especially 437–59; and *The Human Condition*, 2nd ed. (Chicago: University of Chicago Press, 1958), 320–25 and *passim*. One should note in this context Nancy's spirited rejection of the trope that "everything is political," in *The Truth of Democracy*, trans. Pascale-Anne Brault and Michael Naas (2008; repr. New York: Fordham University Press, 2010), 45–51.

23. While Heidegger's name is inserted here, one might also exhibit some skepticism here given more recently revealed works, such as the so-called *Black Notebooks*, translated by Richard Rojcewicz under the title *Ponderings* (Boomington: Indiana University Press), with three volumes so far published in 2016 and 2017.

24. Jean-François Lyotard, "A l'insu (Unbeknownst)," trans. Georges Van Den Abbeele, in *Community at Loose Ends*, ed. Miami Theory Collective (Minneapolis: University of Minnesota Press, 1991), 42–48.

25. Christopher Fynsk, "Contribution 1," Political Seminar, in *Les fins de l'homme: À partir du travail de Jacques Derrida* (Paris: Galilée, 1981), 487–93. This talk and Lacoue-Labarthe's response appear in English translation in Lacoue-Labarthe and

Nancy, *Retreating the Political*, 87–99. It should be noted, nonetheless, that the subsequent development of a more overtly political thinking after Cerisy and with the establishment of the Center did not diminish the critique of "deconstructive politics" and its presumed Heideggerian foundations, most notably Nancy Fraser, "The French Derrideans: Politicizing Deconstruction or Deconstructing the Political?," *New German Critique* 33, no. 3 (1984): 127–54; and Simon Critchley, "Re-tracing the Political: Politics and Community in the Work of Philippe Lacoue-Labarthe and Jean-Luc Nancy," in *The Political Subject of Violence*, ed. David Campbell and Michael Dillon (Manchester: Manchester University Press, 1999), 73–93. Also see, responses to these critiques by Ian James, *The Fragmentary Demand: An Introduction to the Philosophy of Jean-Luc Nancy* (Stanford, Calif.: Stanford University Press, 2006), 168–73; and Morin, *Jean-Luc Nancy*, 102.

26. Derrida, *Specters of Marx*, trans. Peggy Kamuf (New York: Routledge, 1994), and *Politics of Friendship*, trans. George Collins (London: Verso, 1997), appear to suggest a more political turn in his writing, although one can also readily find the seeds of this "turn" even in his earliest works.

27. See Simon Sparks' remarks on the "political" dimension of Derrida's essay in Lacoue-Labarthe and Nancy, *Retreating the Political*, xviii–xix.

28. One might compare these comments once again with Nancy's resolute critique of the trope that "everything is political," in Nancy, *Truth of Democracy*, 45–51.

29. "Opening address," Lacoue-Labarthe and Nancy, *Retreating the Political*, 107.

30. Lacoue-Labarthe, "In the name of . . . ," in Lacoue-Labarthe and Nancy, *Retreating the Political*, 71.

31. Note the symmetry of terms between *the* philosophical and *the* political, which themselves contrast with the terms "philosophy" and "politics," to form a complex homology that exceeds the apparent and oft-discussed distinction between politics and the political, or to respect the more minimal distinction in French between *la politique* and *le politique*. Much has been written on this celebrated distinction dating to Carl Schmidt, and I will not rehearse the particulars here, but refer to the detailed and insightful discussions to be found in Paul Ricoeur, "The Political Paradox," in *History and Truth*, trans. David M. Rasmussen (1965; repr. Evanston, Ill.: Northwestern University Press, 2007); Jacques Rancière, *On the Shores of Politics*, trans. Liz Heron (London: Verso, 1995); Oliver Marchart, *Post-Foundational Political Thought: Political Difference in Nancy, Lefort, Badiou and Laclau* (Edinburgh: Edinburgh University Press, 2007); Chantal Mouffe, *The Return of the Political* (London: Verso, 1993), and *On the Political* (London: Routledge, 2005); Emily Apter, *Unexceptional Politics: On Obstruction, Impasse, and the Impolitic* (London: Verso, 2019). And one should note Nancy's later skepticism about the efforts to distinguish between *le* and *la politique*, the political and politics: "A seemingly incurable schizophrenia affects the use of the word. It only conveys the fact that the thing itself can no longer know what it is nor what it should and can do"; Nancy, *Doing*, trans. Charlotte Mandell (2016; repr. London: Seagull, 2020), 13–14.

But within this context of *la politique* vs. *le politique*, I also note the apparent lack of symmetry with *la philosophie* and *le philosophique*. Doubling the complexity of discussions regarding politics and the political by a paired set of *philosophic* terms does not fail to arouse some confusion and skepticism, even among the most ardent participants of the Center's monthly meetings. During one of the Center's very last recorded sessions, Denis Kambouchner, among others, still remarks that the distinction between the philosophical and philosophy "seems scarcely more convincing than the distinction between the political and politics"; Lacoue-Labarthe and Nancy, *Retreating the Political*, 136. In some sense, the distinctions seem to track out a difference between an institution and the ostensible concerns that would underlie that institution. Indeed, the model of politics with which we've become most familiar since the late '70s as the reigning neoliberalism features a simultaneous reduction of politics to spectacle while (de)concealing power relations as mere management and bureaucratic efficiency. This model then buries or represses deep social divisions as irrelevant in a market-driven world, thus *withdrawing* or brushing away the very ground, the very specificity, the very sense of the political in its antagonistic energy.

Similarly, a line seems to be drawn between philosophy as an institutionalized discipline with its set of protocols (literature, traditions) for thinking and, on the other hand, the philosophical as "a general historico-systematic structure," which is "actually the same thing as metaphysics" but by another name. That other name is deployed specifically "to put to one side" the "apparent simplicity" or "homogenization" of the term's delimitation, even as elaborated by the likes of Kant or Heidegger—that is, "to try to escape" what is in effect "an entire code" and "an entire language" built around the word "metaphysics." Thus, "the philosophical designates a "general historico-systematic structure—which, up until recently, one could have called the West—of which philosophy is each time the thematization, the prefiguration or the anticipation, the reflection (critical or not), the contestation, etc., but which largely overflows the basically restricted field of operations of actual philosophizing"; Lacoue-Labarthe and Nancy, *Retreating the Political*, 124. Other possible concepts or "quasi-concepts" could also have been used to name what they are calling the "philosophical." Lacoue-Labarthe and Nancy list civilization, culture, ideology, mentality, representation, and symbolism, among others, but they are all rejected for being, like the term "metaphysics," already "heavily marked (philosophically)" and "having served in discourses or contexts so foreign or so barely attentive (when not outright hostile) to philosophical phenomena." These so-called "irrecuperable" terms not only evidence Lacoue-Labarthe and Nancy's general suspicion of regional sciences and the so-called social sciences in particular, but the terms themselves would fail to address the broader question of the relations between "the philosophical" and "the political," limited as they are by their ontic perspective. Thus, the insistence on "the philosophical" (as well, of course, as "the political") would seem to offer a more properly ontological analysis of the relations in question: philosophy/philosophical; philosophy/politics; politics/political; philosophical/political; etc.

But these distinctions are themselves slippery and unsure in some of Lacoue-Labarthe and Nancy's own explications, such as when by the use of the term "political," their avowed intent is "not to designate *politics*," such as that indicated by the examples "of the Chinese Emperors, the Benin kings, of Louis XIV or of German social democracy" only to offer then the rather unhelpful qualification that "even though in these last two examples politics and the political are not totally alien to each other"; Lacoue-Labarthe and Nancy, *Retreating the Political*, 125. It is not altogether clear what would distinguish the latter two from the others beyond their European context, but then the political, and for that matter, the philosophical, remain solely derivative of what might generally be called *Western* metaphysics but that would be either to toss the non-European into the irrelevance of so-called prehistory or to ignore that last half-millennium of massive cross-cultural encounters, colonization, and globalization have in effect brought the entire world into the problematic of Western metaphysics or "the philosophical."

32. Richard Terdiman, "On the Dialectics of Postdialectical Thinking," in *Community at Loose Ends*, ed. Miami Theory Collective (Minneapolis: University of Minnesota Press, 1991), 111–20.

33. Arendt, *Human Condition*, 320–25; *Origins of Totalitarianism*, 437–59.

34. One might compare this eerily prescient account of neoliberalism from the early 1980s to Wendy Brown's recent, more expansive work in *Undoing the Demos: Neoliberalism's Stealth Revolution* (New York: Zone, 2015); and *In the Ruins of Neoliberalism: The Rise of Antidemocratic Politics in the West* (New York: Columbia University Press, 2019).

35. One is also reminded of Walter Benjamin's famous distinction between the fascist "aestheticization of politics" and its corollary, the "politicization of aesthetics," in "The Work of Art in the Age of Mechanical Reproduction," in *Illuminations*, trans. Harry Zohn (New York: Schocken, 1968), 242.

36. Jean-François Lyotard, *The Postmodern Condition*, trans. Geoff Bennington and Brian Massumi (Minneapolis: University of Minnesota Press, 1984).

37. Georges Bataille, *The Accursed Share*, vol. 3 (New York: Zone, 1993). Also see Nancy's more ample discussion in *Being Singular Plural*, 36–37: "In one way or another, bare sovereignty (which is, in a way, to transcribe Bataille's notion of sovereignty) presupposes that one take a certain distance from the politico-philosophical order and from the realm of 'political philosophy.' The distance is not taken in order to engage in a depoliticized thinking, but in order to engage in a thinking, the site of which is the very constitution, imagination, and signification of the political, which allows this thinking to retrace its path in its retreat and beginning from this retreat. The retreat of the political does not signify the disappearance of the political. . . . The retreat of the political is the uncovering, the ontological laying bare of being-with."

38. "The political shows itself not within what one names political activity, but within that double movement apparition and occultation of the society's mode of

institution"; Claude Lefort, "La question de la démocratie," in Nancy and Lecoue-Labarthe, *Le retrait du politique*, 74.

39. Jean-François Lyotard, *Enthusiasm: The Kantian Critique of History*, trans. Georges Van Den Abbeele (Stanford, Calif.: Stanford University Press, 2009).

40. Jean-François Lyotard, *The Differend*, trans. Georges Van Den Abbeele (1983; repr. Minneapolis: University of Minnesota Press, 1988).

41. Jean-François Lyotard, "A l'insu (Unbeknownst)," 42–48; *Lectures d'enfance* (Paris: Galilée, 1991); *Postmodern Fables*, trans. Georges Van Den Abbeele (1994; repr. Minneapolis: University of Minnesota Press, 1997).

42. The question of antagonism as inherent to the political is most associated with the work of Ernest Laclau and Chantal Mouffe, *Hegemony and Socialist Strategy: Toward a Radical Democratic Politics* (London: Verso, 1985).

43. As far as I can tell, the term "desertion" never appears in any of the texts or discussions published by the Center, even though the word "dissociation" appears frequently. Perhaps, the word "desertion" and whatever it may imply occurred in informal or unrecorded ways during the Center's existence.

44. Nancy, *Experience of Freedom*, 84. Nancy's suggestion of the political as a set of "networks" is forcefully developed by Armstrong, *Reticulations*.

45. Nancy, *Expectation: Philosophy, Literature*, trans. Robert Bononno (2015; repr. New York: Fordham University Press, 2018).

46. *Dissociation and the Dissociative Disorders: DSM-V and Beyond*, ed. Paul F. Dell and John A. O'Neil (New York: Routledge, 2009). This massive, 900-page tome arose out of an attempt to write a "consensus definition of dissociation" (xix) in preparation for the fifth edition of the American Psychiatric Association's institutionally authoritative *Diagnostic and Statistical Manual of Mental Disorders*, which serves as the taxonomic benchmark for the profession's diagnosis and treatment of psychiatric conditions. Ironically, this attempt to establish a "consensus definition" instead chronicles the very impossibility of consensus. Write the editors in their preface, "We had known at the outset that the term *dissociation* was often used in a vague, overly broad fashion, but we never anticipated that we might be unable to agree upon a definition" (xix). The very vagueness and excessive breadth of the working definition they do finally propose itself points to the problem:

> The essential manifestation of pathological dissociation is a partial or complete disruption of the normal integration of a person's psychological functioning. Dissociative disruptions unexpectedly change the person's usual functioning in ways that the person cannot easily explain. Any aspect of a person's conscious, psychological functioning can be disrupted by dissociation. Specifically, dissociation can unexpectedly disrupt, alter, or intrude upon a person's consciousness and experience of body, world, self, mind, agency, intentionality, thinking, believing, knowing, recognizing, remembering, feeling, wanting, speaking, acting, seeing, hearing, smelling, tasting, touching, and so on. (xxi)

What, one might well ask, would not be a form of dissociation? And what conceivable distinction might one be able to establish between this "pathological" condition and what passes for normal "psychological functioning"? Indeed, it seems much more promising to follow Derrida's lead and to think dissociation as an originary "distension" of being there, as what makes for the very sense of space and time.

47. Freud, *Group Psychology and the Analysis of the Ego*, SE 18:105.

48. The question of the relationality of language, art, and sex (or *logos*, *tekhnè*, and *eros*) are explored by Nancy in a number of places, most notably in *Corpus II: Writings on Sexuality*, trans. Anno O'Byrne (New York: Fordham University Press, 2013; *Sexistence*, trans. Steven Miller (2017; repr. New York: Fordham University Press, 2021); *Immortelle finitude: Sexualité et philosophie*, with Mehdi Belhaj Kacem (Zurich, Paris, and Berlin: Diaphanes, 2020); and *The Deconstruction of Sex*, with Irving Goh (Durham, N.C.: Duke University Press, 2021). We will explore this nexus in Chapter 4.

49. Such a tradition, despite their differences, can be traced from Rosa Luxemburg through Anton Pannekoek, Antonio Gramsci, Henri de Man, Walter Benjamin, and Theodor Adorno, up to Louis Althusser. Tracking the vicissitudes of this tradition is the subject of a forthcoming study.

50. See the essays collected in Lacoue-Labarthe and Nancy, *La panique politique*; also Lacoue-Labarthe and Nancy, *Retreating the Political*, 1–31.

51. Julia Kristeva, "Maux d'amour," *Furor* 4 (1982): 3–22.

52. The obverse of this double emotional tie is the utter dissolution of the group in the moment of "panic" when all ties, horizontal as well as vertical, cease to work, and everyone is suddenly and terrifyingly on their own. As Freud writes in *Group Psychology*, "Anyone who describes a panic as one of the plainest functions of the 'group mind,' arrives at the paradoxical position that this group mind does away with itself in one of its most striking manifestations" (SE 18:97). This making and breaking of the tie is analyzed at length by Nancy and Lacoue-Labarthe in their essay on "La panique politique," 9–60, and Lacoue-Labarthe and Nancy, *Retreating the Political*, 1–31.

53. "We should consider whether . . . an idea, an abstraction, may not take the place of the leader (a state of things to which religious groups, with their invisible head, form a transitional stage), and whether a common tendency, a wish in which a number of people can have a share, may not in the same way serve as a substitute" (SE 18:100).

54. While Freud does acknowledge the need the consider "the different kinds of groups, more or less stable, that arise spontaneously" and that we should guard a "distinction between groups which have a leader and leaderless groups" (SE 18:100), he does not pursue such alternative group possibilities, and indeed his model of the "double tie" of both vertical and horizontal identification leaves little way to account for other collective formations. Spontaneism, on the other hand, has its own history as a political theory and practice, notably associated with the works of Rosa Luxemburg, especially *The Mass Strike* [1906], trans. Patrick Lawin, reprinted

in *Reform or Revolution, and Other Writings*, ed. Paul Buhle (Mineola, N.Y.: Dover, 2006), 101–80, and through the "Socialism ou Barbarie?" and Situationist movements and all the way up to Lyotard's *Enthusiasm*. Spontaneism, of course, drew the special ire of V. I. Lenin in *What Is to Be Done?* (1929; repr. Mineoloa, N.Y.: Dover, 1987).

55. This analysis of life-long dependency also recalls (or more correctly foresees) Lyotard's later concept of "infancy" in *Lectures d'enfance*.

56. The disappearance or "retreat" of the mother may also be a casualty of Nancy and Lacoue-Labarthe's stated move away from Freud, as they indicate without very much in the way of explanation in the "Opening Address" for the Center:

> It is not with Freud that we have pursued the exploration of this question. From this point, psychoanalysis leads back to the philosophical. In our most recent work, the question of the relation and of the retreat has been reformulated: for one of us [Lacoue-Labarthe] in a questioning, via Heidegger, of the retreat of the political in the problematic of the work of art; and for the other [Nancy] in an examination of what, building on Kant, I [who??] would call the ethical prescription of relation. But these are, in all essentials, works in progress, and this is not the right place to speak of them. (Lacoue-Labarthe and Nancy, *Retreating the Political*, 119, my interpolations)

Nancy's indicated project is recognizable as what would appear in 1983 as *L'impératif catégorique* (Paris: Flammarion). In a note preceding the republication of two essays from this period as *La panique politique*, Nancy—this time under his sole signature—also references how their "research moved away from Freud toward other motifs which had led to the still common creation, in 1981, of the *Center for Research on the Political*, whose works were published by Galilée"; Nancy and Lacoue-Labarthe, *Panique politique*, 7. On the other hand, the curious absence of the mother in Nancy's *Ego Sum* is also trenchantly addressed by Derrida in *On Touching—Jean-Luc Nancy*, trans. Christine Irizarry (2000; repr. Stanford, Calif.: Stanford University Press, 2005): "Isn't birth into the world the first ex-pulsion? The word 'mother' does not appear, despite Nancy's obvious, explicit reference to her (at the time of birth and nursing)" (28). As for the exclusively male membership of the Center, it should be noted that at least one prominent feminist thinker, Sarah Kofman, did attend the group's meetings but there is no record of her having presented, or even being asked to present, a contribution to the Center's research.

57. Derrida's *Politics of Friendship*, trans. George Collins (London: Verso, 1997), while not based in any specific contribution by him to the Center and not specifically addressing the friendship/collaboration between Nancy and Lacoue-Labarthe, does nonetheless offer itself "as a sign of gratitude, a modest and belated contribution to work that was important for my own" (137). In the headnote for *La panique politique*, Nancy refers to the writing of texts "in common" with the following assessment, which of course does little to clarify the specific contributions of each author without, for that matter, asserting an undifferentiated collaboration that would

reduce the two writers to a single functional author: "[These essays] were written on different occasions but thanks to a single research project conducted also in common within the context of university teaching. The editing was sometimes in common, sometimes separately, without it being possible to distinguish between them, even when (in the second text), the first person was used" (7). As Philip Armstrong astutely observes, while the Center's actual research production may have been brief and not all that impactful in and of itself, the resonances of its work in the ensuing theoretical work of its members is almost incalculable, most notably in the major works in the '80s and '90s by Lyotard, Lefort, Étienne Balibar, Jacques Rancière, and, of course, Derrida, as shown previously; Armstrong, *Reticulations*.

58. One can see the possible answers to this question as guiding much of contemporary debates over abortion and reproductive rights, especially in those iterations where it is a question either of prioritizing the mother or the child's right over her (or his?) "own" body.

59. "The Intruder," in *Corpus*, trans. Richard Rand (New York: Fordham, 2008), 166.

60. Freud, *Three Essays on Sexuality*, SE 7:191, 231–39; see also Norman O. Brown, *Love's Body* (New York: Vintage, 1966).

61. According to Lacoue-Labarthe and Nancy, Lyotard is said to have found this designation of the 'mother" as "risky" (Lacoue-Labarthe and Nancy, *Retreating the Political*, 133), although I can find no independent corroboration of any such statement by him. On the other hand, as already indicated, Lyotard would also subsequently develop a parallel line of thought from the side of the child in *Lectures d'enfance*.

62. Giorgio Agamben, *Homo Sacer: Sovereign Power and Bare Life*, trans. Daniel Heller-Roazen (Palo Alto, Calif.: Stanford University Press, 1998).

63. This understanding is also at the heart of Nancy's argument in *Truth of Democracy*.

64. Lyotard, "A l'insu (Unbeknownst)."

65. Martin Heidegger, *Introduction to Metaphysics*, trans. Gregory Fried and Richard Polt, 2nd rev. ed. (New Haven: Yale University Press, 2014), 163–68. Cf. Lacoue-Labarthe, "In the Name of . . . ," in Lacoue-Labarthe and Nancy, *Retreating the Political*, 72–74). The strange, uncanny confluence of Freud and Heidegger also beckons to Jacques Lacan's Seminar X on "anxiety." While acknowledging in *La panique politique* the value of "the entire work of Jacques Lacan" in articulating "a discourse woven from Freud, from Heidegger," Lacoue-Labarthe and Nancy do engage there the fraught question of the "distant proximity" between Freud and Heidegger in a passage that is worth quoting at length to the extent that it calls once again upon the "singular logic of the retreat":

> Freud and Heidegger's distant proximity is thus established around the only question which forms the *limit* of the entire metaphysical egology. It is the insurmountable solipsism, or perhaps one would have to say the *ipseism*, of

the thought of the Subject, which both Freud and Heidegger have in sight. But from then on the difficulty is so considerable that it doubtless explains both the reciprocal exclusion, at this very point, of psychoanalysis and of philosophy, and the interruption, in both Freud and Heidegger, of the (at least direct) questioning of this difficulty. . . .

What clearly poses a problem is that if it is indeed a question of a *limit*, a discourse can hold itself at this limit only by virtue of holding itself at the limit of discourse: henceforth, Freud and Heidegger's *retreat* on either side of this limit should not be considered as simply a failure. We do not have to occupy the space of a radical science with a more powerful discourse, whether this be called analysis or philosophy. We do not have to identify the limit of identification, nor to relinquish discourse either. . . . This space is thus clearly that of another politics, of another politics of discourse as well as of the rest; Lacoue-Labarthe and Nancy, *Retreating the Political*, 19–20.

4. Corpus interruptus: Uncommon Sense and the Singular Crossings of Eros, Logos, and Tekhnè

1. The key Nancy texts here will be *Corpus*, trans. Richard Rand (New York: Fordham University Press, 2008); *Corpus II: Writings on Sexuality*, trans. Anne O'Byrne (New York: Fordham University Press, 2013); *Corpus III: Cruor and Other Writings*, trans. Jeff Fort (New York: Fordham University Press, 2022); *Coming* (with Adèle Van Reeth), trans. Charlotte Mandell (2014; repr. New York: Fordham University Press, 2017); and *Sexistence*, trans. Steven Miller (2017; repr. New York: Fordham University Press, 2021); along with their precursor analyses in "Shattered Love," trans. Lisa Garbus and Simona Sawhney, in Nancy, *The Inoperative Community*, trans. Peter Connor (1983; repr. Minneapolis: University of Minnesota Press, 1991), 82–109; and *The Muses*, trans. Peggy Kamuf (1994; repr. Stanford, Calif.: Stanford University Press, 1996).

2. Francis Guibal, "Ouverture," in *Sens en tout sens*, ed. Francis Guibal and Jean-Clet Martin (Paris: Galilée, 2004), 9.

3. Alain Badiou, "L'offrande réservée," in Guibal and Martin, *Sens en tout sens*, 21; Catherine Malabou, "Pierre aime les horranges," in Guibal and Martin, *Sens en tout sens*, 39–57.

4. Nancy, *A Finite Thinking*, trans. Simon Sparks (1990; repr. Stanford, Calif.: Stanford University Press, 2003), 6.

5. Paul Valéry, *M. Teste*, trans. Jackson Matthews (Princeton: Princeton University Press, 1973), 21.

6. Gottlob Frege, "On *Sinn* and *Bedeutung*," in *The Frege Reader*, ed. Michael Beaney (Oxford: Blackwell, 1997), 151–71.

7. Nancy, *Corpus*, 119.

8. Aristotle, *On the Soul*, trans. J. A. Smith, in *The Complete Works of Aristotle*, ed. Jonathan Barnes (Princeton: Princeton University Press, 1984), II.676–78:425b, 25–30, 426b, 10–30.

9. Aristotle, *On the Soul*, II.679:427a, 16–20.

10. René Descartes, *Discourse on Method*, in CMS I:111. The slippage here between "good sense [*bon sens*]" and common sense signals the moment when the latter term begins to emerge as the sign of baseline human rationality per se rather than the more archaic sense of what would coordinate our perceptions from various senses into a subjective understanding of the world.

11. Nancy, "The 'There Is' of Sexual Relation," in *Corpus II*, 12.

12. Nancy, *Sexistence*, 108.

13. "The Birth of Breasts," in *Corpus II*, 48; trans. modified.

14. Ferdinand de Saussure, *Course in General Linguistics* (New York: McGraw-Hill, 1965), 113.

15. G. W. F. Hegel, *Phenomenology of Mind*, trans. J. B. Baillie (New York: Harper & Row, 1967), 153.

16. Hegel, *Phenomenology of Mind*, 160.

17. Nancy, *The Fragile Skin of the World*, trans. Cory Stockwell (2020; repr. New York: Fordham University Press, 2021).

18. With regard to such a deflation of the "supposedly" thick sense of the body down to the linearity of skin, one is reminded of Jean-François Lyotard's edgy opening chapter on "The Great Ephemeral Skin," in *Libidinal Economy*, trans. Iain Hamilton Grant (Bloomington: Indiana University Press, 1993), 1–6ff.

19. Nancy and Federico Ferrari, *Being Nude: The Skin of Images*, trans. Anne O'Byrne and Carlie Anglemire (2013; repr. New York: Fordham University Press, 2014).

20. Nancy, "Cosmos Basilius," in *The Creation of the World, or Globalization*, trans. François Raffoul and David Pettigrew (Albany: SUNY Press, 2007), 109–12. Also see Georges Van Den Abbeele, "*Fabula est Mundus*: On the Plurality of Fontenelle's Worlds," *Biblio 17* (*Actes de Columbus*) 17 (1990): 165–80.

21. Nancy, "Shattered Love," 88.

22. Nancy, *Je t'aime un peu, beaucoup, passionément* (Paris: Bayard, 2008), 81.

23. Nancy's critique of time as flow would seem to be much indebted to the tradition inspired by Husserl and critically rearticulated by Paul Ricoeur in his three-volume *Narrative and Time*, trans. Kathleen McLaughlin et al (Chicago: University of Chicago Press, 1990); and by Jean-François Lyotard in a number of works, from *Phenomenology*, trans. Brian Beakley (1954; repr. Minneapolis: University of Minnesota Press, 1991), to *Sur la composition du temps par la couleur dans les oeuvres récentes d' Albert Ayme* (Paris: Édition traversière, 1980), and *The Inhuman: Reflections on Time*, trans. Geoff Bennington and Rachel Bowlby (Stanford, Calif.: Stanford University Press, 1991). For a fuller discussion, see Georges Van Den Abbeele, "A Matter of Time: Color, Affect, and the Suffering of Thought," in *Lyotard and Critical Practice*, ed. Kiff Bamford and Margret Grebowicz (New York: Bloomsbury, 2023), 51–63.

24. Nancy's use of the term hearkens back to Michel de Montaigne, whose *Essays* play on the sense of thought as weighing as a form of experimental thinking that tries, or "essays," to measure the value of any given thoughts in the "balance" of skeptical inquiry, as dramatized in Montaigne's own emblem of a pair of scales over the words "What do I know?"; Montaigne, "Apology for Raymond Sebond," in *The Complete Essays*, ed. and trans. Donald Frame (Stanford, Calif.: Stanford University Press, 1943), II.xii, 393). And with regard to such "gravity" of thought, its weight or ponderousness, one wonders then if there can be a black hole–level of thought that collapses space-time? Such a thought could only be either the sense of death or the absolute death of sense, its untimely end as catastrophic implosion of all perception/intellection and an infinite stop to any referral or sending, an abolition of relation itself, which is to say the canceling of the sense of sense itself. Such an end is literally unimaginable, at best a figuration of the unfigurable, the end of discontinuity and interruption as the very heartbeat of existence, the collapse of bodily differences into senseless indifference. Death, writes Nancy, is not interruption or discontinuity but continuity itself, the "cessation of relation" (*Sexistence*, 87). The iterability of the singular, the interruption or discontinuity constitutes the very continuity of existence as world creation in its areality, but discontinuity is the essence of existence; death is the only continuity.

25. Even self-sensing, even touching oneself, hand to hand as in Merleau-Ponty's famous example, yields symmetry but not identity, such as the difference between left and right brain. Even touching oneself yields a sense of touching that is inalterably other, not so much ipseity as "hecceity." The question of intimacy resides in ecstasy or extimacy, not the touching of one's own hands but touching the other as innermost exteriority, the impossible limit of penetration.

26. Despite Nancy's explanation and the sense of the term "pulsar," that astronomical object does not technically "pulse" from some internal dynamism like a beating heart, but its observed periodic fluctuation is actually a function of its spinning on its axis so that its in-fact consistent radiance in one direction looks to us to be flashing on and off, much the same way a lighthouse lamp works by rotating a single beam of light. Such a "pulsar" arises from the extreme density of a collapsed star, all the way down to the level of neutrons, hence it's also referred to as a neutron star. Still, this is not as extreme as the singularity of a black hole, where the density is such that not even light can escape, with space-time itself reduced to a single dimension, a point.

27. Nancy, *The Experience of Freedom*, trans. Bridget McDonald (1988; repr. Stanford, Calif.: Stanford University Press, 1993), 159.

28. Nancy, *The Muses*, 22.

29. Jacques Derrida, *On Touching—Jean-Luc Nancy*, trans. Christine Irizarry (2000; repr. Stanford, Calif.: Stanford University Press, 2005).

30. Ernst Mach, *The Analysis of Sensations and the Relation of the Physical to the Psychical*, trans. C. M. Williams, rev. Sydney Waterlow (New York: Dover, 1959), 10n; Gilbert Ryle, *The Concept of Mind* (London: Hutchinson's University Library, 1949), 237.

31. Sense-sensation as sense-meaning defines the phenomenological feedback loop of experience as interpretive calibration of sense as information and of sense-directionality as proleptic, predictive behavior. This is the model of "artificial" intelligence, of intelligence as artifice, artifact, as mere technology.

32. Nancy often returns to this conundrum of plural worlds as plurality within *the* world, citing Ludwig Wittgenstein: "By writing that 'the sense of the world must lie outside the world,' Wittgenstein simultaneously stated two things: that the world in itself does not constitute an immanence of meaning, but that, since there is no other world, the 'outside' of the world must be open 'within it'—but open in a way that no other world could be posited there"; Nancy, *The Sense of the World*, trans. Jeffrey S. Librett (1993; repr. Minneapolis: University of Minnesota Press, 1997), 52; the Wittgenstein quotation can be found in Wittgenstein, *Tractatus Logico-Philosophicus*, trans. D. F. Pears and B. F. McGuinness (London: Routledge, 1961), 6.41, 144–45.

33. More than just a "linguistic contingency," this semantic convergence is also an actual contingency of sense, indeed a kind of *Witz*, that category excluded from philosophy that Nancy wrote about early in his career, evoking again a certain horizon and retreat of the (m)other, of the relation between *Witz* and matrice as "menstruum universalis"; in *The Birth to Presence*, trans. Brian Holmes et al. (Stanford, Calif.: Stanford University Press, 1993), 248–65. Does the play of sense and singularity suggest the advent or the event of a certain *Witz*?

34. Charles Baudelaire, "Correspondences," in *Flowers of Evil*, trans. James McGowan (Oxford: Oxford University Press, 1993), 19.

35. Maurice Merleau-Ponty, *Phenomenology of Perception*, trans. Donald A. Landes (London: Routledge, 2012), 238.

36. The singularity of art as imagined here by Nancy is not without recalling Walter Benjamin's concept of the "aura" linked to the particularity of any given work of art, an aura that disappears under conditions of mechanical reproducibility: Benjamin, "The Work of Art in the Age of Mechanical Reproducibility," in *Illuminations*, trans. Harry Zohn (New York: Schocken, 1968), 217–51.

37. Gérard Lépinlois, "La vallée de la figuration," indicated as a yet "unpublished text," cited by Nancy in *The Muses*, trans. Peggy Kamuf (1994; repr. Stanford, Calif.: Stanford University Press, 1996), 32 and 112n.

38. Many of these poetic forms are given detailed treatment by Nancy in such works as *Portrait*, trans. Sarah Clift and Simon Sparks (2000, 2014; repr. New York: Fordham University Press, 2018); *The Pleasure of Drawing*, trans. Philip Armstrong (2009; repr. New York: Fordham University Press, 2013); with Jérôme Lèbre, *Signaux sensibles, entretien à propos des arts* (Paris: Bayard, 2017); with Abbas Kiarostami, *The Evidence of Film*, trans. Christine Irizarry and Verena Andermatt Conley (Brussels: Yves Gevaert, 2001), and the many essays in *The Muses* and in *Multiple Arts: The Muses II*, ed. Simon Sparks (Stanford, Calif.: Stanford University Press, 2006).

39. The Hegel reference is to *Aesthetics*, trans. T. M. Knox (Oxford: Clarendon, 1975), 2:976. Ian James adroitly tracks Nancy's aesthetics "between Hegel and

Heidegger," which is also to pinpoint the relation between art and technique: James, *The Fragmentary Demand: An Introduction to the Philosophy of Jean-Luc Nancy* (Stanford, Calif.: Stanford University Press, 2006), 202–30; and James, "Jean-Luc Nancy: Poetry, Philosophy, Technicity," in *Philosophy and Poetry*, ed. Ranjan Ghosh (New York: Columbia University Press, 2019), 271–82.

40. Here and elsewhere, one is tempted to describe much of Nancy's work as a kind of neo- or post-existentialism, one whose recurrent Sartrian undertones nonetheless expose a radical revision of Sartre's core humanism and voluntarism. It is not just the *subject* of existentialist freedom that is displaced but the entire phenomenological apparatus that supports existentialism's residual idealism. While Nancy tends to get associated predominantly with Derrida, there is a palpable connection with Sartre (such as the *Inoperative Community*'s invocation of his remarks about the unsurpassable horizon of communism) that would be worth a study in itself. A number of scholars have indeed noted this Sartrian dimension in Nancy's thinking: Paul John Gorre, "Sartre, Jean-Paul," in *The Nancy Dictionary*, ed. Peter Gratton and Mare-Eve Morin (Edinburgh: Edinburgh University Press, 2015), 207–8; Tommaso Tuppini, *Jean-Luc Nancy: Le forme della communicazione* (Rome: Carocci, 2012), 133–73; and in more guarded ways: James, *The Fragmentary Demand*, 173; and Frédérique Neyrat, "*No/us*: The Nietzschean Democracy of Jean-Luc Nancy," *Diacritics* 43, no. 4 (2015): 67–72.

Bibliography

Note: This is not meant as a comprehensive list of everything written by or about Jean-Luc Nancy, only of those works consulted or cited for this study. Whenever possible, English translations of works written in other languages are referenced, with the original publication date in brackets. Nancy's solo works are listed in chronological order. All other works are listed alphabetically by author.

Works by Jean-Luc Nancy

As Solo Author

[1973] 2001. *The Speculative Remark: One of Hegel's Bons Mots*. Translated by Céline Surprenant. Stanford, Calif.: Stanford University Press.

[1975] 2007. *The Discourse of the Syncope: Logodaedalus I*. Translated by Saul Anton. Stanford, Calif.: Stanford University Press.

1977. "Larvatus pro deo." Translated by Daniel Brewer. *Glyph* 2, 14–36.

1978. "*Dum scribo*." Translated by Ian McLeod. *Oxford Literary Review* 3, no. 2: 6–21.

1978. "Mundus est fabula." Translated by Daniel Brewer. *MLN* 93, no. 4: 635–53.

[1979] 2016. *Ego Sum: Corpus, Anima, Fabula*. Translated by Marie-Eve Morin. New York: Fordham University Press. [ES]

1979. "Monogrammes I." *Digraphe* 20: 131–37.

1979. "Monogrammes II." *Digraphe* 21: 133–38.

1980. "Monogrammes III." *Digraphe* 22–23: 221–29.

1980. "Monogrammes IV." *Digraphe* 24: 131–40.

1980. "Monogrammes V." *Digraphe* 25: 199–208.

[1982] 2019. *Dies Irae*. Translated by Angela Candello. London: University of Westminster Press.

1982. *Le partage des voix*. Paris: Galilée.

[1983] 1991. *The Inoperative Community*. Translated by Peter Connor. Minneapolis: University of Minnesota Press. [IC]

1983. *L'impératif catégorique*. Paris: Flammarion.

1986. *L'oubli de la philosophie*. Paris: Galilée.

[1988] 1993. *The Experience of Freedom*. Translated by Bridget McDonald. Stanford, Calif.: Stanford University Press.

[1990] 2003. *A Finite Thinking*. Translated by Simon Sparks. Stanford, Calif.: Stanford University Press.

[1992] 2008. *Corpus*. Translated by Richard Rand. New York: Fordham University Press. [C]

1993. *The Birth to Presence*. Translated by Brian Holmes et al. Stanford, Calif.: Stanford University Press.

[1993] 1997. *The Sense of the World*. Translated by Jeffrey S. Librett. Minneapolis: University of Minnesota Press. [SW]

1992. *Monogrammes VI*. Futur Antérieur 10, no. 2.

1992. *Monogrammes VII*. Futur Antérieur 11, no. 3.

1992. *Monogrammes VIII*. Futur Antérieur 12–13, no. 4–5.

1992. *Monogrammes IX*. Futur Antérieur 14, no. 6.

1993. *Monogrammes X*. Futur Antérieur 15, no. 1.

1993. *Monogrammes XI*. Futur Antérieur 16, no. 2: 141–44.

1993. *Monogrammes XII*. Futur Antérieur 17, no. 3.

1993. *Monogrammes XIII*. Futur Antérieur 18, no. 4.

1993. *Monogrammes XIV*. Futur Antérieur 19–20, no. 5–6.

1993. "'You Ask Me What It Means Today . . .': An Epigraph for *Paragraph*." *Paragraph* 16: 2. Special Issue on the Work of Jean-Luc Nancy, edited by Peggy Kamuf.

1993. *Sur l'ex-Yougoslavie, Actes de la journée du 6 mars 1993*. Paris: Collège International de Philosophie.

[1994] 1996. *The Muses*. Translated by Peggy Kamuf. Stanford, Calif.: Stanford University Press.

[1996] 2000. *Being Singular Plural*. Translated by Robert D. Richardson and Anne E. O'Byrne. Stanford, Calif.: Stanford University Press.

[1997] 2002. *Hegel: The Restlessness of the Negative*. Translated by Jason Smith and Steven Miller. Minneapolis: University of Minnesota Press.

[2000] Rev. ed. 2010. *L'intrus*. Paris: Galilée (English translation in *Corpus*).

[2000, 2014] 2018. *Portrait*. Translated by Sarah Clift and Simon Sparks. New York: Fordham University Press.

2001. *"Un jour, les dieux se retirent. . . ."* Paris: William Blake.

2001. *La communauté affrontée*. Paris: Galilée.

2001. *L'"il y a" du rapport sexuel*. Paris: Galilée. (Translation in *Corpus II*).

2001. *La pensée dérobée*. Paris: Galilée.

[2002] 2007. *The Creation of the World, or Globalization*. Translated by François Raffoul and David Pettigrew. Albany: SUNY Press. [CW]

[2002] 2007. *Listening*. Translated by Charlotte Mandell. New York: Fordham University Press.
[2002] 2012. "In Place of Utopia." Translated by Patricia Viera and Michael Marder. In *Existential Utopia: New Perspectives on Utopian Thought*, edited by Patricia Viera and Michael Marder. New York: Continuum.
[2003] 2008. *Noli me Tangere: On the Raising of the Body*. Translated by Sarah Clift, Pascale-Anne Brault, and Michael Naas. New York: Fordham University Press.
[2004] 2008. *Philosophical Chronicles*. Translated by Franson Manjali. New York: Fordham University Press.
2004. *Résistance de la poésie*. Paris: William Blake.
2005. *The Ground of the Image*. Translated by Jeff Fort. New York: Fordham University Press.
2005. *Sur le commerce des pensées*. Paris: Galilée.
[2005] 2008. *Dis-Enclosure: The Deconstruction of Christianity*. Translated by Bettina Bergo, Gabriel Malenfant, and Michael B. Smith. New York: Fordham University Press.
2006. *La naissance des seins*, suivi de *Péan pour Aphrodite*. Paris: Galilée. (Translation in *Corpus II*).
2006. *Multiple Arts: The Muses II*. Edited by Simon Sparks. Stanford, Calif.: Stanford University Press.
2007. *À plus d'un titre: Jacques Derrida*. Paris: Galilée.
[2007] 2009. *The Fall of Sleep*. Translated by Charlotte Mandell. New York: Fordham University Press.
2008. *Le poids d'une pensée, l'approche*. Strasbourg: Le Phocide.
[2008] 2010. *The Truth of Democracy*. Translated by Pascale-Anne Brault and Michael Naas. New York: Fordham University Press.
2008. *Je t'aime un peu, beaucoup, passionément*. Paris: Bayard.
[2009] 2011. *God, Justice, Love, Beauty: Four Little Dialogues*. Translated by Sarah Clift. New York: Fordham University Press.
[2009] 2013. *The Pleasure of Drawing*. Translated by Philip Armstrong. New York: Fordham University Press.
2010. *Identité: Fragments, franchises*. Paris: Galilée.
[2010] 2013. *Adoration: The Deconstruction of Christianity II*. Translated by John McKean. New York: Fordham University Press.
2011. *Maurice Blanchot: Passion politique*. Paris: Galilée.
[2012] 2015. *After Fukushima: The Equivalence of Catastrophes*. Translated by Charlotte Mandell. New York: Fordham University Press.
[2013] 2016. *Intoxication*. Translated by Philip Armstrong. New York: Fordham University Press.
2013. *Monogrammes XV. L'Impossible* 10 (February).
2013. *Monogrammes XVI. L'Impossible* 12 (April).
2013. *Monogrammes XVII. L'Impossible* 13 (Summer).

2013. *Corpus II: Writings on Sexuality*. Translated by Anne O'Byrne. New York: Fordham University Press.

[2015] 2017. *The Banality of Heidegger*. Translated by Jeff Fort. New York: Fordham University Press.

2015. *Journal des Phéniciennes*. Paris: Christian Bourgois.

[2015] 2018. *Expectation: Philosophy, Literature*. Translated by Robert Bononno. New York: Fordham University Press.

[2016] 2020. *Doing*. Translated by Charlotte Mandell. London: Seagull.

[2017] 2021. *Sexistence*. Translated by Steven Miller. New York: Fordham University Press.

[2018] 2020. *Excluding the Jew within Us*. Translated by Sarah Clift. Cambridge: Polity.

2019. *Derrida, suppléments*. Paris: Galilée.

2019. *What Do We Need Art For?* Translated by Martin Turnbull. Cologne: Verlag der Buchhandlung Walther König.

[2020] 2021. *The Fragile Skin of the World*. Translated by Cory Stockwell. New York: Fordham University Press.

[2020] 2021. *An All-Too-Human Virus*. Translated by Cory Stockwell, David Fernbach, and Sarah Clift. New York: Fordham University Press.

[2021] 2022. *Corpus III: Cruor and Other Writings*. Translated by Jeff Fort. New York: Fordham University Press.

2021. *Mascarons de Macron*. Paris: Galilée.

2021. *La vérité du mensonge*. Paris: Bayard.

With Coauthors

Badiou, Alain, and Jean-Luc Nancy. 2018. *German Philosophy*. Translated by Richard Lambert. Cambridge, Mass.: MIT Press.

Bouthors, Jean-François, and Jean-Luc Nancy. 2019. *Démocratie! Hic et Nunc*. Paris: François Bourin.

Cadava, Eduardo, Peter Connor, and Jean-Luc Nancy. 1991. *Who Comes after the Subject?* New York: Routledge.

Ferrari, Federico, and Jean-Luc Nancy. 2005. *Iconographie de l'auteur*. Paris: Galilée.

———, and Jean-Luc Nancy. 2018. *La fin des fins*. Paris: Kimé.

Kacem, Mehdi Belhaj, and Jean-Luc Nancy. 2020. *Immortelle finitude: Sexualité et philosophie*. Zurich, Paris, and Berlin: Diaphanes.

Lacoue-Labarthe, Philippe, and Jean-Luc Nancy, eds. 1981. *Les fins de l'homme: À partir du travail de Jacques Derrida*. Paris: Galilée.

———, eds. 1981. *Rejouer le politique*. Paris: Galilée.

———, eds. 1983. *Le retrait du politique*. Paris: Galilée.

———, eds. 1988. *The Literary Absolute: The Theory of Literature in German Romanticism*. Translated by Philip Barnard and Cheryl Lester. Albany: SUNY Press. Partial translation of *L'absolu littéraire*. Paris: Seuil, 1978.

———. 1991. *Le mythe nazi*. La tour d'Aigues: L'Aube.

———. 1992 [1973]. *The Title of the Letter: A Reading of Lacan*. Translated by François Raffoul and David Pettigrew. Albany: SUNY Press.
———. 1997. *Retreating the Political*. Edited by Simon Sparks. Translated by Simon Sparks, Céline Surprenant, Richard Stamp, and Leslie Hill. Oxon: Routledge.
———. 2013. *La panique politique*. Paris: Christian Bourgois.
———. 2013. *Scène*. Paris: Christian Bourgois.
Nancy, Jean-Luc, Philip Armstrong, and Jason E. Smith. 2011. *Politique et au-delà*. Paris: Galilée.
Nancy, Jean-Luc, and Jean-Christophe Bailly. 1991. *La comparution*. Paris: Christian Bourgois.
Nancy, Jean-Luc, and Arélien Barrau. [2011] 2015. *What's These Worlds Coming to?* Translated by Travis Holloway and Flor Méchain. New York: Fordham University Press.
Nancy, Jean-Luc, and Peter Engelman. [2005] 2019. *Democracy and Community*. Translated by Wieland Hoban. Cambridge: Polity.
Nancy, Jean-Luc, and Federico Ferrari. [2003] 2014. *Being Nude: The Skin of Images*. Translated by Anne O'Byrne and Carlie Anglemire. New York: Fordham University Press.
Nancy, Jean-Luc, and Irving Goh. 2021. *The Deconstruction of Sex*. Durham, N.C.: Duke University Press.
Nancy, Jean-Luc, and Pierre-Philippe Jandin. [2013] 2017. *The Possibility of a World*. Translated by Travis Holloway and Flor Méchain. New York: Fordham University Press.
Nancy, Jean-Luc, and Abbas Kiarostami. 2001. *The Evidence of Film*. Translated by Christine Irizarry and Verena Andermatt Conley. Brussels: Yves Gevaert.
Nancy, Jean-Luc, and Jérôme Lèbre. 2017. *Signaux sensibles, entretien à propos des arts*. Paris: Bayard.
Nancy, Jean-Luc, and Marcia Sá Cavalcante Schuback, eds. 2013. *Being With the Without*. Stockholm: Axl.
Nancy, Jean-Luc, and Adèle Van Reeth. [2014] 2017. *Coming*. Translated by Charlotte Mandell. New York: Fordham University Press.

Works on or about Jean-Luc Nancy

Alexandrova, Alena, Ignaas Devisch, Laurens Ten Kate, and Aukje Van Rooden. 2012. *Re-treating Religion: Deconstructing Christianity with Jean-Luc Nancy*. New York: Fordham University Press.
Armstrong, Philip. 2009. *Reticulations: Jean-Luc Nancy and the Networks of the Political*. Minneapolis: University of Minnesota Press.
Badiou, Alain. "L'offrande réservée." 2004. In Guibal and Martin, *Sens en tout sens*, 13–24. Paris: Galilée.

Birnbaum, Antonia. [1992] 2008. "To Exist Is to Exit a Point." In Nancy, *Corpus*, translated by Richard Rand, 145–49. New York: Fordham University Press.
Conley, Verena Andermatt, and Irving Goh, eds. 2014. *Nancy Now*. Cambridge: Polity.
Critchley, Simon. 1999. "Re-tracing the Political: Politics and Community in the Work of Philippe Lacoue-Labarthe and Jean-Luc Nancy." In *The Political Subject of Violence*, edited by David Campbell and Michael Dillon, 73–93. Manchester: Manchester University Press.
Derrida, Jacques. [2000] 2005. *On Touching—Jean-Luc Nancy*. Translated by Christine Irizarry. Stanford, Calif.: Stanford University Press.
Fraser, Nancy. 1984. "The French Derrideans: Politicizing Deconstruction or Deconstructing the Political?" *New German Critique* 33, no. 3: 127–54.
Goh, Irving, ed. 2014. "The Prepositional Senses of Jean-Luc Nancy (1)." *Diacritics* 42, no. 2.
———. 2014. *The Reject: Community, Politics, and Religion after the Subject*. New York: Fordham University Press.
———. 2019. *L'existence prépositionnelle*. Paris: Galilée.
———, ed. 2022. *Nancy among the Philosophers*. New York: Fordham University Press.
Gratton, Peter, and Mare-Eve Morin, eds. 2015. *The Nancy Dictionary*. Edinburgh: Edinburgh University Press.
Gratton, Peter, and Mare-Eve Morin, eds. 2015. *Jean-Luc Nancy and Plural Thinking: Expositions of World, Ontology, Politics, and Sense*. Edinburgh: Edinburgh University Press.
Guibal, Francis, and Jean-Clet Martin, eds. 2004. *Sens en tout sens*. Paris: Galilée.
Guyer, Sara. "Buccality." 2007. In *Derrida, Deleuze, Psychoanalysis*, edited by Gabriele M. Schwab. 77–104. New York: Columbia University Press.
Hutchens, B. C. 2005. *Jean-Luc Nancy and the Future of Philosophy*. Montreal: McGill-Queen's University Press.
Hutchens, B. C., ed. 2012. *Jean-Luc Nancy: Justice, Legality and World*. London: Continuum.
James, Ian. 2006. *The Fragmentary Demand: An Introduction to the Philosophy of Jean-Luc Nancy*. Stanford, Calif.: Stanford University Press.
James, Ian. 2019. "Jean-Luc Nancy: Poetry, Philosophy, Technicity." In *Philosophy and Poetry*, edited by Ranjan Ghosh, 271–82. New York: Columbia University Press.
Jandin, Pierre-Philippe. 2012. *Jean-Luc Nancy: Retracer le politique*. Paris: Michalon.
Kamuf, Peggy, ed. 1993. *Paragraph* 16, no. 2. Special Issue on the Work of Jean-Luc Nancy.
Lèbre, Jérôme, and Jacob Rogozinski, eds. 2017. "Jean-Luc Nancy: Penser la mutation." *Les cahiers philosophiques de Strasbourg* 42, no. 2.
Librett, Jeffrey. 2014. "On an Intermittent Subject in Jean-Luc Nancy." *Diacritics* 42, no. 2: 36–58.

Malabou, Catherine. 2004. "Pierre aime les horranges." In Guibal and Martin, *Sens en tout sens*, 39–57. Paris: Galilée.
Marchart, Oliver. 2007. *Post-Foundational Political Thought: Political Difference in Nancy, Lefort, Badiou and Laclau*. Edinburgh: Edinburgh University Press.
Miami Theory Collective (G. Van Den Abbeele, P. Kamuf, J. Creech, Mitchell Greenberg, Britton Harwood, Marie-Claire Vallois, and Stephen Nimis). 1991. *Community at Loose Ends*. Minneapolis: University of Minnesota Press.
Morin, Marie-Eve. 2012. *Jean-Luc Nancy*. Cambridge: Polity.
Murray, Timothy, ed. 2015. *The Prepositional Senses of Jean-Luc Nancy (2)*. *Diacritics* 43, no. 4.
Neyrat, Frédérique. 2015. "*No/us*: The Nietzschean Democracy of Jean-Luc Nancy." *Diacritics* 43, no. 4: 67–72.
Sheppard, Darren, Simon Sparks, and Colin Thomas, eds. 1997. *On Jean-Luc Nancy: The Sense of Philosophy*. London: Routledge.
Tuppini, Tommaso. 2012. *Jean-Luc Nancy: Le forme della communicazione*. Rome: Carocci.
Van Den Abbeele, Georges. 1993. "Singular Remarks." *Paragraph* 16, no. 2: 180–86.
———. 1997. "Lost Horizons and Uncommon Grounds: For a Poetics of Finitude in the Work of Jean-Luc Nancy." In *On Jean-Luc Nancy: The Sense of Philosophy*, edited by Darren Sheppard, Simon Sparks, and Colin Thomas, 12–18. London: Routledge.
———. 2014. "*Monograms*: Then and 'Now.'" In *Nancy Now*, edited by Verena Andermatt Conley and Irving Goh, 59–89. Cambridge: Polity.

Other Works Cited

Agamben, Giorgio. 1998. *Homo Sacer: Sovereign Power and Bare Life*. Translated by Daniel Heller-Roazen. Palo Alto, Calif.: Stanford University Press.
Apter, Emily. 2019. *Unexceptional Politics: On Obstruction, Impasse, and the Impolitic*. London: Verso.
Arendt, Hannah. 1958. *The Human Condition*. 2nd ed. Chicago: University of Chicago Press.
———. 1968. *The Origins of Totalitarianism*. Rev. ed. New York: Houghton Mifflin.
Aristotle. 1984. *The Complete Works of Aristotle*. Edited by Jonathan Barnes. 2 vols. Princeton: Princeton University Press.
Baillet, Adrien. 1691. *La Vie de Monsieur Des-Cartes*. Paris.
Bataille, Georges. 1993. *The Accursed Share*. New York: Zone.
Baudelaire, Charles. 1993. *Flowers of Evil*. Translated by James McGowan. Oxford: Oxford University Press.
Benjamin, Walter. 1968. *Illuminations*. Translated by Harry Zohn. New York: Schocken.
———. 1998. *The Origin of German Tragic Drama*. Translated by John Osborne. London: Verso.

Blanchard, Marc E. 1990. *Trois portraits de Montaigne: Essai sur la représentation à la Renaissance*. Paris: Nizet.
Boehm, Rudolph. 1976. *La métaphysique d'Aristote, le fondamental et l'essentiel*. Translated by Emmanuel Martineau. Paris: Gallimard.
Brown, Norman O. 1966. *Love's Body*. New York: Vintage.
Brown, Wendy. 2015. *Undoing the Demos: Neoliberalism's Stealth Revolution*. New York: Zone.
———. 2019. *In the Ruins of Neoliberalism: The Rise of Antidemocratic Politics in the West*. New York: Columbia University Press.
Céard, Jean. 1977. *La nature et ses prodiges: L'insolite au XVIe siècle*. Geneva: Droz.
Dell, Paul F., and John A. O'Neil, eds. 2009. *Dissociation and the Dissociative Disorders: DSM-V and Beyond*. New York: Routledge.
Derrida, Jacques. [1967] 1978. *Writing and Difference*. Translated by Alan Bass. London and New York: Routledge.
———. 1976. "Pas." *Gramma*, no. 3/4: 111–215.
———. [1978] 1987. *The Truth in Painting*. Translated by Geoff Bennington and Ian McLeod. Chicago: University of Chicago Press.
———. [1978] 2007. "The *Retrait* of Metaphor." Translated by Peggy Kamuf. In *Psyche: Inventions of the Other*, edited by Peggy Kamuf and Elizabeth Rottenberg, 1:48–80. Stanford, Calif.: Stanford University Press.
———. [1980] 1980. *The Postcard*. Translated by Alan Bass. Chicago: University of Chicago Press.
———. 1981. "Sur un ton apocalyptique naguère adopté en philosophie." In Lacoue-Labarthe and Nancy, *Les fins de l'homme*, 471–78.
———. 1983. "Le retrait de l'apocalypse." Radio interview, Montreal 1983. Tape recording Critical Theory Archives, UC Irvine, box 40, folder 2.
———. 1988. *Limited Inc*. Translated by Samuel Weber and Jeffrey Mehlman. Evanston, Ill.: Northwestern University Press.
———. *Specters of Marx*. 1994. Translated by Peggy Kamuf. New York: Routledge.
———. 1997. *Politics of Friendship*. Translated by George Collins. London: Verso.
Descartes, René. 1963–73. *Oeuvres philosophiques*. Edited by Ferdinand Alquié. Paris: Garnier. [Alquié]
———. 1964–76. *Oeuvres de Descartes*. Edited by Charles Adam and Paul Tannery. Rev. ed. Paris: Vrin. [AT]
———. 1984. *The Philosophical Writings of Descartes*. Translated by John Cottingham, Robert Stoothoff, and Dugald Murdoch. Cambridge: Cambridge University Press. [CSM]
Eco, Umberto. 1986. *Travels in Hyperreality*. San Diego: Harcourt.
Foucault, Michel. [1961] 2006. *History of Madness*. Partial edition by Jean Khalfa; translated by Jonathan Murphy. London and New York: Routledge. Complete French edition: *Folie et déraison: Histoire de le folie à l'âge Classique*. Paris: Plon, 1961.
Frege, Gottlob. 1997. "On *Sinn* and *Bedeutung*." In *The Frege Reader*, edited by Michael Beaney, 151–71. Oxford: Blackwell.

Freud, Sigmund. 1940–52. *Gesammelte Werke*. London: Imago. [GS]
———. 1953–74. *The Standard Edition of the Complete Psychological Works*. Translated by James Strachey London: Hogarth. [SE]
Fynsk, Christopher. 1981. "Contribution 1." Political Seminar. In Lacoue-Labarthe and Nancy, *Les fins de l'homme*, 487–93. This talk and Lacoue-Labarthe's response appear in English translation in Sparks, *Retreating the Political*, 87–99. Oxon: Routledge, 1997.
Gilson, Étienne. 1947. *René Descartes: Discours de la méthode; Texte et commentaire*. Paris: Vrin.
Hawking, Stephen W. 1988. *A Brief History of Time*. New York, Bantam.
Hegel, Georg Wilhelm Friedrich. 1911. *Grundlinien der Philosophie des Rechts*. Leipzig: Felix Meiner.
———. 1952. *The Philosophy of Right*. Translated by T. M. Knox. London: Oxford University Press.
———. 1967. *Phenomenology of Mind*. Translated by J. B. Baillie. New York: Harper & Row.
———. 1975. *Aesthetics*. 2 vols. Translated by T. M. Knox. Oxford: Clarendon.
Heidegger, Martin. 1967. *What Is a Thing?* Translated by W. B. Barton Jr. and V. Deutsch. South Bend, Ind.: Gateway.
———. 1968. *What Is Called Thinking?* Translated by J. Glenn Gray. New York: Harper and Row.
———. 1971. *On the Way to Language*. Translated by Peter D. Hertz. San Francisco: Harper and Row.
———. 1977. *Basic Writings*. Translated by David Farrel Krell. New York: Harper and Row.
———. 1982. *Nietzsche*. Edited by David Krell. Translated by F. A. Capuzzi. Vols. 3 and 4. New York: Harper and Row.
———. 1996. *Being and Time*. Translated by Jane Stambaugh. Albany: SUNY Press.
———. 1997. *Kant and the Problem of Metaphysics*. Translated by Richard Taft. Bloomington: Indiana University Press.
———. 2014. *Introduction to Metaphysics*. Translated by Gregory Fried and Richard Polt. 2nd rev. ed. New Haven: Yale University Press.
———. [2016] 2017. *Ponderings (The Black Notebooks)*. Translated by Richard Rojcewicz. Bloomington: Indiana University Press.
Henry, Michel. 1983. *Marx: A Philosophy of Human Reality*. Translated by Kathleen McLaughlin. Bloomington: Indiana University Press.
Hintikka, Jaako. 1963. "Cogito, Ergo Sum as an Inference and a Performance." *Philosophical Review* 72, no. 4: 487–96.
Kant, Immanuel. 1999. *Critique of Pure Reason*. Translated and edited by Paul Guyer and Alan Wood. Cambridge: Cambridge University Press.
Kaufmann, William J. III. 1979. *Black Holes and Warped Spacetime*. New York: W. H. Freeman.

Kermode, Frank. 1966. *The Sense of an Ending: Studies in the Theory of Fiction.* Oxford: Oxford University Press.

Kristeva, Julia. 1982. "Maux d'amour." *Furor* 4: 3–22.

Lacan, Jacques. [2004] 2014. *Anxiety: Seminar X.* Edited by Jacques-Alain Miller. Translated by A. R. Price. Cambridge: Polity.

Lacoue-Labarthe, Philippe. 1997. "In the Name of. . . ." In Sparks, *Retreating the Political,* 72–74. Oxon: Routledge.

Laclau, Ernesto, and Chantal Mouffe. 1985. *Hegemony and Socialist Strategy: Toward a Radical Democratic Politics.* London: Verso.

Lee, Kyoo. 2011. "*Cogito Interruptus*: The Epistolary Body in the Elisabeth-Descartes Correspondence, June 22, 1645–November 3, 1645." *philoSOPHIA* 1, no. 2: 173–94.

Lefort, Claude. 1983. "La question de la démocratie." In Lacoue-Labarthe and Nancy, *Le retrait du politique,* 71–88. Paris: Galilée.

Lenin, V. I. [1929] 1987. *What Is to Be Done?* Mineoloa, N.Y.: Dover.

Lépinlois, Gérard. [unpublished]. "La vallée de la figuration." Indicated as a yet "unpublished text." Cited by Nancy in *The Muses,* 32 and 112n.

Lewis, Philip E., 1981. "Vers la traduction abusive." In Lacoue-Labarthe and Nancy, *Les fins de l'homme,* 253–61. A modified translation of this text appears as "The Measure of Translation Effects," in *Difference in Translation,* edited by Joseph F. Graham, 31–62. Ithaca: Cornell University Press, 1985.

Luxemburg, Rosa. 2006. *Reform or Revolution, and Other Writings.* Edited by Paul Buhle. Translated by Patrick Lawin, 101–80. Mineola, N.Y.: Dover.

Lyotard, Jean-François. [1974] 1993. *Libidinal Economy.* Translated by Iain Hamilton Grant. Bloomington: Indiana University Press.

———. 1979. *The Postmodern Condition.* Translated by Geoff Bennington and Brian Massumi. Minneapolis: University of Minnesota Press.

———. 1980. *Sur la composition du temps par la couleur dans les oeuvres récentes d' Albert Ayme.* Paris: Édition traversière.

———. [1983] 1988. *The Differend.* Translated by Georges Van Den Abbeele. Minneapolis: University of Minnesota Press.

———. [1986] 2009. *Enthusiasm: The Kantian Critique of History.* Translated by Georges Van Den Abbeele. Stanford, Calif.: Stanford University Press.

———. 1991. "A l'insu (Unbeknownst)." Translated by Georges Van Den Abbeele. In *Community at Loose Ends,* edited by Miami Theory Collective, 42–48. Minneapolis: University of Minnesota Press.

———. 1991. *The Inhuman: Reflections on Time.* Translated by Geoff Bennington and Rachel Bowlby. Stanford, Calif.: Stanford University Press.

———. 1991. *Lectures d'enfance.* Paris: Galilée.

———. [1994] 1997. *Postmodern Fables.* Translated by Georges Van Den Abbeele. Minneapolis: University of Minnesota Press.

Mach, Ernst. 1959. *The Analysis of Sensations and the Relation of the Physical to the Psychical.* Translated by C. M. Williams. Revised by Sydney Waterlow. New York: Dover.

Markovitz, Dan. 2008. "Cogitus interruptus: The Case for Focus." https://www.socialmediatoday.com/content/cogitus-interruptus-case-focus.
McCarthy, Mary. 1965. *Birds of America*. New York: Harcourt Brace Jovanovich.
McLuhan, Marshall. 1964. *Understanding Media*. New York: McGraw-Hill.
Merleau-Ponty, Maurice. 2012. *Phenomenology of Perception*. Translated by Donald A. Landes. London: Routledge.
Montaigne, Michel de. 1943. *The Complete Essays*. Edited and translated by Donald Frame. Stanford, Calif.: Stanford University Press.
Mouffe, Chantal. 1993. *The Return of the Political*. London: Verso.
———. 2005. *On the Political*. London: Routledge.
Rancière, Jacques. 1983. "La représentation de l'ouvrier ou la classe introuvable." In Lacoue-Labarthe and Nancy, *Le Retrait du politique*, 89–111.
———. 1995. *On the Shores of Politics*. Translated by Liz Heron. London: Verso.
Ricoeur, Paul. [1965] 2007. "The Political Paradox." In *History and Truth*, translated by David M. Rasmussen. Evanston, Ill.: Northwestern University Press.
———. 1990. *Narrative and Time*. Translated by Kathleen McLaughlin et al. 3 vols. Chicago: University of Chicago Press.
Rimbaud, Arthur. 1963. *Poésies complètes*. Edited by Pascal Pia. Paris: Livre de Poche.
Ryle, Gilbert. 1949. *The Concept of Mind*. London: Hutchinson's University Library.
Saussure, Ferdinand de. 1965. *Course in General Linguistics*. Translated by Wade Baskin. New York: McGraw-Hill.
Schildgen, Brenda, and Georges Van Den Abbeele, eds. 2003. *A World of Fables*. Berkeley, Calif.: Pacific View Press.
Schlegel, Karl Wilhelm Friedrich von. 1978. *Athenaeum Fragmenten*. In *L'absolu littéraire*, edited by Jean-Luc Nancy and Philippe Lacoue-Labarthe. Paris: Seuil.
Sedlmayr, Hans. 1957. *Art in Crisis: The Lost Center*. London: Hollis and Carter.
Shakespeare, William. *Hamlet* (I.ii.65).
Terdiman, Richard. 1991. "On the Dialectics of Postdialectical Thinking." In *Community at Loose Ends*, edited by the Miami Theory Collective, 111–20. Minneapolis: University of Minnesota Press.
Valéry, Paul. 1973. *M. Teste*. Translated by Jackson Matthews. Princeton: Princeton University Press.
Van Den Abbeele, Georges. 1990. "*Fabula est Mundus*: On the Plurality of Fontenelle's Worlds." *Biblio 17* (*Actes de Columbus*) 17: 165–80.
———. 1992. "Duplicity and Singularity in André Thevet's *Cosmographie de Levant*." *L'Esprit Créateur* 32, no. 3 (Fall): 25–35.
———. 1998. "Fabel." In *Historisch-Kritisches Wörterbuch der Marxismus*, edited by Wolfgang Fritz Haug (Berlin: Argument-Verlag, 1999); English translation in *Historical Materialism* 16, no. 4 (2008): 233–38.
———. 2019. "What Does It Mean to be Human in a Time of Rapid Technological Change?: Questions and Provocations." *Chinese journal of Marxist Aesthetics* (October). https://mp.weixin.qq.com/s/Nm3mNeGJmW589zKZtohh8g.

———. [forthcoming]. "A Matter of Time: Color, Affect, and the Suffering of Thought." In *Lyotard and Critical Practice*, edited by Kiff Bamford and Margret Grebowicz. New York: Bloomsbury.

Volosinov, V. N. 1973. *Marxism and the Philosophy of Language*. Translated by Ladislav Matejka and I. R. Titunik. Cambridge, Mass.: Harvard University Press.

Weber, Samuel. 2014. *Inquiétantes singularités*. Paris: Hermann.

Wittgenstein, Ludwig. 1961. *Tractatus Logico-Philosophicus*. Translated by D. F. Pears and B. F. McGuinness. London: Routledge.

Index

actuality, 51, 54–55, 65, 73, 177n6. *See also* *Wirklichkeit*
Adorno, Theodor, 3, 103, 188n49
aesthetics, 4–5, 20, 55, 115, 139, 153, 157–58, 161, 186n35, 194n39. *See also* arts; poetry
Agamben, Giorgio, 190n62
Alquié, Ferdinand, vii, 41, 45, 171n4, 172n7
Althusser, Louis, 103, 188n49
anima, vii, 171, 179n2. *See also* Aristotle
apocalypse, 1–2, 18, 167n3
apperception, 41, 66–67, 124
Apter, Emily, 184n31
Aquinas, St. Thomas, 119
areality, 9–10, 19, 28–30, 31, 42–44, 47–48, 79, 117, 120, 158, 161, 172n13, 175n29
Arendt, Hannah, 20, 88–89, 92, 94, 96, 183n22, 186n33
Aristotle, 83, 111, 118–19, 123, 127–28, 140, 144–45, 148. *See also* *anima*
arts, 21, 115, 142, 144–45, 151–58. *See also* aesthetics

Badiou, Alain, 116–17, 152, 169n18, 180n5, 184n31
Baillet, Adrian, 173n16
Bailly, Jean-Christophe, 17
Balibar, Etienne, 190n57
Barrau, Aurélien, 17
Bataille, Georges, 3, 39, 46, 89, 97, 103, 107, 186n37
Baudelaire, Charles, 125, 147, 194n34

Being/being, 7, 10, 15–17, 34, 37, 79, 93, 110, 126–28, 134, 136, 180–81n6
Benjamin, Walter, 11, 80, 103, 141, 164, 169n19, 181n7, 188n49
Benveniste, Emile, 35
Bergson, Henri, 103
Birnbaum, Antonia, 47, 175n24, 176n35
black hole, 14–16, 132–33, 169n23, 193n24, 193n26. *See also* cosmos/cosmology; pulsar
Blanchot, Maurice, 81, 180n6
Boaistuau, Pierre, 13
Boehm, Rudolph, 174n21
Bouthors, François, 17
Brown, Norman O., 109, 190n60
Brown, Wendy, 186n34

capitalism, 74
Cartesian, 24–25, 28, 33, 42–44, 47, 52, 63, 78, 115, 155, 172n12, 174n21, 175n25. *See also* Descartes, René
Celan, Paul, 141
Cerisy Conference on *Les fins de l'homme*, 91–93, 113–14, 163, 184n25
Cervantes, Miguel de, 57, 68
cogito, 19, 24–48, 78, 100, 115, 122, 131, 155, 172n8, 172n12, 172–73n14. *See also* Descartes, René
cognition, 41, 45, 61, 122–23
community, 7–18, 32–33, 36–37, 39, 84–85, 90, 96, 101–12, 159, 169n22, 180n6. *See also* inoperative

209

concept, 7, 11, 14–15, 19–20, 25, 27, 34, 40, 56, 60–62, 71, 75, 81–82, 93, 96–97, 100, 106, 108–9, 113, 115, 117, 130, 132, 143, 154, 156, 158, 172n13, 172–73n14, 175n27, 189n55
consciousness, 19, 33, 100, 106, 123, 131–32, 140, 156, 173n14, 187n46
corpus, v, vii, 9, 16, 20–21, 40, 42, 107, 115–16, 169n14, 170n36, 171n2, 175n24, 175n26, 179n2, 181n6, 188n48, 190n59
cosmos/cosmology, 12–18, 121, 169n21, 192n20. *See also* black hole; pulsar; world
creation, vii, 181n6, 192n20
Critchley, Simon, 184n25

Dasein, 16, 25, 34, 41, 100, 177n6
de Man, Henri, 103, 188n49
deconstruction, 2, 3, 8, 12, 19, 25, 32, 46, 78, 92, 117, 146, 150, 151, 168n11, 174n21, 184n25, 188n48. *See also* Derrida, Jacques
Deleuze, Gilles, 2, 175n28
democracy, 32, 180n5, 181n6, 183n22, 184n28, 190n63
Derrida, Jacques, 1–2, 4, 11, 20, 23–24, 26, 47, 79, 81–86, 88, 90–93, 97, 99–101, 103, 107, 109, 113, 116, 148, 167n1, 167n2, 170n33, 170n35, 171n3, 172n13, 175n27, 175n28, 177n8, 180n4, 181n7, 182nn9–12, 183n14, 183n16, 183n25, 184n26, 188n46, 189n56, 190–91n57. *See also* deconstruction
Descartes, René, v, vii, 5, 16, 18–19, 23–48, 50–52, 60, 73, 78, 100–1, 117, 119, 122, 131, 164n33, 171nn4–6, 172n7, 173n14, 173n16, 174n18, 174n23, 175nn25–27, 176n30, 178n16; *Meditations*, 24–27, 30, 38, 40–41, 51, 172n7, 174n20, 176n30. *See also* Cartesian; cogito
dialectic, 41, 87–88, 123, 130–31, 139
Dickinson, Emily, 141
difference, 9–10, 48, 63, 90, 118, 123, 128, 143–44, 151, 188n49
discourse, 4, 7, 12–13, 28–29, 31, 35, 63–64, 70, 72, 82, 84, 98, 111, 135, 167n3, 168n6, 171n5, 174n21, 190–91n65
disenclosure, 1–2, 7–8, 13, 37, 52, 158, 174n21
dissociation, 90, 93, 99–101, 106–10, 113–14, 187n43, 187–88n46
Duns Scotus, John, 14

Eco, Umberto, 173n14
ego, vii, 19, 23–28, 29–31, 33–34, 35–39, 40–47, 49, 79–80, 100–1, 104–6, 122, 170n33, 171n2, 172nn7–8, 174n20, 174n23, 175n27, 179n2, 180n6, 188n46. *See also* Freud, Sigmund; psychoanalysis
Elizabeth, Princess of the Palatinate, 41, 173n14
Entzug/Entziehung, 82–83, 85, 86, 90
epistemology, 62
eros, 20, 115, 126, 133–34, 136, 141–42, 158, 160, 188n48
essence, 25, 27, 37, 75, 85, 93, 97–99, 101–3, 105, 112–15, 125–26, 128, 130, 138, 148, 160, 177n6, 179n21
extension, 40–44, 149, 154, 175n26

fable, 33–40
faculty, 42, 61, 64, 119, 130–31
Ferrari, Federico, 18, 124, 168n6
finitude, 1, 6–8, 18, 21, 25, 46–48, 53, 62, 75, 76, 99, 117–19, 133, 144, 145–47, 161. *See also* infinity
Foucault, Michel, 2, 175n27
Fraser, Nancy, 184n25
freedom, 16, 21, 33, 46, 80, 158–61, 176n34
Frege, Gottlob, 191n6
Freud, Sigmund, 20, 68, 81, 88, 100–6, 113, 134, 140, 142–43, 160, 179n18, 182n9, 183n21, 188n47, 188n52, 188n54, 189n56, 190n60, 190–91n65; Freudian, 104, 109–10, 172–73n14. *See also* ego; psychoanalysis
Fukushima, 20, 74–76, 168n12, 170n34, 176n4, 179n27
Fynsk, Christopher, 91–92, 183n25

Gassendi, Pierre, 176n30
Gilson, Etienne, 173n16
Goh, Irving, 172n10, 172n11, 179n1, 188n48
Gramsci, Antonio, 103, 188n49
Guibal, Francis, 116, 191n2, 191n3
Guyer, Paul, 175, 178n13

Hamacher, Werner, 116
Hawking, Stephen, 15–16, 169n20, 169n24
Hayek, F. A., 95
heart, 108–9, 129–35, 147. *See also* intruder; pulsar
Hegel, Georg Wilhelm Friedrich, 2, 16, 23–24, 47, 50, 63, 68, 76, 87–88, 93, 96, 100, 123, 139, 154, 168n5, 170n1, 177n7, 178n15; Hegelian, 6, 56, 87–88, 112, 130, 177n6
Heidegger, Martin, 4, 23–24, 47, 66–67, 69, 78, 82, 84–86, 88–90, 100, 103, 109, 113,

INDEX

170n1, 171n6, 173n17, 176n34, 178n17, 179n22, 179n1, 182n13, 183n14–15, 183n23, 185n31, 190–91n65, 195n39; Heideggerian, 82–83, 86–88, 120, 140, 184n25
Henry, Michel, 88, 183n20
Hintikka, Jaako, 172n12
history, 55–58, 63–65, 94
Hölderlin, Friedrich, 4
Hume, David, 73
Husserl, Edmund, 103, 174n23

identity, 8–9, 12, 16–17, 31, 43, 51, 70, 102–4, 107, 111, 118, 124, 143, 160–61
immanence, 8–12, 33, 94, 96, 131, 139, 143, 149, 151, 155–59. See also transcendent; transcendental; trans-immanence
implosion, 9, 15, 56, 95
infinity, 8, 12, 62, 76, 78, 85–86, 161. See also finitude
inoperative, vii, 7, 11, 23, 27, 32–33, 39, 51, 79, 90, 96, 107, 131, 136, 164, 168n13, 180n3, 180n6, 181n6, 191n1. See also community
intruder, 108–9. See also heart
Islam, 34

Kambouchner, Denis, 110, 185n
Kamuf, Peggy, 81, 164, 168n7, 169n22, 170n35, 180n4, 182n13, 184n26, 191n1
Kant, Immanuel, 1, 3, 16, 19, 23–24, 28, 47, 50, 60–61, 65, 67, 69, 71, 76, 119, 139, 143, 147, 159, 161, 169n18, 171n5, 177n7, 178n13, 178n17, 179n22, 189n56; Kantian, 30, 59, 61–62, 69, 76, 117, 159, 163, 169n18, 187n39. See also schema
Kermode, Frank, 1, 167n1
Kiarostami, Abbas, 17
Kleist, Heinrich von, 141
Kristeva, Julia, 103, 108, 188n51

Lacan, Jacques, 32, 103, 131, 140, 190n65
Laclau, Ernesto, 17, 170n28, 187n42
Lacoue-Labarthe, Philippe, 17, 71, 79, 81–82, 86–89, 90–99, 101–4, 106–7, 110–14, 163, 167n3, 169n15, 181n7, 182n19, 183n17, 183–84n25, 184n27, 184nn29–30, 185–86n31, 188n50, 188n52, 189nn56–57, 190n61, 190–91n65
language, 3, 5, 10–11, 14, 30–31, 63, 66–67, 79, 82, 84, 88, 92–93, 97, 110, 113, 120, 122, 134–36, 141, 150, 153–54, 157–58, 161. See also discourse; logos; poetry

Lèbre, Jérôme, 18, 194n38
Lefort, Claude, 96–97, 180n5, 184n31, 187n38, 190n57
Leibniz, Gottfried Wilhelm, 52, 73
Lemaître, Georges, 170n27
Lenin, V. I., 189n54
Lépinlois, Gérard, 152
lexical, 82–84, 98, 143
Librett, Jeffrey, 170n31, 172n12, 173n17, 181n6
Locke, John, 119
logos, 136–41, 188n47; See also discourse; language; poetry
Luxemburg, Rosa, 188n49, 188n54
Lyotard, Jean-François, 2, 4, 89, 96–98, 103, 112, 163, 171n5, 177n10, 183n24, 187nn30–41, 189n55, 190n57, 190n61

Mach, Ernst, 140, 193n30
Macron, Emmanuel, 20, 74, 76–77, 170n34, 176n4, 179n27
Magritte, René, 175n29
Malabou, Catherine, 116–17, 191n3
Mann, Herbie, 134
Martin, Jean-Clet, 116
Marx, Karl, 87–88, 92, 96, 181n6, 183n20, 184n26
Marxism, 92, 94–95, 182n7; Marxist, 56, 88, 103
McCarthy, Mary 67–69, 179n19
Merleau-Ponty, Maurice, 147, 193n25, 194n35
metaphysics, 5, 9, 76, 82, 93, 117, 150, 171n5, 177n7, 182–83n13, 185–86n31; metaphysical, 21, 99, 117, 138–39, 183n13, 190n65
Miller, Henry, 141
Minerva, 2, 70, 168n5, 178n15
mitsein/being together, 10, 20, 33, 37, 48, 75, 78–79, 102–12, 115, 137, 159
Mitterand, François, 94
modernism, 2, 157
modernity, 96, 157
Monnier, Mathilde, 17
Montaigne, Michel de, 57, 68, 193n24
mother, 67–70, 101–12, 115–16, 143, 158–61, 189n56, 190n58, 190n61
Mouffe, Chantal, 17, 170n28, 184n31, 187n42

Narcissus, 108
neoliberalism, 186n34
neologism, 79–80, 131, 133
Nietzsche, Friedrich, 3–4, 10, 25, 47, 69, 93, 171n6, 180n5

Neyrat, Frédéric, 195n40
nominalism, 14

ontology, 35, 37, 81, 86, 88, 135, 140, 156; ontological, 6, 24–25, 29, 32, 81, 86, 88, 97–98, 100, 150, 161, 168n6, 172n7, 185n31, 186n37

Pannekoek, Anton, 188n49
paradox, 33, 46, 54, 78, 81, 95–96, 127–28, 139
philosophy, 3, 5, 25, 70–71, 164, 168n5, 169n18, 170n32, 171n15, 174n23, 177n7, 179n21, 182n7, 183n20, 184–85n31, 186n37
Plato, 139
Plutarch, 174n22
poetry, 10–11, 21, 116, 134, 148, 149, 153–55, 160
polis, politics/political, 8–10, 20, 33, 75, 77, 78–114, 115, 177–78n12, 180–81n6, 182n10, 183n22, 183–84n25, 184nn26–30, 184–86n31, 186n35, 186n37, 186–87n38, 187n42, 187n44, 189n56, 190–91n65
postmodern, 3–4, 9, 96, 177n10, 186n36, 187n41
psychoanalysis, 104, 106, 128, 160, 189n56, 191n65. *See also* Freud, Sigmund; Lacan, Jacques
pulsar, 134, 145, 193n26. *See also* black hole; cosmos/cosmology; heart
Pythagoras, 174n22

Rancière, Jacques, 87, 183n18, 184n31, 190n57
Rand, Richard, 120, 175n24
reflection, 19, 29, 50, 53, 59, 63, 68, 86, 115, 121, 185n31
reinscription, 82–83, 97, 106, 152
relation, 83, 90, 99–100, 115, 133, 136, 145, 185n31
retrait, 4, 14, 18, 19–20, 36, 44, 51–52, 62–63, 65, 78–114, 151, 152, 159, 170n35, 180n4, 181n6, 182–83n13
Ricoeur, Paul, 184n31, 192n23
Rimbaud, Arthur, 4, 11, 169n17
Romanticism, 62, 67, 143, 151
Rousseau, Jean-Jacques, 67
Ryle, Gilbert, 140, 193n30

Sartre, Jean-Paul, 6, 46, 94, 168n13
Saussure, Ferdinand de, 122, 192n14
schema, 19, 30, 48, 60–62, 64, 66–69, 71, 105, 178n17, 179n22. *See also* Kant, Immanuel
Schlegel, Karl Wilhelm Friedrich von, 62, 178n14
Schmidt, Carl, 184n31

sciences, 47, 97, 175n27, 185n31; social sciences, 58–59
Sebond, Raymond, 195n24
sense (common), 20, 29, 115, 118–19, 123, 140, 192n10
sense/sensation, 3, 5, 19–21, 45–47, 116–19, 122, 124–25, 133, 140–41, 147, 149, 155, 194n31; sensory, 29–30, 45, 62, 118–19, 123, 140, 145, 147
senselessness, 4, 10, 145, 193n24
sensibility, 60
series, 19, 43, 49, 54–55, 58–59, 63, 68–69, 72–74, 76–77, 79, 100, 115, 158, 182n13
sexistence, 20, 122, 124–26, 129–30, 133–36, 139–44, 148, 159, 161, 170n36, 188n48, 192n12, 193n24
sexuality, 5, 18, 20, 115, 126, 170n36, 188n48, 190n60
Shakespeare, William, 57, 68, 179n20
signature, 24, 51–52, 171n15, 189n56
signification, 4, 8, 10, 17, 61, 116, 121–22, 126, 138, 147, 150, 186n37; signifying, 9, 150, 156
singularity, 12, 14–15, 113, 132–33, 169n21; singularities, 13–17, 21, 34, 47, 75, 99, 114, 116, 136, 150–51, 160, 180–81n6. *See also* black hole
situation, 7, 10, 32, 55–56, 58, 82, 105, 121, 160, 177n6
skepticism, 92, 94, 135, 139, 142, 183n23, 184–85n31
socialism, 189n54, socialist, 170n28, 187n42
sociality, 59, 102, 104, 106–7, 110–11, 181n6
Soulez, Philippe, 100, 103, 109
Sparks, Simon, 20, 87, 89, 164, 176n32, 182n10, 184n27, 191n4, 194n38
spatial, 9–10, 28, 150, 161
Spinoza, Baruch de, 156
Stalinism, 94, 96
Stellungnahme, 101–2, 104–5, 107. *See also* Freud, Sigmund
Strasbourg, 70, 72
structuralism, 2, 168n6
subjectivity, 19, 27–29, 31–33, 72, 78, 98, 104, 106–7, 119, 123, 139, 172n12

technique, 59, 125–26, 141–42, 151–56, 158, 195n39
technology, 5, 21, 115–16, 125–28, 139, 145, 194n31; techno, 56, 58, 98; technological, 95, 108, 128, 144, 151–52, 157, 175n25
tekhnè, 20, 115, 125–26, 133, 139, 141–42, 158, 160
Terdiman, Richard, 186n32

theology, 8, 28, 143, 174n21
Thevet, André, 13, 169n21
totalitarianism, 93–94, 97, 110, 112
trans-immanence, 143, 147, 149, 151, 155, 155, 157, 158. *See also* immanence; transcendent; transcendental
transcendent, 97, 99, 120, 128–29, 143, 149
transcendental, 1, 28, 96, 99, 146, 167n3
translation, 82–83, 136–41
Tuppini, Tommaso, 195n40

uncanny, 54–55, 113–14
unum quid, 40–46, 61–63, 78, 84, 99–100, 115, 117, 122, 125, 131, 141–42, 175n29

Valéry, Paul, 118, 191n5
Van Reeth, Adèle, 18
virus, 74, 76, 168n12, 170n34, 175n25, 176n4, 177n11, 179n27
Volosinov, V. N., 182n7

Weber, Samuel, 170n27, 172n13
Williams, William Carlos, 141
Wirklichkeit, 6, 177n6. *See also* actuality
Wittgenstein, Ludwig, 152
world, 11, 28, 33–34, 37–40, 47–48, 50, 121, 125, 140, 152, 154–61, 174n20, 174nn22–23, 181n6, 194n32. *See also* cosmos/cosmology

Georges Van Den Abbeele is Professor of Humanities at the University of California at Irvine. He is the author of *Travel as Metaphor: From Montaigne to Rousseau*, the translator of five books by Jean-François Lyotard and others, and the editor or coeditor of numerous books and journal issues.

www.ingramcontent.com/pod-product-compliance
Lightning Source LLC
Chambersburg PA
CBHW020407080526
44584CB00014B/1217